THE CAGE BIRD

QUESTION AND ANSWER MANUAL

DAVID ALDERTON

BARRON'S

Contents

First published for United States and Canada
in 2000 by Barron's Educational Series, Inc.

AN ANDROMEDA BOOK

Copyright © 2000 Andromeda Oxford Limited

Planned and produced by
Andromeda Oxford Limited
11–13 The Vineyard, Abingdon,
Oxfordshire OX14 3PX, England

Edited and designed by Derek Hall & Associates

All inquiries should be addressed to:
Barron's Educational Series, Inc.
250 Wireless Boulevard
Hauppauge, New York 11788
http://www.barronseduc.com

Advisory Editors
ARTHUR FREUD (US), APRIL ROMAGNANO
(US), DR. JIM COLLINS (UK)

Editor	Derek Hall
Designer	Alyson Kyles
Project Manager	Peter Lewis
Picture Research Manager	Claire Turner
Production Director	Clive Sparling
Publishing Director	Graham Bateman

ISBN 0-7641-5237-8

Library of Congress Card Number: 99-069965

Cover photographs: *front top* Jörg and Petra Wegner/
Bruce Coleman Collection, *front center* Hans Reinhard/
Bruce Coleman Collection, *back* Cyril Laubscher

Film origination by Omniascanners, Milan, Italy
Printed by Polygraf Print, Prešov, Slovakia

9 8 7 6 5 4 3 2 1

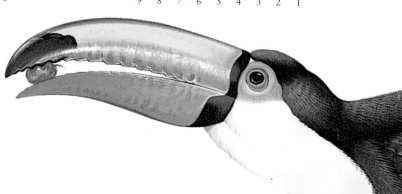

Introduction

Birdkeeping is a pastime which offers tremendous scope. There are many species available for aviculture, varying in size, shape, color, and requirements. In addition to the enjoyment of keeping birds for their attractive plumage, song, or fascinating behavior, they offer opportunities through breeding and exhibiting to extend your interest in the hobby still further.

If you want a pet bird that will become tame and can be taught to talk, then a member of the parrot family is the obvious choice, or perhaps the Hill Mynah. Remember, though, that not all parrots are talented mimics. Some talking birds, such as Amazons, are also likely to be far noisier than, say, Cockatiels or Budgerigars. This is a major consideration, especially if you have neighbors nearby. Finches and most softbills are a better choice for an urban aviary, since they are much quieter.

If you live in a temperate climate, then the relative hardiness of the birds that appeal to you also needs to be considered. As a general rule, virtually all parrots and parakeets are hardy, but smaller birds such as finches are at risk from hypothermia during the winter, partly due to the cold and partly due to the shorter day length, which reduces the opportunity to feed.

▲ ▶ *Military Starlings, Amazon parrots, and sugar-birds are attractive and interesting cagebirds but may be rather challenging for the beginner.*

▲ ▶ *Lovebirds, Zebra Finches, Canaries, and Budgerigars are among the least demanding and least expensive of all the popular cage and aviary birds.*

Bird feeding is now greatly simplified thanks to the availability of modern foodstuffs, although some types of birds, such as nectar-feeding softbills, will be more demanding than seed-eating species. More time is also likely to be required in caring for them during the breeding period.

With such a wide range of species available, it is not surprising that the costs of birdkeeping can vary enormously. Building and stocking an aviary of destructive parrots such as cockatoos is far more expensive than housing a mixed collection of finches, say. Costs will rise still further if your birds need to be accommodated in an outdoor birdroom that requires heating and lighting over winter. The cost of birds them- selves is another important factor. Prices for popular birds such as Canaries and Budgerigars vary widely between a brightly colored songster bought as a house pet and a bird purchased from a specialist with the intention of exhibiting and possibly breeding from it. The price difference reflects the bird's pedigree and its show potential.

The aims of this book are to help the beginner choose the right bird and make looking after it straightforward and enjoyable, to answer many of the questions that birdkeepers ask about birds and their care, and to introduce more experienced birdkeepers to new species and broaden their knowledge.

DAVID ALDERTON

Bird Care

WHEN STARTING OUT IN THE BIRDKEEPING HOBBY, IT IS VERY easy to focus simply on the birds themselves. In reality, however, you must first consider their housing needs, as well as the amount of time needed to look after them, before committing yourself to purchasing stock. Often these considerations will balance themselves out. For example, softbills generally require more time spent on their daily care than most finches, but some types are able to spend winter outdoors without the need to provide artificial heating or lighting, and so will be easier to accommodate.

Your choice of bird has a direct impact on the type of accommodation you will need to provide. Fortunately, you do not have to be an experienced builder to erect an aviary, since a number of companies specialize in building such structures and will even put them up on site for you. Even so, you will need to be patient once the aviary has been built, for it will take time for the birds to settle down and start breeding, and also for the planting scheme inside the flight—and possibly outside as well—to develop to its full extent. Within a year, though, birds and plants should be well established, and you will have an attractive feature in the garden.

It is obviously easier to start out with a single household pet, but again, it pays to research the types of cages available before selecting the most appropriate design for your bird. Like a poorly planned aviary, an unsuitable purchase may prove to be a costly mistake. The guidelines set out in this section of the book will help you avoid the most common pitfalls.

The advice that follows will also help you understand the feeding and breeding requirements of cage and aviary birds, and show you how to keep them healthy.

▶ *Seeds of various kinds form the basis of the diet of many pet and aviary birds. These Budgerigars are feeding on millet sprays.*

What Is a Bird?

THE CHARACTERISTIC THAT SETS BIRDS APART from all other living creatures is the presence of feathers. These provide birds both with the means to fly and a way of helping them maintain their body temperature by trapping air close to the skin. Feathers may also be used for display purposes to attract mates. In some species, the coloration of their feathers helps them to remain concealed from enemies. Most birds molt their feathers annually, over several weeks, enabling damaged feathers to be replaced. Unlike the bony tails of other vertebrates, the tails of birds are also comprised essentially of feathers.

Bills and Feeding

Instead of having jaws with teeth, like mammals and reptiles, birds have evolved bills. Although still strong, bills are lighter than teeth, which aids flight. Depending on the species, the bill may be used to crack seeds, break off pieces of food for easy swallowing, filter food from water, grab flying insects, or probe flowers for nectar. The bill may also be used for display or for fighting, as well as for grooming plumage to keep it sleek.

The absence of teeth has meant that other associated components have been lost—such as the muscles used for chewing food in the mouth. Instead of being chewed, food is swallowed down whole and passes into a saclike structure called the crop, located at the base of the neck. (The crop is particularly apparent in chicks before they feather up.) From the crop, food passes through an organ known as the proventriculus, and then into the gizzard. This is a muscular, thick-walled organ in the case of seed-eating birds. Here, seed and other foodstuffs are ground

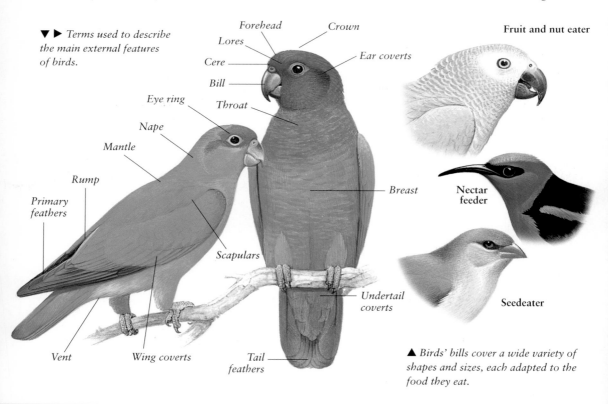

▼ ▶ Terms used to describe the main external features of birds.

Forehead
Crown
Lores
Ear coverts
Cere
Bill
Eye ring
Throat
Nape
Mantle
Rump
Primary feathers
Breast
Scapulars
Undertail coverts
Vent
Wing coverts
Tail feathers

Fruit and nut eater

Nectar feeder

Seedeater

▲ Birds' bills cover a wide variety of shapes and sizes, each adapted to the food they eat.

The Structure of Bone

Internally, the body of the bird has undergone a number of changes to lighten it for flight. For example, the main bones are honeycombed, as the section through a wing bone below shows.

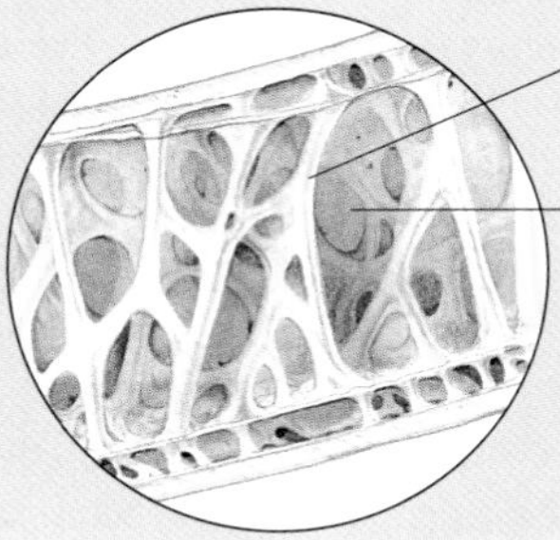

Supporting strut

Air space

up by the action of the gizzard.

Within this organ, grit helps abrade the particles of food, and the mixture then continues through into the small intestines where the absorption of nutrients takes place. In contrast, nectivores have thinner gizzards, because their food is more fluid.

Birds do not have a large bladder where urine collects, because this weight would hamper their ability to fly. Instead, their kidneys produce a highly concentrated nitrogenous waste in the form of uric acid. This semisolid matter travels down the ureter, into the cloaca, and is joined by the feces. These are then voided from the body together. The condition of a bird's droppings can tell much about its overall state of health.

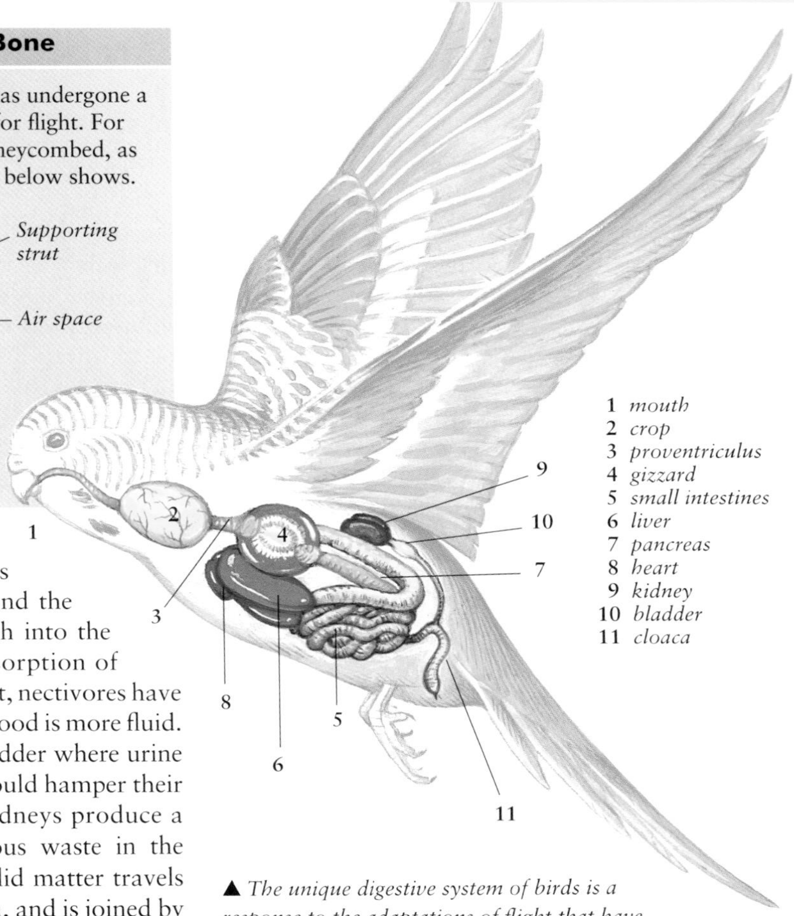

1 mouth
2 crop
3 proventriculus
4 gizzard
5 small intestines
6 liver
7 pancreas
8 heart
9 kidney
10 bladder
11 cloaca

▲ *The unique digestive system of birds is a response to the adaptations of flight that have caused them to lose the jaws and teeth found in other bony animals. Some of the other major internal organs are also shown here.*

Q&A...

● *My vet tells me there is a problem with one of my bird's air-sacs. What are these structures?*

The air-sacs form a vital part of the bird's respiratory system. There are four pairs of air-sacs on each side of the body, plus one unpaired air-sac. A bird's lungs do not expand greatly as air passes through them, so the air-sacs act as bellows, pushing air through the respiratory system. Unfortunately, fungal spores such as *Aspergillus* may be inhaled and then develop in the airways, causing a bird to experience breathing difficulties.

● *Which sense is most important to birds?*

The sense of sight is most important, enabling birds to hunt, avoid predators, and allowing them to judge

distances accurately during flight. Birds possess binocular vision, enabling them to pinpoint objects in front of them with great accuracy. Thanks to the position of their eyes, they also have a wide field of view around their heads.

● *Do birds have other senses?*

By gently ruffling the feathers just behind the eyes, you will see a hole on each side of the head. These mark the entrances to the bird's ears. Birds have no ear flaps to help them capture the direction of the source of sound (although owls use special feathers for this purpose) and, overall, their sense of hearing is less acute than that of most mammals. The bird's sense of taste is also weak, since they have relatively few taste buds over the surface of their tongue. Most birds do not use a sense of smell.

Buying a Bird

THERE ARE SEVERAL WAYS TO DECIDE ON THE bird you want. The second section of this book describes the features of many popular species, and pet stores and even zoos and wildlife parks will enable you to see many birds in real life. Or perhaps you know someone who keeps birds who will let you see his or her collection. Another way is to visit a bird show. This will help you gain an insight into what sets show stock apart from ordinary pet birds. It is also an invaluable

▲ *Healthy birds, like this handsome Toco Toucan, are inquisitive and alert.*

way of seeing a wide range of excellent specimens of different species and can help you decide which bird appeals to you.

Having decided which type of bird you are interested in keeping, the next step is to locate a supplier. There are a number of possibilities, depending partly on the type of bird you are seeking. Pet stores typically stock the most popular species—such as Canaries, Budgerigars, Cockatiels, and various other finches and parakeets—but it may not always be possible to obtain much information about the birds on offer. Furthermore, once birds have molted into their adult plumage, it is virtually impossible to

▶ *When seeking exhibition stock, visiting as many shows as possible is an excellent way to make contact with breeders and gain an insight into good specimens.*

determine their age with any degree of certainty unless they have been banded with a closed ring.

Another possibility is to visit a specialist bird farm, where a much wider variety of birds will be on offer. These establishments are also likely to have a greater range of avian accessories and equipment in stock. Many bird farms often have a good selection of hand-reared parrot chicks available. These birds have usually been bred and reared in the farms' own set-ups.

Selecting a Bird

● Are you seeking a pet bird or an aviary occupant?

● How important is talking ability?

● Is the bird's coloration or its character more important?

● Are you interested in breeding your bird?

● Are you keen to exhibit your bird regularly?

● How much time do you have to look after your bird?

● Would you be concerned about feeding your bird live invertebrates?

● Would a noisy bird disturb your neighbors?

● How much do you want to spend on your bird and its housing?

▲ *A group of healthy waxbills, firefinches, and mannikins suitable for a mixed aviary. Finches in particular can be housed in groups made up of different species, but try to obtain birds from one source for this.*

Breeders

The other alternative is to locate a breeder, either through the advertisement columns of birdkeeping magazines or via a local bird club. National organizations also exist for different groups of birds, and since many of these now have websites, it is quite easy to contact breeders this way.

This does not guarantee that you will be able to obtain the bird of your choice instantly, however, especially if you are seeking a youngster as a pet. Availability depends largely on the time of year. Some birds—such as Canaries—have a closely defined breeding period, whereas others—such as Cockatiels—may breed most of the year.

It is definitely recommended that you go to a breeder if you are seeking exhibition stock. Here you are likely to receive advice on the best pairings, based on personal knowledge of the birds concerned and their ancestries. It is important in this case not only to look for healthy stock but also to find birds of suitable quality.

Health Checklist

Birds should be in tight feather. Bald patches may indicate feather-plucking or the viral disease seen in parrots known as psittacine beak and feather disease (PBFD).

Feathering around the vent should be clean. Staining here usually indicates that the bird is suffering from a digestive disorder.

Eyes should be clear and bright.

Bill should be of the correct shape for the species and not distorted in any way.

All claws should be present (at least in the case of birds which you hope to exhibit), and there must be no swelling of the feet or toes, which may indicate a foot infection.

Breastbone, running down the center of the body in the vicinity of the lower chest, should be well covered on each side with muscle, rather than feeling very prominent.

Droppings should be well formed, except those of nectar-feeding birds, which are very watery.

Cage Considerations

CHOOSING THE CORRECT HOUSING FOR BIRDS at the outset is vital, because any mistakes may have serious consequences. Plan the accommodation carefully, taking into account the needs of the birds that appeal to you, and remember that you may wish to expand in the future.

When choosing a cage, do not be seduced by a superficially stylish design, since many of the more ornate cages are not suitable. In particular, avoid tall, vertical designs that offer relatively little flying space. Rectangular designs afford more opportunity for exercise. The widest selection of suitable cages can usually be found at bird farms and similar outlets.

Decide where in the home you will want to keep your bird. An area where you spend much of your time when at home is recommended. Areas to avoid include the kitchen, not just on

grounds of hygiene but also because the toxic fumes given off by overheating non-stick cooking utensils are likely to prove fatal to a bird.

Positioning the Cage

The location in the room is also significant, in order to give your bird a sense of security. Never position a bird directly in front of a window. The heat from the sun coming through the glass could cause your bird to rapidly succumb to heat stroke and die. The best location is along a wall. Protect the wall from bird droppings and food deposits by suitable screening.

You may also need a stand—if the cage is relatively low in height—to ensure that the bird is located at, or near, eye level. A better alternative is to place the cage on a chest or similar piece of furniture to achieve the correct height. This is also likely to be more secure than a stand— which is a particularly important consideration if you have young children or boisterous dogs in the home. Protect the surface of the furniture by standing the cage on a wipe-clean board. It is a good idea to measure the area intended for the cage beforehand, to ensure that the cage you are considering will fit in the available space.

Many larger cages are supplied in flat-pack form, and it is advisable to wash the component

External perch

Good-quality mesh

Perches

Securely locking door

Slide-out floor tray

Castors for ease of movement

Glazed parrot bowl

Budgie toy

Drinking bottle

◀ A good-quality cage is a worthwhile investment. It will provide a safe and enjoyable environment for your pet. Perches can be repositioned as required.

parts of any cage before assembly to ensure that they are thoroughly clean. Check the sections to ensure that there are no sharp or distorted edges.

Perches

Plastic perches supplied with cages are easy to keep clean, but many birds find their constant diameter uncomfortable. It is much better to discard these perches and cut fresh branches from non-poisonous trees such as sycamore and apple. These should be scrubbed off, in case they have been soiled by wild birds, and must not be cut from trees recently sprayed with pesticides.

The perches can be cut and trimmed so that

▼ *A wide range of accessories is available for use with cages. These include food bowls, drinking bottles, and toys. Those designed to fix onto the mesh are usually supplied with clips or hooks for easy attachment.*

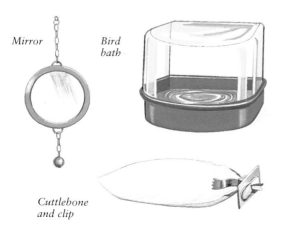

Mirror

Bird bath

Cuttlebone and clip

they fit snugly into the perch holders supplied with the cage. Be prepared to replace perches regularly, because some birds will soon destroy them with their bills. This is normal behavior and helps keep bills in trim, so don't be tempted to offer an indestructible artificial substitute. If you want to place one long-lasting perch in your parrot's quarters, you can buy lengths of tough manzanita wood from specialist outlets.

Food and Water Containers

Many cages come equipped with food and water containers, but these may not be up to the task—particularly in parrot cages. Containers that just hook onto the sides of cages can be pulled out of place by birds and their contents spilled.

You may need to buy a drinking bottle for the cage as well, since these are rarely supplied. Open water containers encourage birds to bathe, but their contents are easily soiled by droppings and debris if left in place for any length of time. Bacteria here will multiply quickly, presenting a possible health hazard. The best type of bottle is therefore either a plastic-style tubular bottle for smaller birds such as Budgerigars, or a large bottle with a spout—often the preferred choice for parrots. A bottle guard will hold the bottle in place and also keep it out of reach of the sharp bills of birds like parrots.

Q&A...

● Would our long hallway be a suitable location for a flight cage for our parrot?

Hallways are not recommended, because they are often drafty, which can be harmful to a bird's health. If your pet is out of its quarters, an outside door opening unexpectedly may result in it escaping from the home. There is also a greater risk that a bird located here may be upset by a dog or a cat sharing your home.

● Will a second-hand cage be safe?

It depends on what happened to the previous occupant! If the bird died, the likelihood is that it may have had an infectious disease, and under these circumstances it is probably better to start with a new cage to avoid any risk of the disease being passed on. In any event, you should strip the cage down and disinfect it very thoroughly, using a special avian product designed for this purpose.

Planning an Aviary

THERE ARE A NUMBER OF FACTORS THAT NEED to be considered carefully when deciding where to place an aviary. You will need to consider the overall layout of your yard, preferably from a good vantage point such as an upstairs window. The aviary structure should complement the existing garden design features, however, rather than obscuring them. The size and shape of the aviary you are planning is also significant, since these factors may place limitations on the most suitable site in the yard. It is definitely not a good idea to locate the aviary in a front yard, where it can become a target for thieves and vandals and where the headlights of passing vehicles are likely to disturb the birds at night.

Naturally, you will want to be able to get good views of the aviary from the yard, but you should choose a site where an attractive aspect of the aviary can also be seen from inside your home, aiming to conceal the safety porch (which prevents birds escaping when you enter). This can be achieved by planning the design so that the entrance is in back of the structure, with the flight area in front being most obvious. Another benefit of having the aviary relatively close to the home is that it will then be easier to run an external power supply to heat the aviary, which will be vital for many finches and softbills if they are to live outdoors during a cold winter.

Avoid choosing an area beneath overhanging trees, however, because their leaves will prevent light reaching the structure in the summer. Later on in the year, their leaves are likely to accumulate on the aviary roof and block the guttering, leading to severe flooding of the interior, while any branches breaking off may result in damage to the aviary structure itself.

Consider the views of your neighbors, particularly if any of them are likely to be affected by your plans. Consultation will help avoid future grievances that could escalate into costly legal disputes. Planning permission is unlikely to be necessary for a small structure, but check the local planning regulations before you start building the aviary.

Choosing Materials for an Aviary

Aviary suppliers advertise in birdkeeping magazines, and it is worthwhile reading catalogs to compare designs as well as prices. For example, not all panels are necessarily covered in mesh of the same size or gauge, and some manufacturers quote for supplying untreated frames, whereas others use tanalized timber which is exceedingly durable and requires no further treatment.

If possible, visit the manufacturers nearest to you so you can look at their products, or visit one of the major shows where a range of aviaries and birdrooms are likely to be on display. This will give you a sound basis for comparison.

Mesh Sizes

● The gauge of the mesh is measured by the thickness of the individual strands. The higher the number, the thinner the mesh.

● Non-destructive birds such as Budgerigars can be housed behind 19G mesh, but the aviaries of other parakeets should be covered with 16G mesh. The largest parrots require accommodation with 12G or 14G mesh.

● Mesh dimensions are also important, both to prevent birds escaping and to exclude mice from the aviary. Most aviary mesh consists of 1 x 0.5in (2.5 x 1.25cm) strands, although for small finches 0.5in (1.25cm) square mesh is often recommended.

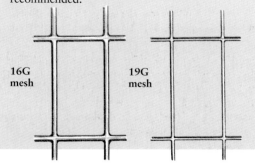

16G
mesh

19G
mesh

▶ *Aviaries can become an attractive focal point in a garden. They can be built in a range of different styles to suit individual preferences and can be blended with natural features like plants.*

◀ *A medium-sized aviary typical of the kind often seen at bird shows. Larger bird shows in particular offer an excellent opportunity to see a wide range of aviaries and to discuss your requirements with manufacturers.*

Q&A...

● **Is the shape of the aviary important?**

Rectangular structures are most common and provide good flying space—especially for more active species such as Australian parakeets. Where space is tight, octagonal flights are often built. These are ideal for small finches and softbills, although they tend not to afford such good protection against the elements. Shielding the most exposed part of the flight with plastic paneling at the back is often a sensible precaution.

● **Are aviaries for some types of birds more expensive than others?**

The larger parrots such as macaws and cockatoos are the most costly birds to house, not just because of their size but also on account of their destructive natures. Timber cannot generally be used in the construction of their aviaries, and so a combination of steel- or aluminum-framed flight panels with brick or blockwork pillars and shelter will be necessary. The increased costs may not just end with the materials—constructing the aviary is far more likely to need professional building expertise.

● **What are suspended aviaries?**

These aviaries, which are especially popular in North America, are designed with the shelter and flight raised off the ground. The cost of building this type of structure is lower compared with a typical walk-through aviary. The flights are constructed using broad mesh on the base, so that the droppings fall through onto the floor out of reach of the birds—as happens in the shelter as well. Cleanliness can still be a problem even in this type of aviary, however, when feathers start accumulating on the mesh base.

Building an Aviary

THE FIRST STEP IS TO CLEAR THE SITE AND MARK out the position of the aviary accurately on the ground. The area should be leveled, and you will then need to excavate down to a depth of about 12in (30cm). A layer of concrete should be laid in the bottom of this trench for the blockwork foundations. These support the aviary and deter vermin from tunneling into the flight. When the foundations are set, build the blockwork up to a height of at least 12in (30cm) above the ground. Above ground, you may prefer to use bricks. Construct similar foundations within the aviary, from the point at which the shelter and aviary outer walls meet, to support the front and sides of the shelter.

Decide on the floor covering now, because it will be much easier to prepare this before the structure is erected, although any planting should be left until the end. Grass is recommended for ground-dwelling birds like pheasants. A concrete base provides the most hygienic option and can be washed and disinfected easily. A third option is a deep gravel bed. This is often favored in parakeet aviaries, combined with paving slabs positioned under the perches where most of the droppings are deposited. These areas can be scrubbed easily, with the rest of the flight remaining clean. Floor areas should be built with a slight slope so that water can drain away through holes at one end of the flight, away from the shelter. Irrespective of the base in the flight, the floor of the shelter is usually concreted over.

▲ *A well-planted aviary provides seclusion, security, nesting sites, and feeding opportunities for many birds. The plants also help to give the aviary a natural look.*

Flight Panels

When you purchase your flight panels (which are obtainable from specialist suppliers), you will need to obtain suitable bolts to anchor the structure together. It is very useful to have assistance when it comes to assembling the panels on site. They are not especially heavy in most cases, but they are cumbersome. Start with adjoining faces, such as the front of the flight and one of the adjacent sides. Position the shortest unit on the base, attaching it here by means of framefixers driven down into the base. Then align the side against this, checking that the frames are positioned the right way round, with the sides clad in mesh always forming the inner face of the aviary.

Apart from helping to protect the timber from the birds' bills, this also means that the panels will be easier to bolt together, standing outside the aviary. Holes located at the top and bottom of the flight panels should be drilled for this purpose and bolts threaded through. They should be fitted with washers before the nuts are applied, and they must then be kept well oiled.

The roof section should extend over the panels forming the sides. This anchors the structure together, with the bolts here being fitted into the frames below. The shelter should be erected in a similar way, taking great care not to split or scuff the roofing felt. Use only top grade roofing felt.

Perches

It may be easier to fit perches into place before the doors are hung. For many parakeets, the perches should be located at either end, with a clear area for flying between them. Do not position the farthest perch too close to the end of the flight, however, because the birds are likely to catch their tail feathers there. For smaller birds, a clear area for flying is also important, with groups of plants to provide cover for nesting.

Finishing Touches

Add plastic sheeting over the roof of the flight nearest the shelter, to provide cover for the birds when the weather is bad. It can be fitted on the sides as well. Next, position guttering along the lower edge of the plastic and at the back of the shelter, to channel rain water away. Incorporate secure locks on all external aviary doors.

Provide a landing platform to give the birds easy access in and out of the shelter, which must be well lit to encourage them to enter. Windows in the shelter must be covered with mesh.

● *Is a safety porch worthwhile?*

Yes. It will ensure that birds cannot escape when you enter the aviary.

The outer door of the safety porch should open outward, and the door leading into the aviary should open inward. A bolt on the inside of the safety porch means you can secure the outer door before opening the aviary door. If a bird escapes from the aviary, it will remain in the safety porch.

● *What is double wiring?*

In adjoining aviaries, mesh must be applied to both sides of the flight panel between them. This stops birds in adjoining flights from reaching, and injuring, each other's toes through the mesh—which would occur if just a single layer of mesh separated them.

● *How does a birdroom differ from an aviary shelter?*

The birdroom may incorporate an aviary shelter at one end, but also provides additional space for breeding cages, possibly an indoor flight, and storage space for seed and other equipment. A snug structure of this type is also valuable for overwintering more delicate birds.

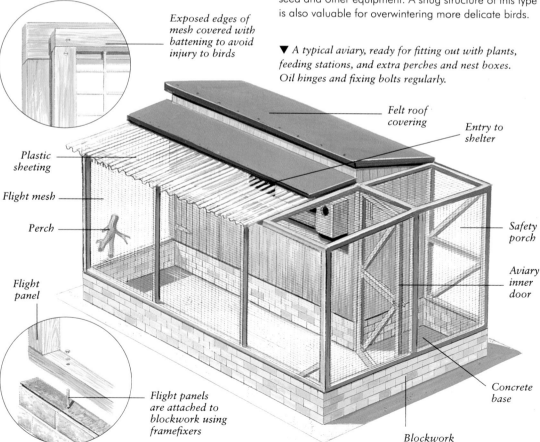

Exposed edges of mesh covered with battening to avoid injury to birds

▼ *A typical aviary, ready for fitting out with plants, feeding stations, and extra perches and nest boxes. Oil hinges and fixing bolts regularly.*

Felt roof covering

Entry to shelter

Plastic sheeting

Flight mesh

Perch

Flight panel

Safety porch

Aviary inner door

Flight panels are attached to blockwork using framefixers

Concrete base

Blockwork

Foods and Feeding

IT IS NO COINCIDENCE THAT THOSE BIRDS ABLE to thrive on a sparse diet comprised of little more than dry seed—such as the Budgerigar—were the first to be successfully domesticated. Today, however, a much wider range of foodstuffs is available, and it is easier than ever for aviculturists to keep and breed species with specialized diets—even the more delicate softbills. This has been brought about mainly because of a greater understanding of the nutritional needs of birds.

The basic requirements of all birds are similar in terms of protein, carbohydrate, and fat, but the way in which they obtain their nutrients differs widely. Many birds also require additional foods throughout the breeding season. These are called rearing foods, and they are important not only to the chicks' development but also in terms of providing extra nutrients to the adults.

How Much Food?

The amount of food a bird requires will depend on the individual, the time of year, and the weather. Replenish food supplies every day, and

◀▼ *Two seed feeders. Hook-on feeders (below) are easy to fix close to perches, but create more wastage, since birds are prone to scatter seed on the floor. When using hoppers (left), check that the seed always flows smoothly.*

always remove any uneaten food at the same time. Adjust the amount according to the bird's appetite to avoid wastage (especially in the case of softfoods). When replenishing seed, brush off the uneaten husks before topping up the bowl. Sieve the seed every few days to remove dust.

Seed

Parrots are traditionally fed on a diet of various seeds. Plain canary seed and millets—recognizable in a mix by their rounded shape—feature prominently in the diet of smaller species. These are called cereal seeds. They have a relatively high carbohydrate content, and they provide a valuable source of energy. Other seeds in this category include groats (dehulled oats) plus corn, which is often kibbled (broken), because in its dry state it is very hard for parrots. Flaked corn is also present in some seed mixtures, making them suitable for a much wider range of birds.

The two main ingredients in a standard parrot mixture are oil seeds, in the form of sunflower and peanuts—the latter also known as groundnuts when sold in their shells. Striped sunflower seed is most commonly used as parrot food, but white sunflower seed is nutritionally superior, having a lower oil content. Take particular care when purchasing peanuts, because they can be infected by *Aspergillus* mold, which will damage a bird's liver. It is very difficult to recognize this contamination by sight, and nuts are frequently tested prior to being sold. It is therefore important to buy seed only from reputable suppliers.

A number of serious avian viruses can contaminate seeds. For this reason, it is better to buy packeted seed if you obtain supplies where birds are also on the premises. There is also less risk that packeted seed will have been contaminated by rodents or fodder mites, both of which may spread disease. Seed should be stored in secure, airtight bins or in similar containers, to prevent attack by pests.

▲ *Many birdkeepers prefer to buy seed already mixed, instead of individual seed varieties which then need to be combined.*

▶ *Seeds contain different nutritional ingredients and often need to be mixed to provide a more balanced diet. Red rape has a high fat and protein content but is low in carbohydrate. Millet has a high carbohydrate content. Linseed is a tonic seed for promoting healthy plumage.*

Q&A...

● *Do large sunflower seeds offer better value?*

Frequently not, because although the casing may appear impressive, the inner kernel, which is what the birds actually eat, is no bigger than in smaller seeds. The same applies when buying groundnuts in their shells, compared with loose peanuts.

● *What are tonic seeds?*

These are seeds which are considered to be especially valuable when added to the diets of birds under stress, typically because they are convalescing or molting. Perilla is a typical example, while others include evening primrose and gold of pleasure. Tonic seeds are traditionally used for Canaries and other finches. It is possible to obtain tonic seed mixes containing ingredients of this type that can be used to supplement the birds' regular seed mix. Other tonic seeds are favored for use when birds are breeding. These include niger, reputed to offer protection against egg-binding.

● *Can I feed my pet parrot nuts packaged for human consumption?*

Not if they are salted or otherwise treated, because this could be very harmful to your bird. Many parrots enjoy nuts such as Brazils, walnuts, or hazelnuts, although only the bills of larger species are strong enough to crack them. However, your parrot will certainly appreciate being offered the kernels of these nuts. But do not be tempted to offer them a Brazil nut encased in chocolate—chocolate is potentially deadly to parrots.

Red rape

Linseed

Millet

Soaked Seed

This is a very valuable rearing food and can also help rekindle the appetite of a sick bird. Millet sprays, Budgerigar seed, and even sunflower seed can be prepared this way. This treatment softens seed, improving its digestibility, and stimulates germination, to add nutritional value.

● Wash in a sieve between a quarter and a half of the daily seed eaten by the birds, and rinse thoroughly under a cold tap. Drain and tip into a bowl.

● Pour hot water over the seed until it is well covered. Place a plate or saucer over the bowl to prevent contamination and leave overnight.

● Rinse off thoroughly in the morning, and tip into a clean feeding container for the birds.

● Remove any uneaten food at the end of the day, before it starts to turn moldy.

Balanced Diet

Seed alone is deficient in a number of the key ingredients that birds require, and without these the health of the birds will suffer, and they are unlikely to breed successfully. It is possible to avoid this risk by offering birds fruit and greenfood as well, and by adding a food supplement to seed. Supplements of this type, marketed in both powder and liquid form, are widely available. Follow the dosage instructions carefully, because over time, an excess can be harmful.

▼ *Seasonal fruit (left) should figure prominently in the diet of parrots. Soaked and sprouted seeds and pulses (right) are also popular with these birds.*

▶ *Greenfood is an important addition to the diet of many seedeaters, providing extra vitamins which are deficient in a diet of dry seed. Damp greenfood also provides an easy way of dispensing powdered tonics.*

High-quality Pellet Diet

The other method is to use a high-quality pellet diet (sometimes called a complete diet). These products are formulated to replace seed, and although they may seem expensive, bear in mind that about half of a parrot's seed intake is discarded as husk. There is also no need to purchase supplements, since these foods contain adequate levels of vitamins and minerals.

The main difficulty with prepared foods of this type for parrots is that not all birds will sample them, despite the fact that they are probably significantly superior in nutritional terms to the foods they are eating. Young birds are most likely to be persuaded to eat such foods, if they are introduced before their feeding preferences are more clearly established. In hand-reared birds, such diets are often used for weaning purposes, being similar to the food the chick was previously eating.

Fruit and Greenfood

Persuading some individuals to eat fruit and greenstuff can be difficult initially. Pomegranates are one of the most popular of all fruits with parrots, although they may only be seasonally available. Regular standbys such as sweet apples and grapes can be offered throughout the year. All these fruits are acceptable to softbills.

By way of preparation, the fruit should be washed thoroughly and may need to be cut into suitably sized pieces to prevent it being wasted. Parrots often use their feet to hold fruit, and pieces of the appropriate size are recommended for them, but grapes can be offered whole. Fruit may need to be diced up into small

● **What is the best way to wean a bird onto a complete diet?**

One way is to suddenly transfer the bird by taking away its regular food and substituting the complete diet instead. The risk, however, is that the bird may simply not eat anything for a time, increasing the possibility that it could fall ill. The other method is to introduce the complete food gradually, mixing it in alongside the regular seed, but it is more likely simply to be ignored, accumulating in the food bowl.

● **Can some types of parrot be persuaded more easily to switch to complete diets than others?**

This appears to be the case. Cockatoos and African Grey Parrots are often the most conservative species in their feeding habits, whereas at the other end of the spectrum, *Pyrrhura* conures will sample unfamiliar foodstuffs very readily, and can usually be persuaded to take complete foods with little difficulty.

● **Can I gather greenstuff in the wild?**

Yes, but it is better to collect this from your yard if possible, because you can then be certain that it will not have been sprayed with any harmful chemicals. Do not harvest wild foods for the birds from roadside fields—these are particularly dangerous collecting sites due to likely contamination with weedkillers.

pieces for softbills, so it can be swallowed whole.

Greenstuff, too, is often eaten by parrots, although rarely by most softbills. Many finches will nibble at greenstuff as well, with chickweed and dandelion leaves often being favorites, along with seeding grasses. Spinach can be offered to parrots for much of the year, but preferably a strain with a low level of oxalic acid, because this chemical can interfere with calcium absorption in the body.

▼ *Many wild plants can be used to supplement the diets of parrots and finches, as well as touracos. Some of the most useful plants are shown here. If you grow these in your yard, make sure they do not come into contact with chemicals. Most of these plants will also thrive if grown in pots.*

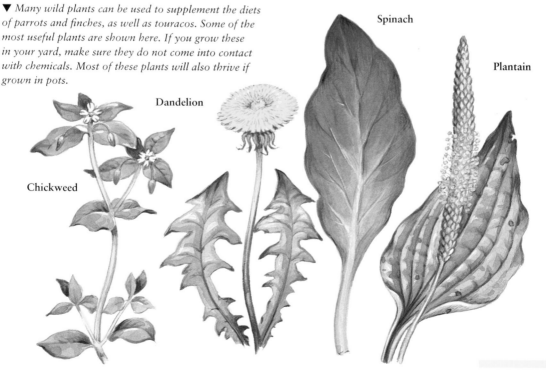

Spinach

Plantain

Dandelion

Chickweed

Softfood and Livefood

Feeding softbills may appear to be complex, but although their food can be more time-consuming to prepare, it is really not difficult to cater to these birds. This is due to the widespread availability of packeted, prepared foods and also due to the ease with which invertebrate livefood can be obtained. These figure prominently in the diet of many species, and are also vital for the successful rearing of young finches such as waxbills.

The diets of softbills usually consist of varying amounts of fruit, livefood, and softbill food or pellets. Some birds also need nectar as part of their diet. Various softbill foods are available, and in the majority of these the most important consideration is the iron content of the food. In small amounts this element is very important, but it is absorbed into the body readily and can rapidly reach toxic levels in the liver, causing the condition known as iron storage disease.

Commercial Animal-based Foods

Mealworms Traditional source of livefood. The larval stage of the Meal Beetle (*Tenebrio molitor*). Ideal for many larger softbills but not recommended for birds with young chicks, since the hard exoskeleton may not be digested.

Waxmoth larvae Suitable for a wide range of softbills. Will pupate into moths if left, so do not over-order stocks.

Pinkies Dead day-old mice, obtainable frozen. Useful for larger softbills. Do not refreeze these once thawed.

Crickets (below) Available in a range of sizes from 0.1–1in (2.5–25mm). Suitable for all birds. Also useful as a rearing food.

Pelleted diets for softbills should also contain low iron levels. These diets are especially useful for birds that have difficulty eating loose softbill food, such as hornbills, as well as for birds such as fruit doves that normally feed on berries. Although these pellets may be eaten dry, it improves their palatability if they are soaked for about ten minutes or so before being offered.

Nectivores rely on sugary nectar food to give them energy, while seeking invertebrates which provide them with protein. When preparing nectar solutions, use a spoon to stir the required amount of nectar into a jug containing the appropriate amount of water. Do not use hot water, for fear of burning the bird's tongue.

Crickets now rank among the most popular livefood, being available in a range of sizes from hatchlings (microcrickets) to individuals about 1in (25mm) or so in length. As in other invertebrates, the calcium:phosphorus ratio is slanted in favor of phosphorus, and therefore a nutritional balancer should be sprinkled over the crickets prior to offering them to the birds.

In the case of mealworms, gut loading is the preferred method of improving their nutritional value. Special food is offered to these invertebrates, which should benefit the birds when they eat them. Mealworms can be stored for weeks if necessary in a ventilated container with chicken meal or bran as a source of food, and a slice of apple. Crickets, in contrast, should be used rapidly or stored in a purpose-built container with greenstuff and moist pieces of sponge to provide them with water.

Eggfood

One of the most important softfoods is eggfood. It is normally offered as a rearing food, although some aviculturists provide it in small amounts all year round. Some birdkeepers still make up eggfood using hard-boiled egg yolks plus ingredients such as finely chopped dandelion leaves, but packeted eggfood is now more widely used. Most blends can be offered straight from the packet, which gives a guaranteed consistency and makes them easy to use. As with all fresh foods, it is vital to prepare, and provide, new supplies of eggfood daily. Always wash out the feeding containers thoroughly before refilling.

▶ *Nectar feeders are available from specialist outlets. Those made from plastic are virtually indestructible, compared with glass designs which are usually tinted to slow the breakdown of vitamins in the nectar solution.*

Q&A...

● **What are the signs of iron storage disease?**

... Affected birds have difficulty in flying at first and will appear fluffed up, although their appetite is unaffected—in fact, they sometimes have a bigger appetite than normal. The abdomen becomes swollen, and by this time, the likelihood of being able to treat the condition satisfactorily will be slight.

● **How should I feed crickets to my birds?**

The best way is to tip the crickets into a bag, and sprinkle the balancer powder over them. It helps if they are chilled for a brief time beforehand, to slow their level of activity. Place the crickets in a steep-sided yet stable bowl for the birds, to prevent them escaping. Don't offer more crickets to the birds than they will eat in an hour or so.

● **Can I collect invertebrates from the yard for my birds?**

Some invertebrates such as aphids can be collected, using a small, clean paintbrush for this, but many, including snails, slugs, and earthworms may prove to be dangerous. This is because they are intermediate hosts for various parasites such as gapeworms, acquired from wild birds. If they are then eaten by an aviary bird, the adult parasites are likely to develop in the cagebird instead.

Red coloration near the spout stimulates birds to feed by mimicking a flower

● **I store my crickets in a tank, but how can I stop them jumping into the water container and drowning?**

You should be able to overcome this problem by using a shallow water container and filling this to the top with a slice of foam sponge, which is kept moist. Alternatively, various products are available that absorb moisture from the air. The moisture is then made available for the crickets to drink.

▼ *Mealworms are available in different sizes, with mini mealworms (left) being more suited to smaller birds. Keep mealworms cool, to slow the rate of development.*

Birds in the Home

MAKE SURE YOU HAVE EVERYTHING READY AT home before you acquire a pet bird. This will mean that you simply have to fill up the water bowl, and then the bird can be allowed out immediately into its quarters. It will take time to settle down there, and it may be beneficial to add a probiotic to the drinking water while the bird spends the first few days in its new surroundings. The probiotic will help stabilize the beneficial bacteria in the intestinal tract and therefore lessens the likelihood of a digestive disturbance. Keep to the diet which the bird has been receiving previously to minimize any risk of digestive upsets, even if you intend to change this later.

Although there will be a great temptation to play with your new pet, you should allow the bird a day or two to settle in its new quarters. If you arrive back quite late in the day with your new bird, leave the room light on for a couple of hours. This will allow the bird an extra opportunity to feed after its journey home. In many cases, your new pet will be able to find its food without any problems, but with young Budgerigars it is advisable to sprinkle a little seed on the floor around the seed bowl if this is a covered type, because they can have difficulty in locating their food initially.

You should not have too much difficulty in winning the bird's confidence, especially if it was hand-reared. You can persuade it to step onto your outstretched fingers by placing your hand

▶ *A favored food item may encourage a pet bird such as this Budgie to step onto the hand, assisting with the taming process.*

Dangers in a Typical Room

Open windows These should be closed and covered with net curtains or similar material to prevent the bird from flying into them.

Open fires All fires can be dangerous. Make sure they are well guarded.

Uncovered fish tank Not only could your bird drown if it falls in, but it could also end up ingesting harmful bacteria in the water if it drinks here.

Cats and dogs They should always be excluded from the room before letting a bird out.

Harmful plants A variety of popular plants such as dumb cane and poinsettia can cause serious illness if eaten. Cacti are hazardous because of their spines.

Q&A...

● *How should I spray my pet bird to keep the feathers in good condition?*

Some cagebirds will bathe in a water bath but others, such as parrots, need to be sprayed regularly. Use a houseplant-type sprayer filled with clean, tepid water for this. Spray gently, allowing the water droplets to fall onto the bird from above. Do not spray into the bird's face, since this may alarm it.

● *I've had my young bird for a month now, but he won't talk. What can I do?*

Be patient. African Greys, which are among the most talented of all avian mimics, can amass a vocabulary of 800 words or so, but it may take six months or more before they utter their first word. Much depends on the individual, however, as some hand-reared birds may be talking virtually by the time they are independent.

● *I recently bought an adult parrot, but he swears. Is there any way to cure him of this?*

This is a difficult problem. Try covering his quarters as soon as he utters the offending phrase and leave the cage covered for ten minutes. This may help to deter him. If you do not repeat the offending phrase to him, it will hopefully fade from his memory—particularly if you can teach him new words. Parrots continue to add to their vocabulary throughout their lives, but they are most receptive to learning new words when young.

alongside the perch. Reward the bird with a treat such as a piece of carrot when it responds as required, but there is no purpose in becoming cross with a bird which fails to react positively, since it will not understand the reason for your annoyance.

Teaching a Bird to Talk

When it comes to teaching a bird to talk, the biggest requirement again is likely to be patience. There are no real shortcuts, but recording the words onto an audio cassette tape with your voice may help. Although compact discs intended to encourage birds to talk are available, these are rarely as successful as teaching the bird directly, partly because your pet will be less ready to respond to the voice of a stranger.

Training sessions, as with taming, should be carried out for periods lasting a few minutes at a time at intervals throughout the day, if possible. This will help you hold your pet's attention, particularly if there are other distractions in the room. You should always repeat the word or phrase clearly. It can be very useful to encourage your pet to learn its name or address. Then, should your bird escape in the future and be caught by someone, it should soon reveal how you can be contacted—hopefully reuniting you quickly. This information can also be useful if a bird is stolen, by settling any arguments about its identity or ownership.

▶ *Allow your pet bird plenty of time outside its cage. A T-stand is an ideal perch in the room, with the bowls offering an opportunity to eat and drink as well.*

25

Aviary Birds

WHEN YOU FIRST ACQUIRE BIRDS FOR THE aviary, do not allow them straight out into the flight, particularly if it is late in the day. They may not be able to find their way back into the shelter and could suffer from night fright if a passing cat or fox disturbs them. This can result in the birds flying around wildly in the dark and possibly sustaining fatal injuries.

Instead, confine the birds in the aviary shelter for the first few days, with their food and water within easy reach. This will allow you to keep a close watch on their feeding behavior, and will enable you to check that they appear healthy before allowing them out into the flight.

▼ *You may sometimes have to hold your bird to examine it. Position its head between the first and second fingers of your left hand (assuming you are right-handed). Keep the wings folded in the palm of your hand.*

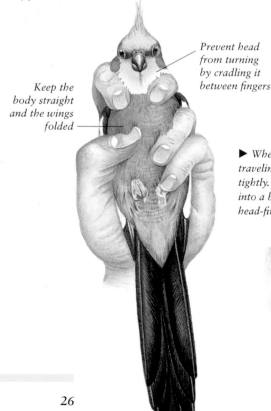

Keep the body straight and the wings folded

Prevent head from turning by cradling it between fingers

Handling a Bird

In a similar way to newly acquired cagebirds, birds intended for the aviary will travel home in a box. They can simply be allowed to come out by opening the lid and leaving it on the floor of the shelter. In the case of birds that do not bite, you can easily take each one out individually. Gently reach into the box with your left hand (if you are right-handed), and place your fingers around its body as shown below. Parrots can inflict a painful bite with their powerful bills, so it will be advisable to wear a stout pair of gardening gloves when handling them. You must take particular care not to grip too tightly, because the gloves will reduce your sensitivity when handling the bird, and you might inadvertently choke it.

There will be times when you need to catch the birds once they are loose in the aviary, and for this, a net is an indispensable tool. It must be both deep and also well padded around the rim. Begin the procedure by lowering all the perches in the flight. This will make it easier to move after the birds, and they will then be forced to rest on the mesh or retreat to the floor, where catching them will be more straightforward. Move the net down gently over the bird you wish to catch, to avoid injury. Once the bird is secure in the net,

▶ *When taking a bird out of a traveling box, do not grip it too tightly. When putting a bird into a box, allow it to go in head-first, as shown.*

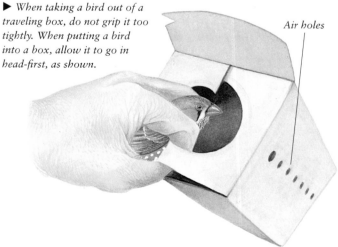

Air holes

Newly Acquired Bird

● Continue offering the food it has been eating at first—particularly in the case of nectivores of all types and softbills—to minimize the risk of a digestive upset.

● Treat all new arrivals with a special avian spray to kill off mites.

● Discuss deworming with your vet, before placing the bird in its permanent quarters.

● Keep the bird confined in its shelter at first.

● Avoid any unnecessary disturbances in the vicinity of the aviary.

● Keep the perches higher in the shelter than in the flight, to encourage the bird to roost under cover.

▶ *Some birds, such as barbets, can be very aggressive toward newcomers. Therefore introductions need to be carried out very carefully to avoid the risk of fighting.*

place your hand over the top to prevent it from flying out again, and gently lower the net to the ground. Then use your other hand to carefully lift the bird out.

Check for Illness
Illness will usually strike within the first few weeks of introducing birds to new quarters, so watch them carefully during this time and look for warning signs (see page 36). If they have previously been kept in a warm environment, they should only be allowed out of doors when the weather is mild and any risk of frost has passed.

▶ *To check for lice, minor injuries, and flight feather damage, carefully extend each of your bird's wings as shown. Hold the wing between thumb and forefinger.*

Q & A ...

● *How should I shut the birds in or out of the shelter?*

The best solution is to construct a sliding door which can be used to close off the entrance hole from outside the aviary. This can be made by cutting a piece of plywood to cover the area and fixing runners to the top and bottom of the shelter opening into which the plywood will fit. The door can then be moved forward or back by pulling on wire or cord extending through the aviary mesh.

● *How should I line the interior of a shelter for softbills?*

The best solution is to insulate it with special quilt, which must be used strictly in accordance with the manufacturer's instructions. This can then be kept out of the birds' reach by fixing oil-tempered hardboard or plywood on the inner surface. The shiny outer surface can be wiped off easily if it becomes soiled.

● *What is the difference between quarantine and acclimatization?*

Quarantine is a period of isolation which all imported or newly acquired birds should go through to ensure that any diseases they may be carrying are not passed to other birds. Quarantine itself usually lasts 30–35 days. Acclimatization is a process during which a bird is slowly accustomed to weather conditions which are different from the ones it experienced previously. Even imported birds which are normally hardy once established may need to be brought inside a birdroom or heated shelter during their first winter. They should then be kept there until the following spring.

Daily Routine in the Aviary

ALWAYS ALLOW ADEQUATE TIME EACH DAY TO carefully examine your birds. Note particularly their general condition and also any unusual behavior. This practice should enable you to spot early signs of health problems before they can develop into something more serious. This is especially important, because early detection may prevent a condition from becoming life threatening.

Feeding Arrangements

Your birds will also need daily feeding and watering. In the case of Budgerigars and some other parrots, it may be possible to provide seed for these birds in a hopper, which will keep it clean and may also incorporate a tray beneath to catch the seed husks. The birds should always be fed in the aviary shelter, rather than the flight. This will ensure that their food remains dry and is less likely to attract rodents.

For softbills, a simple feeding table, rather like a bird table, can be provided. The table should have a top which can be wiped over and disinfected easily, because these birds are quite messy feeders and any deposits of food are likely to turn moldy, threatening the birds' health as they continue feeding here. Alternatively, you can fix a feeding table to the shelter wall, but again, the side of the shelter there must be easy to wipe clean. For birds such as quails, which require their food and water to be placed on the floor, the containers must be carefully positioned so they cannot be soiled by other birds sharing their

Aviary-cleaning Equipment

- Plastic sacks for disposing of stale food and soiled newspaper.
- Long-handled brush for sweeping the floor.
- Dustpan and brush for sweeping up seed husks.
- Shovel for scraping up droppings under the perches in the outside flight.
- Brush and bucket of water for washing off the perches.
- Brush and bowl for cleaning feeding bowls.
- Safe cleaners and disinfectants.

Q & A...

- **What can I do to stop the guttering around the aviary from flooding?**

It could be that the guttering is not fixed properly, allowing water to flow over the rim rather than away along its length. Alternatively, there could be a blockage. Leaves are an obvious hazard, but a plastic bag caught in the guttering can have the same effect. The best solution may be to invest in guttering protectors, which allow rain water to enter easily but exclude leaves and other debris.

- **What is the best way to clean food containers?**

Use a brush that will enable you to reach into the corners easily if you are using plastic, hook-on food bowls. It is equally useful for washing out circular food bowls. Ensure that you rinse the brush thoroughly after use. Keep a washing-up bowl specially for cleaning food containers, which you can also disinfect after use with one of the safe avian disinfectants that are now widely available.

◀ *A humane mouse trap, baited with a small food item such as chocolate and positioned on the aviary floor, will keep the aviary free of potentially harmful rodents.*

▶ *A densely planted aviary will assist in the breeding of several species. However, to allow access for cleaning, be sure to prune the plants and shrubs on a regular basis.*

accommodation perching above. You should always clean up any perishable food that has been spilled on the floor, to avoid it being eaten by birds after it has gone stale.

Cleaning and Maintenance

The floor of the shelter can be lined with sheets of newspaper, taped in place to prevent them from being disturbed by the wind or by birds flying around in this part of the aviary. Newspaper is absorbent and easy to change, so is ideal for this purpose. It is also cheaper and easier to use than materials like bird sand. Avoid using colored paper, however, which may contain toxic inks. As a general guide, the floor of the shelter will need to be changed once or twice a week, depending on the number of birds being housed there and their diet. Spillages of perishable foods should be cleared up each day. Perches must be thoroughly cleaned and disinfected regularly.

At the end of the breeding season, the aviary must be cleaned out more thoroughly. It may be advisable to transfer the birds elsewhere for this task, so that you can move freely through the aviary. If the aviary has a solid base consisting of concrete or paving tiles, this should be scrubbed and disinfected thoroughly before being rinsed off. In a planted aviary, cut back and prune shrubs, taking care to ensure that their weight on the aviary mesh has not created any holes through which the birds could escape. Sweep up any dead leaves as well.

Finally, check the outside of the aviary. If necessary, treat the timber with a safe preservative to prolong its life. Pay particular attention to the parts of the panels that come into contact with the base, because this is where water collects and rot is most likely to start developing.

▲ *Many ground-dwelling birds are at risk from frostbite because of their long toes, and may be afflicted like this lapwing. Ensure they roost under cover if it seems likely that the temperature will fall below zero.*

Breeding Preparations

BIRD PAIRS CAN SOMETIMES BE TOLD APART easily by differences in their plumage or by other features that separate the cock and hen—such as cere coloration in Budgerigars (see page 119). Sometimes, however, sexing may rely on behavioral differences, making it very difficult to identify a pair with certainty when you are choosing birds, since these signs may not be apparent at this stage. DNA technology is used for routinely sexing many aviary birds, particularly the larger parrots. It is easy to carry out from a birdkeeper's standpoint, since all that it requires is a feather sample to be sent to a specialist laboratory.

The other option is surgical (endoscopic) sexing, but this is less popular because it means anesthetizing the bird and cannot be used for young birds. Using this method, a vet views the bird's sex organs through a tiny tube.

Some birds are more ready than others to nest in aviary surroundings. The greatest likelihood of success is with birds such as Zebra Finches and Budgerigars, which will rear their chicks on little more than their usual diet. Generally, the

Requirements for Breeding

● A true, compatible pair (or even occasionally a trio of birds) in breeding condition.

● Seclusion for the birds in their cage or aviary.

● Adequate nesting facilities in terms of foliage, nest boxes, platforms, nesting pans, wicker nesting baskets, or similar receptacles.

● A firm support for nest boxes.

● A suitable supply of nesting material.

softbill species are the hardest to persuade to nest satisfactorily. This is because they usually require a well-planted enclosure and almost unlimited quantities of tiny livefoods for rearing chicks.

It will usually take some time for birds to settle sufficiently after a move to commence breeding in aviary surroundings. Established birds are likely to show signs of nesting activity at an earlier stage than recently imported birds. Most species will come into breeding condition in the spring in temperate areas, even if they originate from the tropics. This is because the increasing day length registers via the pineal gland in the brain, triggering hormonal changes associated with the onset of reproduction, which leads to

▼ *A range of typical nesting receptacles for different birds. These can be obtained from pet stores and bird farms. Nest boxes are available in a wide range of sizes and designs to accommodate all types of species.*

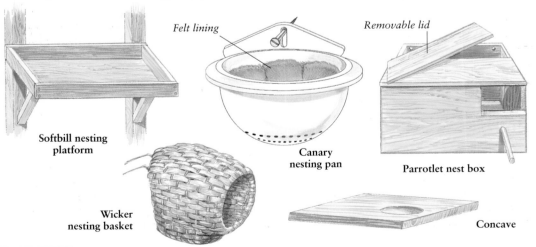

Softbill nesting platform

Felt lining

Canary nesting pan

Removable lid

Parrotlet nest box

Wicker nesting basket

Concave

▲ *Preliminary courtship behavior often entails the cock bird feeding the hen, establishing a bond between them.*

egg-laying. This is the time to put up nest boxes and other nesting receptacles in the aviary. Do not provide these before spring, in case birds begin nesting when the weather is still too cold.

It is vital to offer a choice of nesting sites to pairs that have not nested before, so they can choose the locality that suits them best. If the nesting options are unsuitable, a pair are simply unlikely to show any interest in breeding. This also applies in a mixed collection, where there may be too much disturbance from the other occupants to encourage a pair to nest. Breeding results are usually better if compatible pairs are housed alone, or in colonies comprised of a single species in the case of finches such as nuns.

The Birdroom

Within a birdroom, it is quite common for the breeding cages to be arranged in tiers, but these should be supported on staging rather than being placed directly on the ground, because birds do not feel secure when near the ground, and pairs may be reluctant to nest here. Alternatively, place them on a cabinet (which may even have space beneath for storing show cages and other items). It is often preferable to use double breeding cages, rather than singles, because these are more versatile. You can remove the central partition as the breeding season advances, so these cages can be converted to stock cages for the young birds.

Q & A

● **What sort of cage should I obtain for breeding Zebra Finches?**

... A box-type breeding cage with a foreign finch-type cage front is recommended for these birds. It can be equipped with either an open-fronted nest box or a domed wicker basket which hooks over the cage front, and so can be removed more easily for inspection purposes.

● **What other birds are likely to nest successfully in a breeding cage?**

Bengalese or Society Finches will often nest readily in cages, as may Australian finches such as the Gouldian. Golden-breasted Waxbills and Cut-throats are other possibilities. The narrow bar spacing of the foreign finch front prevents small birds from escaping. Canary breeding cages have slightly larger fronts, with holes to accommodate drinkers, while cages for Budgerigars have even wider spacing between the bars. Breeding cages should be spacious enough to allow the birds to exercise while nesting, to avoid them becoming obese.

● **Where should I site a nest box for parrots?**

The box should always be located under cover, where it cannot become saturated when it rains, because the eggs and chicks could become fatally chilled as a result. It may be better to position the nest box in the shelter, where the degree of seclusion will be greater. Few parrots, with the exception of Australian species, will readily seek to nest in the open. Remember, too, that in hot climates the temperature beneath the aviary roof may become uncomfortable unless shaded.

The Nesting Period

THERE ARE VARIOUS SIGNS THAT INDICATE A PAIR of birds are coming into breeding condition. Cocks of species such as singing finches and Shamas will start to sing more frequently and persistently, while hens become more active and inquisitive as they investigate likely nesting sites within the aviary. Pairs which build nests may be seen hunting for nesting material and carrying it back to their chosen site, so you should ensure that plentiful supplies of twigs, grasses, and other materials are available for this purpose.

Parrots generally become much noisier and more destructive, gnawing away perches as well as cuttlebone—which is especially important at this stage of the year, providing additional calcium for eggshells. Parrots will also start to destroy softwood blocks to form a nest lining, with the hen in particular spending increasing periods of time in the nest box during the day. The larger

▼ Canaries, such as this Norwich hen, incubate the eggs alone. In many other species, including pigeons and doves, incubation is shared between the cock and hen.

Nest Box Tips

● The nest box should be fixed up quite high in the aviary—even though it may be difficult to lift the lid off to see inside.

● The inspection flap must be accessible. This is normally located on the side of the box, approximately 4in (10cm) up from the base. Its position means that if the birds open the flap themselves, there is no risk of chicks or eggs falling out.

● Attach the box to a vertical upright using the metal brackets fixed to the back of the nest box. In the case of a very heavy box, a supporting metal framework beneath may also be needed.

● A perch should be fitted just below the entry hole, to facilitate entry by the birds.

parrots frequently display greater territorial behavior as nesting commences, seeking to drive you away if you approach the box too closely.

Even finches will seek to establish and maintain an area around their chosen nest site. They will drive away any intruders, and outbreaks of aggressive behavior are much more likely to become apparent at this stage. It may even be necessary to remove any birds which appear to be intruding on an established nest site, to prevent serious conflict breaking out.

You should commence offering rearing foods (see pages 22–23) once nesting begins, so that the adults will be used to it when the chicks arrive.

Eggs and Chicks

Just prior to egg-laying, you may notice a change in the hen's droppings. These usually become much larger than normal, and may have a very unpleasant odor associated with them—as is the case with the Budgerigar. Even after egg-laying has started incubation may not begin, and some hens will not sit until they have produced two, or sometimes even three, eggs. Provided the birds

Q&A...

● *What should I watch out for particularly during the egg-laying period?*

Watch hens carefully for signs of egg-binding, since this can rapidly prove fatal if left untreated. This condition results from a hen being unable to expel an egg from her body, which then becomes trapped. The earliest indicators are when a hen is seen off the nest or out of her nest box, looking fluffed up, or often holding her wings down below the sides of her body. She will soon lose the ability to perch if left in this state, and by then her recovery is likely to be in doubt.

● *What should be done with an egg-bound hen?*

A hen in this state should be gently caught up and taken to an avian veterinarian without delay. Handle her carefully at all stages, to avoid any risk of breaking the egg within her body. An injection of calcium borogluconate will usually result in the egg being laid quite quickly, because it increases the contractility of the muscles. In many cases, the egg itself will just be encased in the rubbery shell membranes, rather than having a normal shell.

● *Are there usually any complications following egg-binding?*

There is a slight risk of an accompanying prolapse, caused by the bird straining so hard to pass the egg that the cloaca emerges through the vent as a pink swelling. It can be sutured back into position by your vet. A hen will normally recover uneventfully following egg-binding, but she should be prevented from nesting again until the next breeding season.

◀ *Some birds, such as this tanager, prefer to construct their own nests in the aviary, concealing themselves in the vegetation.*

▲ *Nestlings will need increased amounts of rearing food as they grow. It should be continued until the chicks are weaned.*

are left alone, you should find that everything proceeds normally, however, and that the chicks are of a more even age when they hatch. This increases the chances of their survival.

On occasions, particularly with Budgerigars and some Australian parakeets, the birds may destroy their eggs soon after they are laid. The solution if this happens is to replace them with dummy eggs, which should soon break the birds of this habit. The other possibility is to foster the eggs to another pair, but it is always important to choose a pair which laid at roughly the same time, so that the chicks hatch about the same stage, too. You can check whether the fostered eggs ultimately hatched successfully by marking them very gently with a pencil.

Chick Development

As the time for hatching approaches, the amount of rearing foods you offer the birds should be increased. Their food consumption is likely to grow rapidly once the chicks have hatched. Should there be a sudden decrease in food consumption, however, or if the birds spend more time away from the nest than normal, something is probably wrong. If the birds usually leave their nest when you enter the aviary, you may be able to inspect the nest, but never drive a sitting bird away; this could be catastrophic. If the inspection reveals a dead chick, it must be removed from the nest.

The chicks of pheasants and quails, which are frequently hatched artificially in an incubator, must remain at incubator temperature at first and then be transferred to a brooder to keep them warm. Food and water must be within reach, since they feed themselves. Parrot chicks hatched in incubators are helpless at first, and will need to be hand fed, preferably with one of the specialist foods available. Always wipe the bill after each feed, to prevent food sticking here and distorting the growing tissue.

◀ It may be best to use a teaspoon to hand-feed a chick, rather than a syringe, which may force food down the throat.

One of the best guides to the frequency of feeding is the state of the crop, located at the base of the neck. When this becomes slack, the chick will require feeding again, with the interval between feeds increasing as the youngsters grow older.

The Genetics of Breeding

As with humans, a bird has two sets of chromosomes which carry the genes determining their characteristics—one derived from each parent. It is usually possible to predict characteristics like the color of chicks in species where such varieties are well established.

In most cases, a color variant is recessive to the normal form. As a consequence, this means that pairing, say, a gray Cockatiel with a white-faced Cockatiel, will result in all the chicks being gray in appearance, although they will also carry the white-faced gene. They are described as being heterozygous or "split for white-faced," rather than pure, or homozygous. This is expressed as "gray/white-faced." In due course, if such birds

COLOR VARIANTS		
1.	**Gray x White-faced** *produces*	
	100% gray/white-faced	
2. Gray/white-faced x Gray/white-f. *produces*		
50% gray/ white-faced	25% gray	25% white-faced
3.	**Gray/white-f. x White-f.** *produces*	
50% gray/white-faced		50% white-faced
4.	**Gray x Gray/white-faced** *produces*	
50% gray		50% gray/white-faced
5.	**White-faced x White-faced** *produces*	
	100% white-faced	

are mated together, some offspring are likely to be white-faced, as the table on page 34 shows.

In some cases, the recessive feature is linked to the sex chromosomes, which determine the bird's gender. This means that the pattern of inheritance is slightly different, because the sex chromosomes in the hen are not of even length, unlike the other chromosomes. As a result, in a sex-linked mutation, the appearance, or pheno-type, of a hen of one of these colors—such as lutino or cinnamon—must correspond to its genetic make-up, or genotype. (See table below.)

Relatively few mutations are dominant in genetic terms. Pairing such birds to the normal form will result in this color being likely to emerge in their offspring, although since all pair-ings are random, there is no absolute guarantee that color percentages will correspond exactly to predictions, as these are in effect averages. It may be possible to distinguish between single factor (sf) and double factor (df) dominants by their coloration, as in the case of the dominant silver Cockatiel and spangle, but not the dominant pied mutation of the Budgerigar. In the case of pieds, however, there is no consistency when it comes to inheriting these markings. As a result, young nestlings can vary quite widely with regard to their pied patterning. Pairings and anticipated results are shown in the table below.

You can also use this table to predict the likely percentages of offspring resulting from pairing of dark factor birds, such as the dark green (sf) and olive (df) mutations, which are best known in Budgerigars and Peach-faced Lovebirds.

The Value of Ringing

Accurate records are vital, especially with regard to color breeding, and enable you to identify individual birds. This is easily achieved by using numbered, closed rings, or bands. These can also be used to identify any chick, even if it is not part of a color breeding program. Split rings, which just slip over the leg, can be used for older birds.

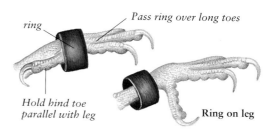

ring

Pass ring over long toes

Hold hind toe parallel with leg

Ring on leg

▲ *A closed ring can only be fitted to the leg of a chick early in its life. After this, its toes become too big. The hind toe should be held back while the ring is passed over the foot, and then released.*

Table of Breeding Results

SEX-LINKED MUTATIONS

1.   Gray cock x Lutino hen *produces*

50% gray/lutino cocks	50% gray hens

2.   Gray/lut. cock x Gray hen *produces*

25% gray cocks	25% gray/lutino cocks	25% gray hens	25% lutino hens

3.   Gray/lutino cock x Lut. hen *produces*

25% gray/lutino cocks	25% lutino cocks	25% gray hens	25% lutino hens

4.   Lutino cock x Gray hen *produces*

50% gray/lutino cocks	50% lutino hens

5.   Lutino cock x Lutino hen *produces*

50% lutino cocks	50% lutino hens

SINGLE FACTOR (SF) AND DOUBLE FACTOR (DF)

1.   Dominant silver (df) x Gray *produces*

100% dominant silver (sf)

2.   Dom. silver (sf) x Dom. silver (sf) *produces*

50% dominant silver (sf)	25% dominant silver (df)	25% gray

3.   Dominant silver (sf) x Gray *produces*

50% dominant silver (sf)	50% gray

4. Dom. silver (df) x Dom. silver (sf) *produces*

50% dominant silver (df)	50% dominant silver (sf)

5. Dom. silver (df) x Dom. silver (df) *produces*

100% dominant silver (df)

General Health Care

Once birds become established in their quarters, the likelihood of them suffering from illness is decreased, but it is still important to be vigilant. One of the most important courses of action when faced with a sick bird is to transfer it to a warm environment. There are special hospital cages available for small birds, while a dull emitter infrared lamp can be suspended over the quarters of large birds. Provide another perch in the cage, however, so that the bird can move here if it starts to feel too warm. Keep hospital cages away from other birds to avoid the risk of any infection passing to them.

Diagnosis and Treatment

The accurate diagnosis of avian illnesses is very difficult without clinical tests, even for an experienced veterinarian, simply because the outward signs of many illnesses are similar. Time is normally vital when it comes to saving the life of a sick bird. As a result, where a bacterial illness is suspected, your vet may treat the bird with an antibiotic injection. This delivers the drug directly into the body, so combating the infection with minimum delay. Always complete a course of antibiotic treatment, even if the bird appears to recover quickly. This safeguards against the infection re-emerging if the bacteria have not been eliminated from the bird's system.

Soluble antibiotics are often prescribed as a follow-up to an injection. They must be mixed in accordance with the instructions, because overdosing can be as harmful as underdosing. Once the bird's condition is clearly improving, the temperature of its recovery surroundings can be lowered, especially once its appetite returns to normal. Do not return the bird to an outdoor aviary again until it is fully fit and the weather is fine and relatively warm, however. A bird which falls ill during the winter may have to be kept indoors until the following spring.

Apart from drugs, nutritional advances have also helped to assist in the recovery of sick birds. Products are now available that can be used to keep birds alive until their treatment starts to have an effect. Subsequently, it is recommended to use a probiotic product (available from your pet store) after a course of antibiotics, to stabilize the beneficial bacteria in the gut.

Typical Signs of Bird Illness

- The bird has a generally dull demeanor.

- Its feathers have a fluffed-up appearance.

- The bird tends to sleep on both legs rather than just one leg.

- The bird suffers a sudden loss of appetite.

- The eyes of the bird are closed.

- Its droppings begin to look different, often becoming greenish.

- The bird seems reluctant to fly away, even when approached.

▶ *The dull and listless appearance of this bird are typical signs of illness. The eyes are partly closed and the bird generally shows little interest in its surroundings.*

▲ *Position a hospital cage in a warm, quiet, draft-free spot, to help aid recovery. An infrared heat lamp at the front of the cage provides additional warmth.*

Sometimes, however, treatment will unfortunately be unsuccessful, and the bird will die. It can nevertheless be valuable to have an autopsy carried out to establish the cause of death. It should also be possible to establish the nature of any infection responsible for its death. This can be particularly significant if the bird was part of a group, because there is the risk that others in your collection could fall ill as well. The tests should also result in the most appropriate treatment being quickly available in future cases.

Health Precautions

It is also important to practice good hygiene after removing a sick bird from an aviary or cage. Wash the food and water containers in a disinfectant solution, rinse off the perches, and clean all surfaces thoroughly. Some infections, such as candidiasis, can be spread by food containers. In this case, the yeast microbes multiply rapidly in nectar solutions and will infect other birds using the drinker. Finally, you should wash your hands thoroughly after dealing with a sick bird.

● **My Budgerigar has a swollen eye. Is this likely to be serious?**

If just one eye is affected, then it is likely to be a localized, rather than a generalized, infection, which will probably respond to treatment with drops or ointment. It is very important that the medication is given several times daily, because the bird's natural tear fluid will rapidly wash the medication out of the eye.

● **Can some bird diseases be spread to people?**

As with all pets, there is a very slight possibility that you could acquire infection from your birds. The most significant of these is probably chlamydiosis (psittacosis). This is also sometimes known as parrot fever, although it occurs in a wide range of animals, including cats. Chlamydiosis can cause a flu-like illness but usually responds well to antibiotics. Birds can now be screened for chlamydiosis and treated.

● **What is enteritis? Talking to breeders at the local bird club, it seems a common problem.**

"Enteritis" is a term used for any problem that affects the digestive tract, usually resulting in green, and sometimes in severe cases even blood-stained, droppings. Enteritis literally means "inflammation of the digestive tract." It has many causes, not all of which are necessarily infectious, although often bacteria such as E.coli are responsible.

Bird Parasites

PARASITES CAN BE DIVIDED BROADLY INTO TWO categories. There are those which live outside the body, such as red mites, and those which live within the body, such as roundworms and microscopic protozoan parasites. Many parasites can spread rapidly through a group of birds. Since they can often be hard to spot, regular treatment aimed at preventing them from becoming established is important.

Red Mites (*Dermanyssus gallinae*) are a particular hazard for Budgerigar and Canary breeders, because these parasites will multiply rapidly in a birdroom environment and can quickly become established in the breeding cages. Worse still is the fact that Red Mites can survive there for possibly a year or more without feeding, so they will remain a hazard in the following year. These mites prefer dark surroundings, often invading nest boxes. Here they feed on the birds' blood, causing feather irritation and often anemia, too, in young chicks. There are special avian aerosol products available to enable you to treat the birds and their nest boxes, and these can be used routinely for preventive purposes.

Roundworms are a very common problem, especially in Australian parakeets, which spend more time foraging on the ground for food than other parakeets and are at greater risk of encountering the infective worm eggs there. The lifecycle of these parasites is direct. The eggs pass straight to another bird host by being eaten, and they are almost immediately infective after being voided from the bird. The eggs can survive for a long period, especially in damp soil. Young parakeets can become infected in the nest by the droppings of their parents. Symptoms tend to be much more severe at this stage, with intestinal worms being a relatively common cause of death in this age group. Your vet will prescribe drugs to treat roundworms and tapeworms.

Tapeworms can also infect birds, although the risk to parrots is far less. This is because the tapeworm eggs must pass through an intermediate host, typically an invertebrate such as a snail, before they can enter a bird by being eaten. Softbills that appear slightly dull and underweight may well be infested, since their diet makes them particularly prone to these parasites.

Adult roundworms
live and reproduce
in bird's gut

Eggs eaten
by host bird

**Roundworm
lifecycle**

Eggs voided
in bird's
droppings

Eggs can remain
infective for several
years under suitable
conditions

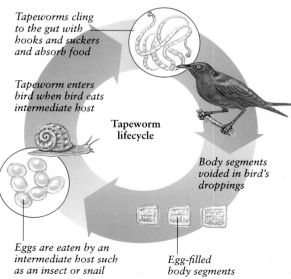

Tapeworms cling
to the gut with
hooks and suckers
and absorb food

Tapeworm enters
bird when bird eats
intermediate host

**Tapeworm
lifecycle**

Body segments
voided in bird's
droppings

Eggs are eaten by an
intermediate host such
as an insect or snail

Egg-filled
body segments

▲ ▶ *Intestinal worms can be a serious hazard to many kinds of parrots and softbills.*

Controlling Parasites

● Deworm Australian parakeets as necessary —usually prior to breeding and again in the fall. Your vet can examine fecal samples to determine whether your birds are infected.

● Remember that parasite eggs will survive for much shorter periods on a concrete, rather than a soil, floor, and solid surfaces of this type will also be easier to disinfect thoroughly.

● There is little to be gained by treating the birds themselves for roundworms when they can reinfect themselves easily from the aviary floor. Control and treatment should go hand in hand.

● Avoid feeding slugs and snails to softbills. Many such invertebrates are the intermediate hosts for avian parasites such as tapeworms.

● While they are still in isolation, treat all newly acquired birds with an aerosol designed to kill mites and lice.

● Wash all breeding cages after use with a special mite-killing product, paying particular attention to the nest box and joins in the cage. Repeat again just before the breeding season. Spray and wash the staging on which the cages are supported.

Q & A...

● **What is scaly face?**

This unpleasant mite infestation is most common in Budgerigars, but it can also affect other birds, particularly kakarikis. The mites bore into the tissue of the bill, causing marks that look rather like miniature snail tracks at first. If left untreated, these develop into the typical coral-like encrustations which spread to the sides of the bill as well. Affected birds should be removed from the aviary. They can be treated with a proprietary remedy or even petroleum jelly smeared over the affected area, which will suffocate the mites.

● **Can I use my dog's flea spray to kill mites?**

No, because this may be fatal for the birds. Use only a special product sold in pet stores for this purpose.

● **Is it possible to treat air-sac mites?**

These tiny parasites localize within the bird's airways and cause breathing distress. They are especially prevalent in Gouldian Finches and Australian grassfinches. The parasites are spread by adult birds to their chicks in the nest. Treatment in the past has been difficult, but now a drug called ivermectin, diluted to the appropriate strength, can eliminate these parasites.

◄ *Lovebirds can be prone to mites and other feather infestations.*

Other parasites are found in birds, particularly in ground-dwelling species such as quails, where they often cause digestive illnesses. *Trichomonas* is relatively common in Budgerigars, finches, pigeons, and doves, and often localizes in the crop where it may cause no apparent signs of illness. But it will be spread to young birds and can rapidly prove fatal. Loss of condition soon after fledging is a common sign in such cases. In adult Budgerigars, trichomoniasis may cause swelling of the crop and results in the regurgitation of mucoid material—not to be confused with the feeding behavior of cocks. Affected individuals often spend longer at the food bowl, dehusking the seed rather than eating it. A sulfur-based drug from your vet can be used for treatment.

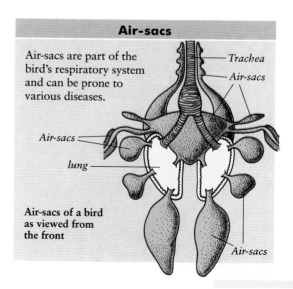

Air-sacs

Air-sacs are part of the bird's respiratory system and can be prone to various diseases.

Trachea
Air-sacs

Air-sacs

lung

Air-sacs of a bird as viewed from the front

Air-sacs

Claws, Bills, and Feathers

IT IS ALWAYS VERY IMPORTANT TO CHECK THE condition of claws, bills, and feathers before buying a bird. Problems affecting the claws and bill may require attention throughout the bird's life, and successfully treating feather ailments is often impossible.

Claws

Smaller finches in particular can suffer from overgrown claws, and you should cut these from time to time. If the claws are left too long, the birds could become caught up around their quarters or may drag youngsters out of the nest. The inclusion in the aviary of sharp grasses, sedges, and bamboo can help keep claws in trim.

A stout pair of nail clippers, as sold for dogs and cats, can also be used for birds. These are much safer than scissors, which often split the nail instead of cutting it cleanly. Clipping the claws needs to be carried out in a good light.

Trimming a Bird's Claw

Before trimming a claw, locate the blood supply running down it. This appears as a pink streak in a light-colored claw, but is harder to see in dark claws. Do not cut into the blood supply.

Blood supply to the claw

Cut claw at this point

Nail clippers

Should you cut the claw in the region where the blood supply is still present, there is a risk of causing bleeding. If this occurs, gently pressing on the tip of the claw will soon cause the blood loss to stop. Alternatively, use a styptic pencil.

Bills

The bill may sometimes need to be trimmed as well, particularly in pet Budgerigars. This can be carried out in a similar fashion to cutting claws. Take great care not to cut into the blood supply by trimming the tip of either part of the bill too short. Have an expert demonstrate this before you try it yourself.

Feathers

Feather problems can also arise, especially with parrots. Pet birds are particularly likely to suffer from feather-plucking. This is a distressing problem, not least because it can be very difficult to overcome successfully. Although there are bitter-tasting sprays marketed for this purpose, they fail to address the underlying causes which have given rise to this behavior. These include boredom, a poor diet, a frustrated desire to breed, illness, and a lack of proper bathing facilities. It is therefore important to seek the advice of an experienced avian vet who can try to pinpoint the reasons before the disorder becomes habitual.

However, feather loss may not be due to behavior problems but to the serious viral illness known as psittacine beak and feather disease (PBFD). It was first recorded in cockatoos, and although this group of parrots is vulnerable, others are equally at risk. The virus is spread through feather dust and can be transmitted easily. It attacks the immune system, resulting in a loss of feathers and a progressive weakening of the tissue of the bill and claws. Most birds suffering from PBFD die from a secondary infection, if they are not euthanased first. Sadly, no really effective treatment is yet available for this distressing condition.

● *How can I distinguish between feather-plucking and PBFD?*

In the case of a parrot kept alone, if areas such as the back of the head or the cheeks start to lose their covering of feathers, then this strongly suggests that PBFD is involved, since these are not parts of the body that the bird can pluck itself.

● *What is French molt?*

The cause of this feather disease was unknown for many years, but it has now been shown to be caused by a virus. It affects Budgerigars primarily, causing their flight and tail feathers to be lost. Some individuals are affected more severely than others; in mild cases, these feathers will regrow more or less normally, but you will still be able to see traces of dried blood in the shafts of birds which have suffered from French molt.

● *How can I control French Molt?*

This is not easy, particularly if you are breeding your Budgerigars on a colony basis, since there is no way of keeping affected pairs apart. In a birdroom, however, isolating affected pairs and using separate cleaning tools and concaves to line the nest can help. An ionizer will also help, by destroying the viral particles in the air currents and lessening the potential for the spread of infection. Affected chicks should also be kept separate after fledging.

▲ *Feather plucking is often difficult to resolve properly, because it is often hard to identify the cause at first, and the problem can soon become habitual.*

◄ *French molt afflicts young Budgerigars about the time they are leaving the nest, preventing them from flying. There is no cure yet.*

How Disease Can Enter a Collection of Birds

New birds Never introduce new birds without first screening them for parasites or disease.

Contaminated food Prepare fresh bird food with clean hands and wash fresh foods thoroughly.

Stale food This is a potent breeding ground for bacteria and fungi. Fresh foods such as eggfood and soaked seed are especially hazardous.

Wild birds Loose food in the flight will attract wild birds. Their droppings can also be hazardous.

Rodents If rats or mice enter the aviary, they will soil the birds' food and water. They must be eliminated without delay, by means of humane traps which will not harm the birds themselves.

Dirty food pots and containers These are another possible health hazard. Regular cleaning will help prevent disease from spreading.

Contaminated livefood Snails and slugs can spread parasites to softbills and may even have been poisoned. Larger softbills may also catch and eat small rodents that may have been poisoned.

Bird Species

THIS SECTION OF THE BOOK DESCRIBES OVER TWO HUNDRED
different species of birds and provides detailed advice on their
care and breeding. The species include many of the most popular
cage and aviary birds available today and are drawn from the
major groups most familiar to the hobby—finches, parrots, and
softbills. Among the finches are the ever-popular Canary and many
other seed-eating varieties, such as weavers and waxbills. The parrot
group includes the Budgerigar, parakeets, lories, and, of course, the
many species of parrots themselves. Typical members of the softbill
group featured here include thrushes, toucans, and starlings.

Many of the species are depicted in color photographs and other
illustrations, and size ranges, differences in appearance between sexes,
and other descriptive features are also provided. Nevertheless, it should
be remembered that individuals can sometimes vary in appearance—
particularly where different subspecies or races occur within separate areas
of a bird's range. Since there is also frequently more than one common
name for a species but always just a single scientific one, scientific names
are used here to help identify a bird easily when you are seeking further
information—in a field guide, for example.

A standard system of classification has been used in this book, which
works as follows. All birds are grouped in the class Aves. This is then
divided into various orders, which in turn are divided into families.
Below the family level is the genus, which embraces birds that display
discernibly similar characteristics to one another. Individual members
of a genus are described as species. Where there is some distinct
divergence in appearance within a species, subspecies are recognized.
By convention, genus and species names are usually written in italics.
Throughout this book, the use of initial capitals is used to denote
individual species—for example, Grey Parrot. The use of lower case
indicates a whole group—for example, parrots. Finally, in the
illustrations following, ♂ denotes a cock, or male
bird, and ♀ denotes a hen, or female bird.

▶ *A Green-naped Lorikeet* (Trichoglossus
haematodus haematodus) *see page 152.*

Domestic Canary SPECIES: SERINUS DOMESTICA

THE ORIGINS OF THE DOMESTIC CANARY CAN be traced to the Canary Islands, off the coast of Africa, where the ancestors of today's breeds are found. The species is also present on the Azores and on Madeira. These Wild Canaries (*Serinus canarius*) differ markedly in appearance from domesticated ones, being a dull, brownish-green with dark patterning on the wings. They are now protected and rarely seen in aviculture, although they are not uncommon in areas of parkland on islands such as Tenerife and Gran Canaria.

The first Wild Canaries were brought to Europe in the 1500s, and soon became very popular. At this stage, the Spaniards tried to restrict the trade to cocks only, but the difficulty in sexing these birds by sight meant that by the 1600s Canaries were being bred in mainland Europe as well, and it may have been then that the first color varieties began to emerge in Italy.

Development of the Domestic Canary
From Italy, Canaries were taken to Germany and Austria, and in the mining communities of the Tyrol, Canary breeding began in earnest. The birds were valued as a means of detecting a lack of oxygen in mine shafts, being taken underground in special cages for this purpose.

This practice spread throughout much of Europe and was still widely used until recently.

Demand for Canaries across Europe continued to grow, and by 1675 it was widely agreed that the song of the Domestic Canary was more musical than that of its wild relative. Although yellow and variegated Canaries were joined by white varieties during this period, the singing abilities of Canaries were considered to be much more important than coloration. When some Tyrolean miners moved to the Harz Mountain region in the 1700s, they took their Canaries with them. It was in this part of Europe that the best-known singing variety of the Canary, the Harz Mountain roller, was developed.

Not only were these Canaries trained to mimic the sounds of mountain streams, but they were sometimes also taught the beautiful song of the Nightingale.

Interest in breeding Canaries for their appearance began in the Low Countries, France, and Britain, where Canaries had first been seen during the early 1600s. These evolved into the so-called type breeds. From the early 1900s onward, particular interest focused on colored Canaries, prized more for the coloration of their plumage than for any other feature.

Fact File

Family name:	Fringillidae
Length:	4.5–8in (11.5–20cm)
Distribution:	Not represented in the wild.
Color variant availability:	Good
Compatibility:	Cocks can be quarrelsome, but otherwise unlikely to be aggressive.
Pet potential:	Cocks are highly valued for their singing prowess.
Diet:	Canary seed mixture, comprised mainly of Canary seed and red rape, along with a little hemp, niger, gold of pleasure, and egg biscuit, depending on the mix. Greenstuff such as chickweed also important. Grated carrot can be offered, but this may affect the birds' coloration during their molt.
Health problems:	Digestive problems. Feather cysts can also be a problem in some breeds.
Breeding tips:	Remove cock when the hen starts to lay.
Nesting needs:	Canary nesting pan lined with felt.
Typical clutch size:	4 eggs
Incubation:	14 days
Rearing requirements:	Eggfood essential, plus greenstuff. A special soaked seed mix can also be offered.
Fledging:	Young ready to leave the nest at 14 days.
Lifespan:	May live for 8–10 years or more.

Short-capped gold

Clear-capped silver

Non-capped silver

Over-capped silver

Clear-capped gold

Broken-capped silver

▲ *A particular feature of the lizard variety is the presence or absence of a clear area of plumage on the head, known as the cap. There are capped, broken (meaning divided), and non-capped forms. These occur in both silver and gold feather types.*

Popular Varieties

The earliest attempt to classify the different types of Canary was undertaken in 1709 by Hervieux, who identified some 29 different types—although these were really variants, rather than the distinctive breeds recognized today.

Lizard. This is the oldest surviving Canary breed and quite different in appearance from other breeds. It is so called because of the markings on its body, said to resemble the scales of these reptiles. Lizards have also been described as "mooned 'uns," because of the crescent-shaped patterning on their wings. A unique feature of lizards is the presence or absence of a clear area of plumage, known as the cap. In lizards, the brighter yellow feather type is known as the gold, with the buff form being known as the silver. There is also a well-established blue variant of this breed.

Frilled. There are a number of distinctive frilled breeds that are particularly popular in mainland Europe. The Parisian frill is the largest, reaching

Q & A ...

● *What is yellow and buff?*

Yellow and buff are used primarily to describe feather type, rather than coloration. Because buff feathers are relatively soft, this creates the impression that such Canaries are slightly larger than their yellow counterparts. There is also a difference in pigmentation, and buff birds appear paler because the pigment does not extend right to the edge of individual feathers, as it does in yellow feather type Canaries.

● *What is double-buffing?*

Ideally, pairs should be comprised of birds of each feather type, but in some cases, breeders have tended to pair buffs together—a process known as double-buffing. This makes the offspring more predisposed to feather cysts, however, and so can be harmful.

● *Can you explain some of the other terminology associated with Canaries?*

"Clear" describes a Canary with no dark melanin pigment, such as a white bird. A "self," such as a blue, has no clear areas on its body. A small area of dark plumage on an otherwise clear bird means it is described as "ticked," but if the proportion increases, it becomes known as "variegated." A self bird with clear areas on the wings or tail is referred to as "foul."

▲ *A white Padovan or crested frill. The ancestral form of all the frilled breeds is thought to be the North Dutch frill, developed as a mutation in about 1800. Frilleds are generally rather nervous birds.*

▼ *In common with other Canary breeds, many of which are localized today, the Norwich reflects its area of origin—being named after the town in England where it was developed.*

8in (20cm) in length. This feature is emphasized by the upright stance of these Canaries. There are three main areas of frilled plumage: with the mantle extending over the back; with the jabot on the front; and with the so-called fins evident at the sides of the body. Other frilled breeds include the Padovan or crested frill, the Milan or color frill (bred in clear white, blue, or red-orange forms) and the Gibber Italicus, which has very sparse plumage.

Norwich Fancy. These are very stocky Canaries with large heads. Unfortunately, repeated double-buffing has meant that feather lumps used to be a particular problem in this breed, but they are less commonly seen today. Norwich hens are often crossed with European finches such as goldfinches, creating hybrids known as mules. These are popular for their song and appearance,

although they usually prove to be infertile.

Belgian Fancy. This breed has played a major part in the development of other posture breeds, especially the Scotch fancy. Both breeds are now far less common, possibly because not only must they excel in type for exhibition purposes, but they must also be trained to move back and forth readily in front of a judge—a movement known as traveling. Breeding also proved a problem, with strains of these Canaries losing vigor.

Yorkshire Fancy. This British breed has altered dramatically in its appearance since Victorian times, when it was reputedly slim enough to slide through a wedding ring! While still measuring about 6.75in (17cm) in length, Yorkshire fancies are now much more rounded.

Border Fancy. These Canaries first became popular in the Border area between England and Scotland, with a standard being drawn up for them at the end of the 19th century. Borders have since built up a strong international following, with often fierce competition in classes for these Canaries.

Fife Fancy. Concern about the increasing size of the Border led Scottish fanciers to redefine the standard in 1957. Here it was agreed that the Fife should not exceed 4.25in (11cm)—about 1in (2.5cm) shorter than the Border.

Gloster Fancy. This breed was created by combining Border fancy and crested roller stock during the 1920s. Pairs should be comprised of one of each type for genetic reasons. Feather cysts have started to become a problem in this variety as well.

Red Factor. These brightly colored Canaries came about as the result of a breeding program begun during the 1920s with the aim of creating Canaries with entirely red plumage, and entailed hybridization with the South American Black-hooded Red Siskin (*Carduelis cucullatus*). The terms "yellow" and "buff" have been replaced by the descriptions "non-frosted" and "frosted" in this case, with the frosted variants having very evident whitish edging to their plumage.

New Colors. A group of Canaries derived from color mutations developed during the 20th century have become very popular today. Yellow, white, and red ground colors form the basis for these varieties, with other changes also visible.

Self cinnamon Border

Clear yellow Border

Eye-, wing-, and tail-marked buff Border

Clear yellow Fife

▲ *The Border fancy is one of the most popular of all Canary breeds and is ideal for beginners. It is also inexpensive and easy to obtain. The Fife is one of the smallest breeds and has also become very popular.*

The ivory mutation, for example, lightens the ground color, turning red to rose, and when this characteristic is combined with yellow and white feathering, it results in gold and silver ivory, respectively. The impact of the red ground color is significant not only in the case of red factor Canaries; it has also been transferred to many other varieties in the new color category.

Buying a Canary

Only cocks sing effectively, and if you want a singing Canary it is best to choose from birds that are four to six months old. This is because it is impossible to sex Canaries by differences in their plumage, so you must wait until they reach the age at which cocks will be starting to sing.

Frosted gold agate opal

Frosted rose-brown ino

Apricot

Frosted rose

Silver isabel ino

Red-orange

▲ *Among the popular new Canary colors available today, inos can be recognized by their red eyes. This is due to a reduction of dark melanin pigment in their genetic makeup. Agates are also common, being a dilute form of green, whereas the isabel is the paler form of brown. An ivory mutation turns red to rose.*

This means that the best time to acquire a pet Canary is likely to be late summer in northern temperate areas, because Canaries have a fairly tightly prescribed breeding season, with early April usually marking the start of their nesting period. Since all cock Canaries sing, the choice of the variety is not generally very significant in this respect, although rollers are still unchallenged in terms of their song.

If you are seeking aviary stock, you must first decide which variety most appeals to you. You will then need to find a breeder, because most pet stores only offer "mongrel" Canaries. These are birds of no fixed variety, or ones that may be healthy but simply will not make the grade on the show scene due to poor coloration or lack of type, for example.

The seasonal nature of Canary breeding means that the best time to seek out aviary stock is likely to be in the early fall, after the breeding period and molt, yet well before the onset of the breeding period at the start of the following spring, when stock becomes very hard to obtain. The price asked for Canaries can differ widely, depending partly on the variety, the show potential of the birds, and their bloodline. Clearly, those from a top show stud will command a much higher price than those bred by a novice starting out in the hobby. Concentrate your efforts on obtaining a few birds of high quality, rather than a larger number of lesser individuals.

Care and Conditions

Canaries will not climb around their quarters like Budgerigars, so whether the bars of the accommodation are horizontal or vertical is not a matter of concern. Canaries do require a relatively large flight cage, however, because they are not frequently allowed out to fly around the room, since they display little, if any, homing instinct and are unlikely to return voluntarily to their cage. If you do decide to let your pet Canary out, however, then it is a good idea to position perches around the room where the bird can rest. These can be held in position with rubber suction cups at their ends and removed when not required.

Within the cage, a sandsheet covering on the floor and a bottle of fresh water will also be required. Canaries can be very messy feeders, scattering their seed in search of favored items in the mix. It is therefore best not to fill the seed container to the top, in order to minimize wastage. Any fresh food such as chickweed—a particular favorite of Canaries—will need to be removed each day, before it can turn moldy. Canaries are quite susceptible to digestive disturbances, and sour food of any kind represents a serious threat to their health.

▲ *The variations in color and appearance that exist in the Domestic Canary are illustrated by this group of birds. Breeders have sought to create distinctive breeds that emphasize particular features such as these.*

Breeding Canaries

While it is possible to breed Canaries successfully in aviary surroundings, serious exhibitors house them in breeding cages for this purpose, where pairings can be carefully supervised. Double breeding cages with removable partitions are recommended for this purpose, since this makes it easier to introduce the cock, which does not normally remain with the hen throughout the nesting period. Check the perches are firmly positioned in the cage, so the birds will be able to mate easily.

The hen requires a nesting pan to act as a support for her nest. This is normally made of plastic, but other materials are available. The base should be wiped over with carbolic soap as a deterrent to mites, and then a lining felt should be stitched in place on top, through holes in the

● **What is the best way to locate Canary breeders?**

Breeders can usually be found through advertisements or show reports in the birdkeeping journals, or via specialist breeds clubs or national birdkeeping organizations whose details may be featured in such publications.

● *My Canary seems to find the perches in his cage uncomfortable. What should I do?*

First check there is no injury or sore area on the ball of the foot causing the discomfort. The perches in many cages are plastic ones with a constant diameter and offers birds little opportunity to exercise their toes. Try replacing these perches with branches from unsprayed fruit trees, such as apple—these will offer more variance in grip and are likely to be more comfortable.

● *At what age can Canaries be allowed to breed?*

Usually in the year following hatching. Hens will then breed consistently for four years or so, after which time the number of eggs in a clutch may decline. Cocks are likely to remain fertile for most of their lives.

base. The nesting pan should be fixed onto the back wall of the breeding cage, usually between the two perches here. Special nesting material (available from pet stores) should be provided for the hen to construct a soft nest on top for her eggs. Tease out the fibers of the nesting material so that the hen can select pieces easily, rather than leaving her with a large lump that she must pull apart, because most of this is likely to end up being soiled on the floor of the breeding cage.

Once she is showing signs of nest-building, the cock can be introduced. If he is already in the other compartment of the breeding cage, simply remove the partition. He should be returned to this section again, or transferred elsewhere, once the hen starts to lay her eggs.

It is advisable to have dummy eggs available (these can be easily distinguished from real eggs by their color) to allow you to control when the chicks hatch. Canary hens normally lay each day, in the morning. On the first day of laying, remove the egg, and transfer this to an egg box (this can be any clean container of suitable size lined with cottonwool or a similar soft material). Keep the egg box in a cool area of the birdroom, out of direct sunlight. Then repeat this procedure

every morning until the fourth egg is due to be laid, at which point the clutch will be complete. You can then take away the three dummy eggs that the hen will have been incubating up to that point, and replace the real eggs under her. This will then ensure that the eggs all hatch at approximately the same time, greatly enhancing the likelihood of survival of the chicks. Without this procedure there will be three days' difference between the oldest and youngest chick, and the smallest may well face a difficult struggle for life as it tries to compete with the older nestlings.

It helps to introduce the eggfood you will be using at least several days before the eggs are due to hatch, so the hen can become accustomed to it. Follow the feeding instructions carefully—the majority of brands can be used straight from the packet and will not need to be mixed with water. Young Canaries grow rapidly, and assuming all goes well, they should be ready to leave the nest when they are about two weeks old. Softfood and other similar items such as soaked seed are especially important at this stage, helping the young birds to become accustomed to eating on their own. Sprinkling blue maw seed on top of the softfood is recommended at this stage, as a

◀ *The Scotch fancy is characterized by its elongated form and stooping posture. Like its ancestor, the Belgian fancy, it is judged both on its shape and its movement from perch to perch.*

▶ *A young cock variegated yellow Yorkshire fancy at a show. In the show cage these Canaries must display themselves to their full height.*

● **What is the best way to offer eggfood to breeding Canaries?**

... Offer fresh supplies of eggfood morning and evening, washing out the feeding containers thoroughly with detergent and then rinsing them off before refilling them. Special finger drawers that attach to the front of the breeding cages are ideal for this purpose.

● **Why is it only possible to color feed effectively during the molt?**

Because it is only at this time of the year that the feathers receive a blood supply. The coloring agent is carried in the bloodstream and is incorporated into the growing feather. Start using the coloring agent at the onset of the molt, otherwise the first feathers that regrow may be paler than those emerging later, simply because they were not exposed to the coloring agent.

● **Why has my Canary stopped singing?**

The cock Canary's song is actually a territorial claim, used to attract hens during the breeding period and to deter other cocks from challenging him at the same time. A number of factors, including light exposure, will bring a Canary into breeding condition, with this behavior being under hormonal control. However, Canaries stop singing during the debilitating molting period, when they are not seeking a mate. Your pet should be singing again after completing his molt.

● **What is slipped claw?**

This is fairly common in Canaries and usually occurs in chicks prior to fledging. The single back toe slips forward, making it impossible for the Canary to maintain a firm grip on the perch. It is often the result of injury in the nest. It can be hard to correct but, if recognized early, it may respond to treatment. This usually entails gently taping up the affected toe parallel with the leg for about two weeks, to encourage the toe back into position.

● **How can I tell the age of non-ringed Canaries?**

It is very difficult, but look at the legs of the birds. Heavily scaled legs are generally a sign of old age, although any chalky deposits here could indicate the parasitic ailment known as scaly leg.

● **Is it possible for Canaries to talk?**

While they are talented mimics of song, especially when taught at a young age, Canaries are not able to talk well. They may sometimes pick up an odd word, though, especially when housed next to a chatty Budgerigar.

▲ *The crested form of the Gloster fancy, shown here, is called the corona. The plain-headed form of this breed is known as the consort.*

way of introducing young Canaries to hard seed.

It usually takes a week or so after the young Canaries have fledged before they are fully independent and can be moved to separate accommodation. By this stage, the hen is likely to be showing signs of nesting again, and she should be given another nesting pan for this purpose, with the cock then being reintroduced for a further period.

Color Feeding

After the second round of chicks, the pair will then start to molt and may need to be color fed during this period. This helps to ensure that the coloration of the new plumage is a richer color than would otherwise be the case. Although natural coloring agents exist, such as cayenne pepper and carrot, synthetic derivatives are preferred. Lizard, Norwich, Yorkshire fancy, and red factor Canaries are usually color fed during the molt. The coloring agent itself can either be given via the drinking water or in a softfood, but take care to avoid overdosing the birds, because this will adversely affect the color of the new feathers until these are shed again in the following year's molt.

True Finches

GENERA: SERINUS, PYRRHULA, URAGUS

THE WORD "FINCH" IS USED TO DESCRIBE MOST of the smaller, seed-eating birds with conical bills but, zoologically, only the family Fringillidae are classified as true finches. This family includes the singing finches, the colorful rosefinches, and bullfinches, which are of Eurasian origin.

Popular Varieties

The singing finches are widely kept, but the availability of Asiatic species is more restricted. A number of different species of rosefinch and bullfinch are represented in aviculture.

Green Singing Finch (*Serinus mozambicus*). Distinctive yellow plumage is present on the face, extending onto the throat, with the underparts being greenish-yellow. The wings are a darker shade of green, while the rump is yellower. Hens can be distinguished by the presence of dark spots forming a necklace across the throat and the duller coloration of their plumage overall.

Gray Singing Finch (*Serinus leucopygius*). The plumage is predominantly grayish-brown, being grayer on the head. The rump is white, and there is also a white area in the center of the abdomen.

Gray Singing Finch

Green Singing Finch

▲ *Singing finches are close relatives of the Canary originating from mainland Africa. Both of these species have pleasant songs.*

Hens have darker streaking on their underparts.
Beaven's Bullfinch (*Pyrrhula erythaca*). It is also called the Gray-headed Bullfinch, and this color continues over the cock's upperparts. The area around the face and eyes is black, with the lower chest and upper abdomen being rosy-red.

Long-tailed Rosefinch (*Uragus sibiricus*). This species has delicate, rosy-pink coloration, with silvery-pink markings on the head extending over the wings and flanks. The upper surface of the tail feathers is brown.

Care and Conditions

Singing finches are reasonably hardy once acclimatized, but if they have previously been housed indoors, they should be kept in an indoor flight over the winter months in temperate areas and should only be released into an aviary once the risk of frost has passed. It is not advisable to

◀ *A cock Beaven's Bullfinch. Hens have a slightly reddish-gray area below the black near the upper throat, while the mantle over the back is ash-brown.*

house bullfinches in flight cages for long periods, because they are more vulnerable to obesity in these surroundings, which may shorten their lifespan. Hemp should be restricted in their diet for this reason as well. Greenfood should be offered regularly, with the young leaves of plants such as hawthorn being eaten with relish. Later in the year, berries will also be eaten readily.

The cup-shaped nest is often located low down in a suitable shrub, being made from a variety of materials such as horsehair and moss, although singing finches often prefer a Canary nesting pan as a nesting receptacle.

▶ *A pair of Long-tailed Rosefinches. The name is derived from their pinkish plumage. The hen, on the left, has browner feathering on her back and wings.*

Fact File

Family name:	Fringillidae
Length:	5in (13cm)
Distribution: Singing finches much of Africa; other species China.	
Color variant availability:	None
Compatibility: Cocks can be aggressive toward each other (especially singing finches).	
Pet potential: Cock singing finches are sometimes kept for their singing prowess.	
Diet: Typical canary seed mixture consisting mainly of canary seed and red rape, plus other oil seeds such as hemp, niger, gold of pleasure, and egg biscuit. Greenstuff such as chickweed, buds of fruit trees, plus grated carrot.	

Health problems:	Enteric disorders can arise.
Breeding tips: Privacy is important, so restrain your curiosity unless you suspect that something is wrong.	
Nesting needs: Canary nesting pan lined with felt, or alternatively provide an open-fronted nest box plus nesting material.	
Typical clutch size:	4–5 eggs
Incubation:	12–14 days
Rearing requirements: Eggfood, greenstuff, and soaked seed, plus some livefood.	
Fledging:	14–21 days
Lifespan: Typically 6–8 years, but over 20 years recorded in singing finches.	

● *Do I need to color feed my rosefinches when they molt?*

This is likely to be helpful in maintaining their distinctive pinkish coloration, which will otherwise fade over successive molts. If they will not eat a softfood, you will need to administer the coloring agent in the drinking water. Alternatively, if they will eat grated carrot, this can help maintain their coloration naturally. This may also be beneficial in retaining the plumage color in Beaven's Bullfinch.

● *Can I mix singing finches with waxbills since they both come from the same part of the world?*

Yes, singing finches can be kept and bred quite satisfactorily in the company of waxbills, but remember

they need a typical Canary-type seed mix, rather than a foreign finch diet. Their nesting requirements are also different, but this will present no particular problems. It is not good practice to house rosefinches or Beaven's Bullfinches in these surroundings, however, since they can be more aggressive.

● *Will Beaven's Bullfinches be destructive toward bushes in their aviary?*

In typical bullfinch manner, they are likely to eat the buds of some plants as these start to develop, particularly favoring fruit trees such as apple, but enough should survive to ensure that the shrubs burst into leaf and provide cover in due course. Providing the birds with greenstuff to eat should help to lessen this potential problem.

Golden-breasted Waxbill and Avadavats GENUS: AMANDAVA

THESE WAXBILLS MAKE AN IDEAL INTRODUCTION to the group, since they are probably among the easiest to breed successfully—sometimes even when kept in cages.

Popular Varieties

No color mutations are established but, occasionally, their plumage may vary in color, owing to regional differences in their origins in the wild.
Golden-breasted Waxbill (*Amandava subflava*). The upperparts are grayish-green, with the underparts being orangish. Light grayish barring is visible on the sides of the body. Cocks have a red stripe above each eye; this is absent in hens.
Red Avadavat (*Amandava amandava*). Males have distinctive reddish plumage, with white spots visible on the sides of the body and the wings during the breeding period. At other times, they resemble hens, which are predominantly brown, with red plumage restricted to the base of the tail. Also known as the Tiger Finch, because of its Asiatic origins, and as the Strawberry Finch, because of the cock's coloration.
Green Avadavat (*Amandava formosa*). Shades of green predominate in the plumage, with the

▲ *The Golden-breasted Waxbill is the smallest of the waxbills. Its tiny size means that it needs to be kept in a flight covered with 0.5in (1.25cm) square mesh to prevent it from escaping.*

● *I saw some Red Avadavats recently that had black, rather than red, plumage. Is this a color mutation?*

No, because a color mutation is the result of changes to the genes controlling the bird's characteristics. Sporadic black areas of plumage in Red Avadavats are due to acquired melanism. This may arise when the birds are kept on a diet consisting mainly of dry seed. By offering a more balanced diet, these black areas will be replaced at the next molt by the usual red plumage.

● *Do other members of this group suffer from acquired melanism?*

It can occur in the Golden-breasted Waxbill and, in this case, it will take up to a year for affected individuals to replace these feathers because they do not have an eclipse plumage, unlike the Red Avadavat.

● *What is eclipse plumage?*

This is the color of a cock's plumage when he is out of breeding condition. At this stage, cocks resemble hens.

underparts of the cock being yellowish. A series of white lines runs down the sides of the body and is especially visible when the wing is raised.

Care and Conditions

Warm wintertime accommodation is essential for these birds. It is not unusual for Golden-breasted Waxbills in particular to nest in spacious breeding cages, but it is vital to ensure that these are fitted with foreign finch fronts, to avoid accidental escapes. Red Avadavats may also nest in similar surroundings, again requiring a nesting basket for this purpose, although in an aviary they are more likely to construct their own, pouch-shaped nest. The change in plumage in this species indicates the onset of the breeding period, and the cock will then sing more intensively and display to the hen at this stage. It is not wise to house them with other waxbills which have predominantly red plumage—for example, firefinches—because this may cause disturbances in the aviary, even though avadavats are not especially aggressive.

Green Avadavats can be more reluctant to nest in cages than their red relative, but again, they should not be encouraged to nest outdoors until the summer, because a sudden cold spell can trigger egg-binding, which is likely to prove potentially fatal in these small birds. Another contributory factor may be a lack of dietary calcium, so it is advisable to scrape off slivers of cuttlebone with a knife, which will make it easier for these birds to consume this vital mineral. Livefood is very important in the diet of these particular avadavats, especially when rearing chicks.

Green Avadavat

♂

♀

♂

Red Avadavat

▲ *Green Avadavats are less commonly kept than Red Avadavats, with a reputation for being more delicate. Hen Green Avadavats are grayer, with paler yellow coloration on their underparts.*

Fact File

Family name:	Estrildidae	**Breeding tips:** A planted aviary is recommended.	
Length:	3–4in (7.5–10cm)	**Nesting needs:** Wicker-type nesting basket; birds may construct their own nest.	
Distribution: Golden-breasted Waxbill Africa south of the Sahara; Avadavats India to China.			
		Typical clutch size:	4–6 eggs
Color variant availability:	None	**Incubation:**	12–14 days
Compatibility:	Quite social	**Rearing requirements:** Small livefoods, soaked seed, and greenstuff. Ant cocoons very beneficial.	
Pet potential:	Will not become tame.		
Diet: Millet-based seed mix plus greenstuff and some invertebrates.		**Fledging:** Young will leave the nest at around 21 days old.	
Health problems: Can be vulnerable to egg-binding.		**Lifespan:** Can live for about 5–8 years.	

Blue and Grenadier Waxbills   GENUS: URAEGINTHUS

▶ *The cock Blue-capped Cordon Bleu. This species is also called the Blue-headed Cordon Bleu.*

THESE BEAUTIFUL BIRDS CAN BE DISTINGUISHED from other waxbills by their predominantly blue or violet coloration. Often difficult to acclimatize initially, they can prove to be quite prolific when housed in suitable aviary surroundings.

Popular Varieties

No color mutations have been recorded in these species, although occasionally Red-cheeked Cordon Bleus have been described with orange, rather than red, plumage on the sides of their faces. It is unclear whether or not such birds represent a color mutation, however, owing to a lack of breeding records.

Blue-capped Cordon Bleu (*Uraeginthus cyanocephala*). The cock has stunning, sky-blue coloration on the head and upperparts, with light brown coloration on the neck and wings. Hens have brown plumage extending up to the bill, with blue on the head encircling the eyes and passing under the throat.

Red-cheeked Cordon Bleu (*Uraeginthus bengalus*). Cocks have prominent crimson-red cheek patches, with light brown in the center of the belly extending across the abdomen. Hens lack the red markings below the eyes.

Blue-breasted Cordon Bleu (*Uraeginthus angolensis*). The bill is grayish, rather than red, which helps to separate it from other cordon bleus. Hens are paler, with less blue.

Purple Grenadier (*Uraeginthus ianthinogaster*). Recognizable by deeper violet plumage around the eyes and extensive purple underparts surrounding a small reddish-brown area. This color predominates on the chest and upperparts. Hens are mainly brown, with a very pale bluish area encircling the eyes and streaking on the breast.

Violet-eared Waxbill (*Uraeginthus granatina*). Violet plumage in cocks of this bird is restricted to the cheeks and the base of the tail, with the remainder of the plumage being a rich shade of reddish-brown. Hens are significantly paler.

Fact File

Family name:	Estrildidae
Length:	4.5–5.5in (11.5–14cm)
Distribution: Across much of Africa south of the Sahara, particularly in southern parts.	
Color variant availability:	None
Compatibility: Cocks will frequently quarrel, especially when breeding.	
Pet potential:	None
Diet: Foreign finch seed mix, based on mixed millets, plus small invertebrates and greenstuff such as chickweed.	
Health problems:	Susceptible to the cold.
Breeding tips: Success most likely in a well-planted aviary where cover is available.	
Nesting needs: Provide a covered wicker nesting basket or small nest box.	
Typical clutch size:	3–5 eggs
Incubation:	13–14 days
Rearing requirements: Small livefood essential, with softfood and soaked millet sprays also proving beneficial.	
Fledging: Young will leave the nest at about 21 days old.	
Lifespan:	May live for 8 years or more.

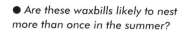

● *Are these waxbills likely to nest more than once in the summer?*

... Pairs will frequently rear two rounds of chicks in succession, but this also depends on when they first started breeding. If it was quite late, they may only breed once. This is most likely when they are introduced to new quarters after the spring. It normally takes about a year for them to settle down before they start nesting.

● *Is it beneficial to feed cheese to waxbills?*

Some breeders offer their birds small amounts of grated cheese. This certainly helps to give a gloss to the plumage, but do not offer large amounts because of its high fat content. A sliver or two should suffice for a pair. Violet-eared Waxbills in particular may also eat pollen granules, sold in health food stores and valued for their protein content. If so, offer a few each day.

● *What type of livefood should be offered to these waxbills when their chicks have hatched?*

The invertebrates required at this stage must be small, easily digested, and nutritionally balanced. Microcrickets, available from specialist suppliers, are a good choice. They can easily be sprinkled with a nutritional balancer to improve their feeding value before being provided to the adults. You can also collect live aphids and tiny spiders from your backyard, but be sure they have not been sprayed with pesticide.

Care and Conditions

The quarters of these birds should be designed so that they have a spacious shelter where they can be kept during periods of bad weather. An infrared lamp (that gives off heat rather than light) suspended over the inside part of the flight will allow them to seek warmth when required.

Once established, pairs can be very prolific, providing sufficient livefood is supplied for their chicks during the rearing period. They may be persuaded to take eggfood as well, which will be very valuable, but this should not be a substitute for the tiny invertebrates that these waxbills, like others of their kind, require in large numbers when there are young in the nest. It is worth supplying a small finch nest box, in case a pair prefer not to construct their own nest in vegetation.

▲ *The characteristic red patches of plumage of the cock Red-cheeked Cordon Bleu distinguish it from the otherwise similar-looking hen.*

Violet-eared Waxbill

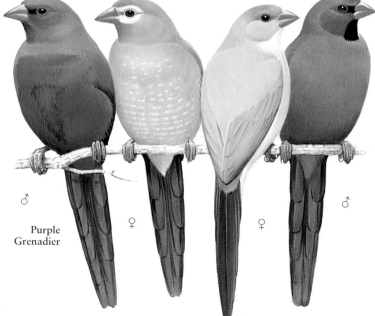

♂

Purple Grenadier

♀

♀

♂

◄ *All Blue and Grenadier Waxbills have a reputation for being delicate. They are sensitive to cold as well as damp, foggy conditions. Their quarters must provide adequate protection from the elements.*

Other Waxbills and Firefinches

GENERA: ESTRILDA, LAGONOSTICTA

THE POPULAR NAME OF "WAXBILLS" STEMS FROM the bill color, which resembles sealing wax in appearance. Firefinches are predominantly red in color. These are all very popular aviary birds. However, as with other members of the group, adequate consideration must be given to wintertime accommodation, because they are not hardy in temperate areas, and they also require artificial lighting to prolong the feeding period during the short and often dull winter days.

Popular Varieties

No color mutations are established, although in mixed collections occasional hybridization may occur. This should be discouraged, however, because these hybrids will have no part to play in future breeding programs. Breeders of these birds now specialize more than in the past, so that instead of keeping mixed collections they often keep small flocks of a particular species. This greatly increases the likelihood of breeding success—especially in the case of those species

Sundevall's Waxbill

Black-cheeked Waxbill

▲ *Like other waxbills, Sundevall's and Black-cheeked need careful acclimatization when first acquired and may not breed during the first year as a consequence. The Black-cheeked is especially insectivorous.*

▼ *Also known as the Common Waxbill, the St. Helena Waxbill will attain adult plumage at about two months of age. Young birds have blackish bills initially.*

where visual sexing is difficult—simply because the likelihood of having true pairs is greatly increased.

St. Helena Waxbill (*Estrilda astrild*). This species has very prominent, dark brown barring across the wings and back, extending onto the flanks as well. Sexing is difficult, but cocks develop more of a pinkish-red hue in breeding condition.

Sundevall's Waxbill (*Estrilda rhodopyga*). Its alternative name of Rosy-rumped Waxbill helps to distinguish this particular waxbill. The wings also have reddish edging on the flight feathers, as a further point of recognition. Sexing is very difficult outside the breeding season. It may be possible to recognize hens because of their paler red markings, however—although this is not always the case because of regional variations. The characteristic dancing display of the cock should help confirm the gender of these waxbills once the breeding season starts.

Black-cheeked Waxbill (*Estrilda erythronotos*). Black coloration on the sides of the head, a gray crown, and pale reddish underparts and rump help to identify this species. The wings are grayish and heavily barred, with the tail feathers being black. Hens have grayish-brown, rather than black, undertail coverts, as well as paler red feathering on the flanks.

Orange-cheeked Waxbill (*Estrilda melpoda*). This species can be recognized very easily, thanks to the prominent orange areas on each side of its face that encompass the eye and extend to the bill. The remainder of the plumage of the head is grayish, with the wings being brown. The rump is reddish, the tail feathers are black, and the underparts are brownish-gray.

Lavender Finch (*Estrilda caerulescens*). These finches are a delicate shade of bluish-gray, with the rump, uppertail coverts, and tail feathers being bright red, with white spotting on the

Q & A...

● *Do I need to remove the young waxbills once they are feeding independently?*

No, this is not normally necessary, since the youngsters will probably not interfere with the nesting activities of the adult birds, and the disturbance entailed in catching them could cause other pairs to abandon their nests.

● *My Red-eared Waxbills have built a large nest, but they don't seem to be using the opening at the top. Instead, they seem to dart in from beneath. Is this usual?*

This is standard survival behavior with these, and most other, waxbills. By not using the obvious upper chamber, the waxbills fool any potential predator looking in here into thinking that the nest is unoccupied whereas, in fact, the birds are safely hidden beneath. The empty part of the nest is often called the cock's chamber.

● *My Orange-cheeked Waxbills seem to be pulling their nest apart with their long claws. Why is this?*

These waxbills often inhabit reedbeds in the wild, and their long claws help them grip onto the thin stems. Unfortunately, however, as you have found, they can be a handicap as well. The best course of action, if the birds do not actually have eggs or chicks, is to catch them and trim the claws back with a pair of nail clippers. Most breeders do this in the early spring before transferring the waxbills back to their outdoor flight after the winter.

◀ *As with many waxbills, visual sexing of Orange-cheeked Waxbills is difficult, although the overall coloration of hens is often paler than that of cocks.*

Fact File

Family name:	Estrildidae
Length:	4.5–5.5in (11.5–14cm)
Distribution: Widely distributed across much of Africa south of the Sahara.	
Color variant availability:	None
Compatibility: Social by nature and can be kept in small groups or as part of a mixed collection.	
Pet potential:	None
Diet: Foreign finch seed mix, based on mixed millets, plus small invertebrates and greenstuff such as chickweed.	
Health problems:	Susceptible to cold weather.

Breeding tips: Require a well-planted aviary where cover is available.	
Nesting needs: A covered wicker nesting basket or small nest box may be used.	
Typical clutch size:	3–5 eggs
Incubation:	12–14 days
Rearing requirements: Must have small livefoods such as microcrickets; eggfood and soaked millet sprays also beneficial.	
Fledging: The young will leave the nest at around 19 days old.	
Lifespan:	May live for 8 years or more.

Lavender Finch

♂

▲ *Also known as the Gray Waxbill, the Lavender Finch is inquisitive and often becomes quite tame. Cocks have an attractive, flutelike call that is likely to be heard frequently at the start of the breeding season.*

flanks. A narrow black band extends on each side from the bill to the eyes. Hens are paler in color. The Black-tailed Lavender Finch (*Estrilda perreini*) is similar, but it has darker plumage as well as black tail feathers and undertail coverts.
Red-billed Firefinch (*Lagonosticta senegala*). The cock has a pinkish-red head and chest, with the underparts being browner. Rump and under-tail coverts are red, with white dots on the sides of the body. Hens, by contrast, are mainly brownish, although the rump and undertail coverts are also red, and there is red plumage around the eye. This species is also called the Senegal Firefinch.
Red-eared Waxbill (*Estrilda troglodytes*). One of several commonly kept species displaying a red stripe extending back from the bill to behind the eyes, with brownish feathering over the wings and paler underparts. The distinguishing features in this case, however, are the relative lack of barring on the wings and sides of the body, as well as the black upper surface to the tail feathers. Pairs are very difficult to distin-guish outside the breeding season, although in the breeding season the underplumage of cocks is much more pinkish than that of hens.

Care and Conditions

Waxbills make a very attractive group of aviary birds, and they can be kept as part of a mixed collection—although breeding results may be

● *I found a young Firefinch chick on the ground. Will it survive if I put it back in the nest?*

There can be no guarantee, but it is certainly a possibility. A young chick can sometimes be dragged out on its parent's foot, particularly if the adult bird is frightened and leaves the nest in a hurry. Hold a chick that has been ejected from the nest gently between the palms of your hands for a few moments, to warm it up. Then, if the young bird is showing signs of life, put it back in the nest without delay.

● *The Lavender Finches I have just bought are badly plucked. Will this be an habitual problem?*

No, unlike the case with most parrots. Their feathering should soon regrow fully once the birds have more space, although their plumage will probably not be immaculate until they have molted properly. As with all newly acquired stock, it is sensible to spray them with a safe avian product to kill any mites or lice that could irritate the birds.

● *What type of plants are most likely to encourage waxbills to construct their own nests?*

Those that offer dense cover and also allow the birds to get into the shrubs easily. Various conifers are good for this purpose, and box (*Buxus* species) is ideal, although bushes in this case are quite expensive, because this is a slow-growing shrub. Climbers can also be useful, particularly by partly covering nest boxes and baskets. Russian Vine (*Polygonum baldschuanicum*) is very vigorous, but beware it does not take over the aviary!

▼ *The decidedly red bill of the Red-billed Firefinch helps distinguish this species from the closely related Blue-billed Firefinch (*Lagonosticta rubricata*).*

Red-billed Firefinch

♀

♂

less satisfactory than if a group of the same species is housed together, partly because of the difficulties in sexing some species. These finches can also be housed with smaller, non-aggressive softbills, as well as Diamond Doves and other doves of similar size.

It is important to ensure that their accommodation is well screened from the elements, however. It is recommended that you use a design that has a solid back and a roof over the top. This will offer greater protection than an aviary with an open, wire-mesh flight. The plants in the flight can be watered as required using a hose. They have an important role not only in providing cover for nesting purposes, but also in attracting small insects such as aphids that will supplement the waxbills' diet.

It is also beneficial to have the flight connected to a warm, birdroom-type structure, in which extra heating can be provided over the winter months. Without this, the birds will need to be

▲ *Red-eared Waxbills can be difficult to breed, but once pairs do start they can produce as many as three broods of chicks in succession. The eye stripes of young birds are paler than those of adults, being decidedly pinkish.*

housed in an indoor flight over this cold period.

When in breeding condition, the cock performs an attractive dance in front of his prospective partner, with a wisp of nesting material in his bill. The difficulty in breeding waxbills successfully is less about persuading them to nest and lay eggs, and more about ensuring that the chicks are reared successfully. While they can be kept quite satisfactorily on a seed-based diet for most of the year, pairs become highly insectivorous when they have chicks in the nest. Without adequate supplies of suitable livefood, chicks will not be reared successfully. This rule applies even if other foods that may actually be of superior nutritional value, such as eggfood, are offered to the breeding birds.

Twinspots and Related Finches

GENERA: PYTILIA, MANDINGOA, HYPARGOS, EUSCHISTOSPIZA, ORTYGOSPIZA

THESE WAXBILLS ARE NOT ESPECIALLY COMMON in aviculture, despite their attractive patterning. Careful acclimatization is essential in all cases.

Popular Varieties

No color mutations have been identified in this group of waxbills. Sexing on the basis of differences in plumage is usually straightforward, however, so recognizing true pairs is not difficult.

Melba Finch (*Pytilia melba*). The head of the cock bird is predominantly gray, with red feathering around the bill, and the back and wings are yellowish-green. As a result, it is also known both as the Crimson-faced Waxbill and the Green-winged Pytilia. There is a yellowish-green area on the chest, with black-and-white barring clearly evident on the underparts. Hens are recognizable by their entirely gray heads.

Aurora Finch (*Pytilia phoenicoptera*). Characterized by a gray head, with reddish suffusion over the back and rump. There is prominent reddish-crimson feathering on the wings, rump, and tail feathers, giving rise to the alternate names of Red- or Crimson-winged Pytilia. The underparts are gray, with attractive, whitish barring. Hens are much browner overall, with wavy, brownish markings on the underparts.

Green-backed Twinspot (*Mandingoa nitidula*). There is some variation in the color of these waxbills depending on the subspecies, but overall cocks are more brightly colored than hens, with dark greenish plumage extending from the top of their heads down over their wings, and with the breast plumage having an orangish hue. Patches of brick-red feathering are present on the sides of the face. The underparts are black, with vivid, white spotting. Hens have much paler coloration overall, particularly on the sides of the head, with this area being of an orangish shade.

Melba Finch ♂ ♀

Aurora Finch ♂

Green-backed Twinspot ♂

Peter's Twinspot ♂ ♀

◀ *These waxbills are not hardy and must be brought inside in winter in temperate areas. They should not be housed in cages through this period, however, because they are more likely to lose condition than if kept in flights. When released back into the outside aviary the following spring, birds kept in cages may take longer to come into breeding condition and may only rear one, rather than two, rounds of chicks during the summer.*

Peter's Twinspot (*Hypargos niveoguttatus*). Cocks have a bright red head and chest, with brown feathering extending from the top of the head over the wings. The underparts are black, broken by relatively large white spots. Sexing is again straightforward, because hens have gray heads, with reddish-orange feathering confined to the throat and upper chest.

Dybowski's Twinspot (*Euschistospiza dybowskii*). Gray plumage extends over the entire head and down onto the breast, with the wings and back being red. The abdomen is black, with white spots. Hens can be distinguished by their dark gray underparts, again with white spotting concentrated mainly on the flanks.

Quail Finch (*Ortygospiza atricollis*). These finches are relatively dull in color, with cocks being mainly dark brown. Black feathering surrounds the bill, and there is a white spot under the chin. Their upperparts have a more grayish tone, while vertical, white banding is visible on the sides of the body. Hens lack the black feathering seen on the face of cocks and tend to be paler in overall coloration.

Care and Conditions

These attractive finches can be difficult to establish at first, and it can be especially useful to give them a daily probiotic when you first acquire them. This can be added to the drinking water and will help stabilize the bacterial population of the intestinal tract, lessening the likelihood of enteritis developing, which can be fatal in small birds. Try to leave these finches to settle down in

● *How compatible are twinspots? I would like to obtain a group of Green-backed Twinspots for breeding purposes.*

It should be quite possible to house these birds together without any risk of serious fighting, even when they start to nest. By starting with a group from the same source, you are more likely to obtain birds of the same subspecies. These particular finches occur in isolated populations, and there can be definite differences in appearance between individuals, unrelated to their gender. Always try to ensure that aviary strains are kept pure when pairing up these birds for breeding.

● *I have just bought some Aurora Finches with red bills, whereas those of my previous birds are black. What is the difference between them?*

The Aurora Finches you have just obtained are of a different subspecies, occurring in the northeastern part of Africa, rather than originating from western and central parts like the more common black-billed form. They are often described as Red-billed Aurora Finches (*P. p. lineata*). Their care is identical.

● *I have noticed that on occasions when I enter the flight, my Aurora Finches seem to freeze. Why is this?*

It has been suggested that this is a defense mechanism, and by also turning its head away to reveal just its tail, the bird becomes less visible. You are likely to find that, once your birds are well established in their quarters, this behavior will become less frequent. In fact, these small birds can become quite steady once they are established in their quarters, with males uttering their attractive song frequently during the breeding period.

Fact File

Family name:	Estrildidae
Length:	4–5in (10–13cm)
Distribution: Represented across much of Africa south of the Sahara.	
Color variant availability:	None
Compatibility: Quite social, but make sure birds are paired up as much as possible in mixed collections.	
Pet potential:	None
Diet: Foreign finch seed mix, comprised mainly of mixed millets and other seeds in smaller amounts, such as canary seed and niger, plus small invertebrates and greenstuff such as chickweed.	
Health problems:	Vulnerable to the cold.
Breeding tips: House in a well-planted aviary with cover.	
Nesting needs: Covered wicker nesting basket or small nest box.	
Typical clutch size:	3–5 eggs
Incubation:	12–14 days
Rearing requirements: Small livefoods such as microcrickets essential; eggfood and soaked millet sprays also beneficial.	
Fledging: Young leave the nest at around 21 days.	
Lifespan:	May live for 8 years or more.

a quiet environment, and never be tempted to place them in an outside flight until the weather is fine and all risk of frost has passed.

Their requirements differ somewhat, with the Melba Finch, for example, often being at home in a less well-planted flight than its relative the Aurora Finch, which inhabits forested areas.

Special conditions will need to be provided for Quail Finches. It is absolutely vital that the ground in their flight is dry and well-drained, with tussocks of grass being included here for the birds also. It may be necessary to cover the

roof of the entire aviary, as well as the back, to give them more protection from the elements. Otherwise, breeding attempts could end up being ruined by the weather, with eggs and even chicks becoming fatally chilled during prolonged cold or damp spells.

When moving around in the aviary where Quail Finches are kept, follow a clearly defined path if possible, and avoid walking through the grass. This is because when feeling threatened, Quail Finches may try to conceal their presence by remaining absolutely still and hoping to avoid

◀ Dybowski's Twinspot is one of the less commonly available species, although it does not differ in its requirements from other members of the group. The bird shown in this photograph is a male.

detection, rather than by flying. You may end up treading on one of the birds. They can also run very fast across the ground in typical quail fashion, seeking cover. Quail Finches are usually very nervous in a cage and may flying upward with considerable force and injure themselves.

All these members of the Estrildidae generally prefer to nest relatively close to the ground, so shrubs with low branches are recommended for inclusion in their aviary for this purpose. Where a group of birds are to be housed together, such shrubs should be spaced out around the aviary, to prevent possible conflicts arising over potential nesting sites. When housed under suitable conditions, these finches are likely to rear two or three clutches of chicks in rapid succession, but small livefoods are absolutely vital for success. If suitable invertebrates are not provided in adequate quantities, the adult birds are simply likely to abandon their offspring. Eggfood in this case will only be useful as a supplementary food, rather than as a mainstay of the rearing diet.

Both adults and young will need to be brought inside into heated accommodation before the onset of winter in temperate areas, with a bird-room equipped with an inside flight being useful for this purpose. It is not advisable to house these birds in cages through this period, however, because they are more likely to lose condition than if kept in flights. When released back into the outside aviary in the following spring, they may then take longer to come into breeding condition. This behavior means a pair may only rear one, rather than two, rounds of chicks during the summer.

● **I want to house some Quail Finches in my aviary. Will they mix well with the Chinese Painted Quails I already have?**

Unfortunately, this combination is not recommended, because the Chinese Painted Quails are likely to upset the Quail Finches, which are very specialized in their habits. Quail Finches hide away and nest in tussocks of grass, and the presence of other birds walking through here is likely to disturb these nervous birds in a relatively small aviary, reducing the likelihood of successful breeding. Quail Finches will, however, benefit from having special bird sand sprinkled in a dry corner of the aviary so they can dust-bathe here. The sand is used to remove excess grease and other debris from their plumage.

● **Is it normal for my pair of Quail Finches to be much noisier than my other waxbills?**

Yes, they do have louder calls, but none of these small finches is likely to offend your neighbors because of their calls. Estrildids are generally quiet, although cocks will sing at the start of the breeding period. In the case of Quail Finches, their calls are probably louder in order to allow the birds to keep in touch with each other, since they spend much of their time hidden. Both the eastern and western populations of Quail Finches are similar in this regard.

● **Which are the most aggressive of this group of finches?**

Although cock Quail Finches may quarrel during the breeding season—particularly if cover on the ground is sparse—problems with aggression are most likely to arise with the Melba Finch. In this species pairs should be accommodated individually, although they can usually be housed and bred harmoniously in the company of other waxbills.

▶ Quail Finches are secretive birds which spend much of their time hidden on the ground. Handfuls of dry moss placed on the floor of their quarters will help give them a sense of security—particularly in the confines of a cage. This bird is a cock.

Zebra Finch

SPECIES: POEPHILA GUTTATA

♂   ♀

◀ *Sexing the normal form of Zebra Finches is easy, thanks to their very distinct plumage. In other forms, sexing is still straightforward, since the hens' bills are always a more orangish shade than those of cocks.*

THE ZEBRA FINCH RANKS WITH THE BENGALESE (see pages 78–79) as one of the most widely kept of all finches. It is an ideal beginner's bird, with pairs usually being very keen to nest. First described in 1805, it is likely that Zebra Finches originally became known in Europe about the same time as the Budgerigar and Cockatiel, around the middle of the nineteenth century.

Popular Varieties

Thanks to the ever-increasing range of colors and varieties that have been developed, there is now also considerable interest in Zebra Finches as exhibition birds.

Normal. This is often also called the gray, to distinguish it from the other color forms. Sexing these finches is very straightforward, particularly in this form. The species is so called because of the black-and-white barring, resembling the stripes of a zebra, evident on the cock's chest. The orangish ear coverts and chestnut markings on the flanks, broken by white dots, are also a feature of cocks of this color, with the wings being grayish-brown. Hens lack these markings, being grayish-brown overall, with paler cream plumage on the lower underparts. There is also a white area bordered by black between the sides of the bill and the eyes on each side of the face. The bill of the hen bird is also significantly paler than the cock's.

White. The first color mutation which came to

prominence was the white. It first appeared in the aviaries of an Australian breeder in 1921. These birds are pure white, but can be distinguished from albinos by their black eyes. Cocks lack their typical distinguishing markings, but they can still be identified easily by their bills—which are a darker shade of red than those of hens.

Albino. Albinos were first recorded during the 1950s in Australia, but they are scarce today. Their plumage should be snow-white, with no hint of barring or other markings. Their eyes are red, with their legs being orange rather than red. This is the only variety of Zebra Finch that is difficult to sex by the color of its bill, although those of cocks again tend to be slightly darker.

Fawn. The fawn mutation has now become widely kept, with such birds displaying light brown, rather than gray, feathering. The throat barring of the cock is also modified, being of a more brownish shade than normal.

Silver. Although not strictly a color, the silver variant of the Zebra Finch is not just significant in its own right but has also led to the creation of other colors. There are two distinctive forms, with differing modes of inheritance. Not surprisingly, the dominant silver has become more popular than the recessive form, because it is easier to breed such birds. This mutation serves to dilute the normal gray coloration, which then results in the creation of paler Zebra Finches, whose coloration resembles silver. There is some variability in the depth of coloration of these birds, however, just as there is with grays themselves, with some individuals being a darker shade than others. This distinction applies also to the cheek patches, which can be any shade between cream and pale orange. If a silver appears unexpectedly as the result of a mating between two grays, then it must be of the recessive type. These birds are very hard to distinguish visually from dominant silvers, however, although they may be of a slightly darker and more even shade.

Pied. The pied mutation was one of the first to occur outside Australia. The markings of such birds can vary widely, with some having just

● **What are Zebra Finches advertised as CFWs?**

... These initials stand for chestnut-flanked white. In this case, although white coloration predominates in the plumage, cocks retain their chestnut flank markings and orangish ear coverts, as well as barring on their breasts and tails, so that sexing is straightforward. Hens of this mutation can be separated from ordinary white hens by the continued presence of black stripes on their faces. This mutation was first recorded in the wild in the state of Queensland, Australia.

● **What is a penguin Zebra Finch?**

In these birds, cocks lack the characteristic barring normally present on the breast, so that their underparts are white, like those of a penguin. This feature is most marked in the case of gray and fawn birds, but can be seen in other varieties as well. It has proved difficult to increase the size of such birds over the generations, with penguin Zebra Finches often tending to be smaller than other varieties.

● **Is it possible to combine the diluting effect of the silver mutations with the fawn?**

Yes, and this has led to the creation of dominant and recessive creams. The dilution in this case has resulted in the gray areas of plumage being replaced by cream, with the markings on the cheeks being grayish, as is the barring on the cock's chest. Recessive creams are unusual compared with the dominant form.

◄ *A crested normal form cock Zebra Finch. The crest should be circular and even in shape. It is possible to combine the crested characteristic with any color. This feature is not especially popular among aviculturists.*

Fact File

Family name:	Estrildidae
Length:	4in (10cm)
Distribution: Australia and the Indonesian islands of Flores, Sumba, and Timor.	
Color variant availability:	Widely bred
Compatibility: Sociable in colonies, or as part of a mixed collection alongside finches of similar size.	
Pet potential: Pairs will breed in flight cages in the home.	
Diet: Seed mixture comprised mainly of mixed millets and some canary seed, plus greenstuff such as chickweed.	
Health problems: Egg-binding can strike hens.	
Breeding tips: Withhold nesting material after hens start laying.	
Nesting needs: Covered wicker nesting basket or open-fronted nest box.	
Typical clutch size:	4–6 eggs
Incubation:	12 days
Rearing requirements: Eggfood and soaked millet sprays recommended.	
Fledging:	Takes place around 21 days old.
Lifespan:	May live for 8 years or more.

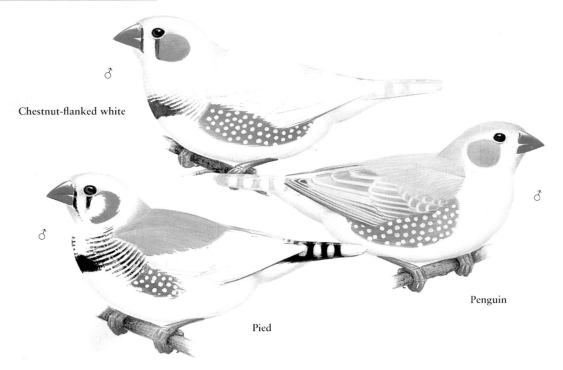

Chestnut-flanked white

♂

♂

♂

Penguin

Pied

small areas of white among their colored plumage, whereas other individuals are predominantly white. Even so, the markings are still usually sufficiently evident for the sexes to be distinguished without difficulty. The pied factor, which is recessive, has been combined with other colors apart from gray, to create pied fawns, for example. When breeding exhibition pieds, there is no guarantee that well-marked adults will produce similar offspring, however.

Black-breasted. The Black-breasted mutation represents the other extreme, where the small area of solid black feathering on the lower breast extends upward to the throat, overlaying the barring here. The tear markings under the eyes, in contrast, are usually much less conspicuous than normal. Zebra Finches which are split for this recessive genetic characteristic can be distinguished by their wider breast bar, compared with normal cocks.

Orange-breasted. This is another variant on this theme which has become quite widely available over recent years. In this variety there is solid orange, rather than black, plumage evident on the breast.

Light-backed. Another of the newer variants is

▲ *These mutations all display an increased area of white plumage compared with the normal gray form, but whereas the coloration of pieds can be very variable, that of the other mutations shown here is fixed.*

the light-backed, in which the head, back, and wings are silver, rather than gray, with the rest of the body plumage being unaffected.

Other Forms. Not all mutations have become popular, however, with the yellow-beaked form now being rare. These birds only differ on the basis of their bill coloration, as their name suggests. This varies from pale yellow through to the more orangish shade associated with cocks.

Crested. Zebra Finches showing this feature should not be paired with each other, but with individuals without crests, because of the possible involvement of a lethal factor.

Care and Conditions

Zebra Finches are lively, active, little birds that will thrive in either a spacious flight cage or an aviary. They are relatively hardy compared with other estrildids, but they must have a well-lit, dry shelter attached to the aviary. It will also be helpful to have an electrical supply here to

▲ *A fawn penguin Zebra Finch. Such changes in the pattern of markings are not uncommon in these finches. They have helped to increase the number of varieties and raise the profile of Zebra Finches at shows.*

provide some extra warmth during prolonged or severe cold spells.

Zebra Finches are more vocal than most other finches, uttering their cheeping calls quite frequently. Although they will not become finger-tame like parrots in the home, they will become quite calm once settled in their surroundings. Pairs will nest readily on a colony basis, although in the case of exhibition stock these birds are usually bred in cages, so the parentage of the offspring can be guaranteed.

These finches are usually shown in matched pairs, comprised of a cock and hen. Odd birds can also be exhibited, although they will not beat a pair of equal quality, simply because it is more difficult to bench a pair in top condi-tion, compared with an individual. The type of the Zebra Finch has been standardized for exhibition purposes, with judging standards also being laid down for the different recognized color varieties.

● **I keep a pair of Zebra Finches indoors as pets. What can I do to stop them from breeding?**

Simply take away their nest box or basket once their chicks have fledged. They will not need this for roosting purposes, and it will cause the hen to stop laying almost immediately. Do not allow Zebra Finches to produce more than two rounds of chicks in succession without a break in any case. Otherwise, hens are likely to suffer from egg-binding, which can be fatal.

● **At what age are Zebra Finches mature?**

Young pairs can be allowed to breed from the age of nine months onward, although they are likely to be mature before this stage. Do not encourage them to breed too soon.

● **My Zebra Finches have carried on building a nest although the hen has already laid. Is this normal?**

Yes, but it is not recommended because the eggs are likely to become buried and chilled as a result. Even if you withhold nesting material, the pair may still carry on using greenstuff for this purpose—which is even worse, because it is likely to turn moldy. As a precaution, therefore, chop up greenfood into small pieces before offering it to the birds.

Grassfinches GENERA: NEOCHMIA, POEPHILA, EMBLEMA

♂

Diamond Sparrow

♂

Bicheno's Finch

♂

Star Finch

ALTHOUGH THEY HAVE NOT ATTAINED THE popularity of the Zebra Finch, grassfinches are relatively straightforward to keep. They can be relied upon to hatch and rear their own chicks without problems, but breeders sometimes use Bengalese as foster-parents, as they do with the Gouldian Finch.

Popular Varieties

This group of finches is relatively well established in aviculture, particularly the species here.
Star Finch (*Neochmia ruficauda*). This species is unmistakable, thanks to its reddish facial coloring, with white spots on the cheeks, extending down across the chest onto the flanks. The wings are greeny-brown, with the underparts being much paler. The tail is reddish-brown, which is why these finches are also called Red-tailed Grassfinches. Hens can be

distinguished by their paler facial coloring. A color variant exists in this species, in which the red facial plumage is replaced by orange.
Bicheno's Finch (*Poephila bichenovii*). Also known as the Owl Finch because of its facial markings, it has a black band encircling the face and throat, which are whitish. There is also a black band across the lower chest, which is otherwise cream. The back is brownish, with white spots on the black wings. The sexes look alike.
Diamond Sparrow (*Emblema guttata*). The top of the head and the wings are brownish-gray, with the cheeks being of a silvery shade. The lower part of the body is white, divided by a black line extending down the sides of the

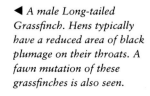

◀ *A male Long-tailed Grassfinch. Hens typically have a reduced area of black plumage on their throats. A fawn mutation of these grassfinches is also seen.*

Fact File

Family name:	Estrildidae
Length: 4–7in (10–18cm); biggest is Long-tailed Grassfinch, with 3in (7.5cm) tail.	
Distribution:	Australia
Color variant availability: Not particularly widespread.	
Compatibility: Long-tailed Grassfinches have a reputation for aggression, particularly when they are nesting. Other species more tolerant.	
Pet potential:	None
Diet: Seed mix comprised of mixed millets and some canary seed, plus greenstuff such as chickweed.	
Health problems: Diamond Sparrows in particular prone to obesity.	
Breeding tips: Birdroom useful for cage-breeding purposes.	
Nesting needs: Covered wicker nesting basket or open-fronted nest box.	
Typical clutch size:	4–6 eggs
Incubation:	12–15 days
Rearing requirements: Eggfood, soaked millet sprays, and greenfood needed.	
Fledging: Will leave the nest at 21–25 days old.	
Lifespan:	Can live for 8 years or more.

◀ *These grassfinches are popular among breeders but are less widely kept and exhibited than their close relative, the Zebra Finch, nor are color variants common. Pairs can be quite prolific, however. They may use a nest box or build their own nest in the aviary.*

Q&A...

● **Why have my Bicheno's Finches produced two chicks with black, not white, feathering on the rump?**

This reflects their origins. There is a subspecies known as the Black-rumped Finch (*P. b. annulosa*), with black plumage on the rump. Cross-breeding in the past between these two forms resulted in chicks that resembled the normal Bicheno's, with the black rump proving to be recessive. When two apparently normal Bicheno's with this characteristic are paired, then black-rumped offspring may appear.

● **How do I sex Long-tailed Grassfinches?**

Look for birds that appear compatible, sitting in close proximity to each other. Also, listen for the cock's rather weak, wheezing song. He often inflates his throat feathers at this stage and subsequently may display by bobbing up and down on the perch to attract the hen.

● **Can I breed Star Finches on a colony system?**

These finches are very social and will usually breed well in such surroundings. Alternatively, single pairs will normally nest readily in spacious flight cages, as well.

● **Could I foster eggs or chicks of grassfinches to a pair of Zebra Finches?**

This can be successful if you need to do so in an emergency, but it is best if the eggs were laid at roughly the same time as those of the Zebra Finches themselves.

body, where whitish spots are apparent. The rump and undertail coverts are red, as is the bare skin encircling the eye. It is almost impossible to distinguish hens by sight, but they may be smaller and less brightly colored than cocks. In the fawn mutation, brown plumage replaces the black areas.

Long-tailed Grassfinch (*Poephila acuticauda*). These grassfinches have relatively long, tapering tail feathers. Brown predominates in their plumage, with a prominent area of black feathering covering the throat and chin. The remainder of the head and neck are bluish-grayish. A prominent black band extends down the sides of the body from the rump, which is otherwise white, and the beak is yellow in the nominate race. The northern Australian subspecies called Heck's Grassfinch (*P. a. hecki*) has a red bill.

Care and Conditions

These grassfinches are generally quite easy birds to keep and breed, particularly since livefood is not essential for the successful rearing of their chicks. Strains are fully domesticated, and it is therefore recommended to start with stock from two separate sources to avoid the risk of any in-breeding at the outset, which could result in poor fertility. While most can be bred in cages, it is better to keep Diamond Sparrows in flights, where they will remain fitter and can usually be relied upon to nest during the warmer months of the year in temperate areas. All these species are relatively hardy, but will benefit from being kept in frost-free accommodation over the winter.

Gouldian Finch

SPECIES: CHLOEBIA GOULDIAE

THESE STUNNINGLY COLORED FINCHES ARE NAMED after the wife of the explorer John Gould and are also known in North America as Lady Gould's Finch. This species is highly unusual, because birds with different head colors live and breed together in flocks within the wild population.

Popular Varieties

Although mutations are now being developed on an increasing scale, few can match the beauty of the wild (normal) form.

Normal. The normal form of the Gouldian Finch has a black band on the throat, narrowing to a stripe around the neck, with a thin, sky-blue area behind. The back and wings are green, the breast is purple, and the underparts are bright canary-yellow. In some individuals the head is entirely black, whereas in others it is bright red. Less commonly seen in wild flocks is the "yellow-headed" form—although this area is actually orange, being a dilute variant of the Red-headed

Gouldian. The sexes are identical in color, but the tip of the cock's bill becomes cherry-red at the start of the breeding period.

Mutations. A number of mutations are now established. They include the white-breasted form in which snow-white plumage replaces the purple coloration of the breast. This feature can be combined with all three head colors. In the lilac-breasted form, the purple coloration is diluted to a paler shade than normal.

There are also several blue forms known, the best-known of which results in blue plumage replacing green, and with the underparts transformed into a variable, creamy-white shade. The breast coloration is also paler than in the normal form, which helps to distinguish such birds from pastels, in which this particular coloration is maintained to its full intensity.

▼ *All three head colors occurring naturally in the Gouldian Finch can be seen here. Genetically, all black-headed variants are dominant to red- or yellow-headed variants, irrespective of the rest of the coloration.*

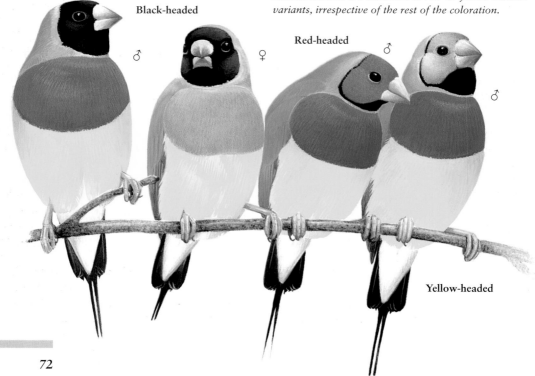

Black-headed ♂ ♀

Red-headed ♂ ♂

Yellow-headed

● *Do I need to foster my Gouldian eggs under Bengalese?*

... This is certainly not essential if your birds will hatch and rear their own offspring. Fostering tends to be used for increasing the likelihood of successful breeding, because by removing the eggs from the Gouldians soon after laying, the hen is likely to lay again soon, effectively doubling her reproductive potential. Another reason for fostering is if your adult birds are suffering from air-sac mites. These parasites are easily passed on in the nest when the young birds are being fed by their parents. By taking the eggs away and hatching them under Bengalese, this cycle of infection is broken.

● *How would I know if my Gouldians were affected with air-sac mites?*

Loss of condition—particularly weight loss—and wheezing are fairly typical signs, with affected birds often perching with their bills slightly open. Treatment is possible using the drug ivermectin, available on veterinary prescription. This needs to be applied in drop form to the skin.

▲ *This cock is one of the newer color variants, a red-headed yellow-backed Gouldian. The yellow-backed characteristic can be combined with any head color.*

Fact File

Family name:	Estrildidae
Length:	5in (13cm)
Distribution:	Northern Australia
Color variant availability:	Now being widely kept.
Compatibility:	Can be kept and bred on a colony system.
Pet potential:	None
Diet: Seed mix comprised mainly of mixed millets, canary seed, and other seeds such as niger and maw. Plus seeding grasses and greenstuff.	
Health problems:	Susceptible to air-sac mites.
Breeding tips: Often prefer to nest during the northern winter, so indoor accommodation needed.	
Nesting needs:	Nest box preferred.
Typical clutch size:	4–6 eggs
Incubation:	16 days
Rearing requirements: Eggfood, soaked millet sprays, and greenfood.	
Fledging: Will leave the nest at about 21 days old.	
Lifespan:	Can live for 8 years or more.

Care and Conditions

These birds are more demanding than most Australian finches, since they require heated indoor accommodation when the temperature falls to 50°F (10°C). Plenty of flying space is also important, thus an indoor aviary is an ideal way to keep them during the winter period, when they may also prefer to nest. Gouldians are frequently bred on a colony system in their homeland, but elsewhere they are more often reared in breeding cages. This method enables the breeding process to be more carefully monitored. Under suitable conditions, they can be quite prolific.

Weaning is a critical period for Gouldians, and it is wise to use a probiotic for at least a fortnight after separating young birds from their parents. This should offset the likelihood of a digestive infection resulting in the condition known as "going light." Never take chicks away until you are certain they are feeding themselves properly, and continue offering them rearing foods, including soaked seed (which is more easily digested than hard seed), to minimize the risk of any losses. A suitable supplement should be offered to young Gouldians when they start molting, since this can also be a debilitating time.

Parrot Finches GENUS: ERYTHRURA

THESE FINCHES ARE SO CALLED BECAUSE OF THE color of their plumage, which is said to resemble that of parrots. Their tail feathers taper toward the tip—a feature especially apparent in the Pin-tailed Parrot Finch.

Popular Varieties

The following three species are the best-known representatives of the group in aviculture.

Pin-tailed Parrot Finch (*Erythrura prasina*). Cocks are distinguished from Blue-faced Parrot Finches by their light cinnamon, rather than green, underparts, and the red plumage in the center of the abdomen. Sexing is also more straightforward, since the heads of hens are green and the underparts dark brownish-gray.

Red-headed Parrot Finch (*Erythrura psittacea*). Red plumage predominates on the head of this New Caledonian species. The remainder of the plumage is mainly green, apart from the rump and undertail coverts which are also red. Some brown feathering is evident over the wings. Hens are duller than cocks. A rare lutino mutation has

▲ *Originating from southeast Asia as well as the islands of Indonesia, the Pin-tailed Parrot Finch is also known as the Pin-tailed Nonpareil. This species resembles the Blue-faced Parrot Finch.*

been recorded in this species, with yellow replacing green feathering and the lores being white rather than black.

Blue-faced Parrot Finch (*Erythrura trichroa*). Dark blue plumage predominates on the head, with the remainder of the plumage being dark green, becoming brownish on the wings—which means these birds can be difficult to spot in a planted aviary. The red coloration of the rump and uppertail coverts helps to explain why it is also known as the Three-colored Parrot Finch. Hens are hard to distinguish, but they may have duller plumage, especially on the head.

Care and Conditions

Some breeders persuade pairs to nest in large, box-type breeding cages, but success is more likely if the birds are housed in a densely planted

♂ ♂

Red-headed
Parrot Finch

Blue-faced
Parrot Finch

◀ *The Blue-faced Parrot Finch is more common in birdkeeping circles than its Red-headed relative. Young birds have much duller coloration than adults but start molting into adult plumage by about five months of age.*

Q&A

● **Which parrot finches are easiest to breed?**

... The Blue-faced has the reputation for being more ready to nest than other species. They also tend to be slightly hardier but, even so, they must not be overwintered in temperate areas without additional heat and light. Other species must be housed indoors over this period.

● **Can I breed parrot finches on a colony basis?**

This is definitely not to be recommended because cocks are aggressive, especially in breeding condition. They can be associated with other finches of similar size, however, and will breed without problems in these surroundings. Once the young are feeding on their own they must be removed from the aviary, however, since cocks are likely to harass their male offspring in particular.

● **At what age can I sex Pin-tailed Parrot Finches?**

It is usually possible to pick out cocks at around six weeks of age by the appearance of odd red feathers on their abdomen, but they will not molt into full adult plumage until they are about six months old.

● **Why is it wrong to offer mealworms when chicks are in the nest?**

This is because its hard, outer covering of chitin means that the mealworm is likely to pass undigested through the chick's digestive system, risking starvation.

flight. As their coloration suggests, they are often to be found in woodland, where their green color enables them to blend in easily against the background. They also show a tendency to nest quite high off the ground, often seeking out a site close to the roof of the aviary. If left to their own devices, parrot finches will construct a fairly bulky nest using a range of materials including leaves, and will line the interior with feathers.

Fruit should be offered, to add variety to their diet. Seeds of dry figs may also be eaten readily if fresh figs are not available. As with most other estrildids, livefood should figure more prominently in their diet when chicks are in the nest, with microcrickets being especially useful at first.

Fact File

Family name:	Estrildidae
Length:	5in (13cm)
Distribution: Southeast Asia, New Guinea, and Indonesian islands to northern Australia. Also found in the Philippines and various Pacific islands.	
Color variant availability:	Very rare
Compatibility: Pairs can be mixed with non-aggressive waxbills.	
Pet potential:	None
Diet: Mixed millets and canary seed, plus seeds such as niger and maw. Seeding grasses, greenstuff, some invertebrates, and fruit also recommended.	

Health problems:	Susceptible to air-sac mites.
Breeding tips: Shy by nature, so a densely planted aviary essential.	
Nesting needs: Nest box needed or may build their own nest.	
Typical clutch size:	4–6 eggs
Incubation:	14 days
Rearing requirements: Eggfood, soaked millet sprays, and greenfood. Pairs may eat more livefood when chicks are in the nest.	
Fledging:	Leave the nest at about 21 days old.
Lifespan:	May live for 7–8 years.

Java Sparrow SPECIES: PADDA ORYZIVORA

ORIGINALLY CONFINED TO JAVA AND BALI, THESE finches have enjoyed a long avicultural history. They have also been introduced successfully to many other parts of southeast Asia and even to east Africa. Their ability to adapt in the wild has led to restrictions on keeping Java Sparrows in some parts of the United States (where they are often better known as Rice Birds).

White

Normal

Popular Varieties

Color forms of this species are now being developed—particularly in some parts of mainland Europe. Those listed below are well established and are widely available to the aviculturist.

Normal. The head is black, apart from extensive white areas on the sides of the face. The rest of the body is grayish, becoming pinkish-gray on the abdomen, with the thighs and undertail coverts being white. The flight feathers, rump, and tail feathers are black. The relatively large bill is pinkish-red. Visual sexing is exceedingly difficult, although the bill of the cock may often appear larger and becomes a deeper shade of red during the breeding period.

White. The origins of the white form appear to be unknown. White birds were reputedly first developed in China hundreds of years ago and have a reputation for being easier to breed than the normal form. There is often no clear-cut delineation between whites and pieds in the case of the Java Sparrow. White individuals often have small areas of gray feathering on their otherwise white bodies. These are typically on the back, but there may be a dark flight feather evident in the wings. Even if they molt out to be

Fact File

Family name:	Estrildidae
Length:	5in (13cm)
Distribution:	Indonesia
Color variant availability:	Increasingly common
Compatibility: Do not mix with smaller waxbills. Weavers of similar size and even Cockatiels are suitable companions.	
Pet potential:	None
Diet: Foreign finch seed mix of assorted millets with a lesser amount of canary seed. Other seeds, including groats and paddy rice, can be offered, plus seeding grasses and greenstuff.	

Health problems: Hens vulnerable to egg-binding.

Breeding tips: Success more likely if kept in a colony.

Nesting needs: Budgerigar-type nest box needed, or may build their own nest.

Typical clutch size:	4–7 eggs
Incubation:	13 days

Rearing requirements: Eggfood, soaked millet sprays, and greenfood. Pairs may also eat livefood at this stage.

Fledging: Young leave the nest when they are about 25 days old.

Lifespan: Can live for 10 years.

◀ *One of the larger mannikins, Java Sparrows are lively, active birds which show to best effect when kept in groups. The normal variety is also known as the gray.*

▶ *Java Sparrows, such as this cinnamon variety, normally have immaculate, glossy feathering. For this reason they are popular subjects for exhibition.*

pure white, young Java Sparrows of this type invariably have gray backs at first, although their bills are pinkish, rather than black, at this stage.

Cinnamon. The other well-established color is the cinnamon, also sometimes described as the fawn. It originated in the aviaries of an Australian breeder in the 1950s. As the name suggests, these birds have cinnamon feathering replacing the gray in their plumage, with brown instead of black coloring on the head and tail. Pied cinnamons are also known and, as with the gray form, the precise markings vary extensively between individuals, with some being predominantly white.

Care and Conditions

Java Sparrows make very attractive occupants for an aviary—thanks to their plumage, which invariably looks sleek and immaculate. They are relatively hardy, although they must have a dry, well-lit shelter forming part of their aviary.

For breeding purposes, most reliable results can be achieved by housing these finches in small flocks. Once they are settled in their quarters, cocks can be distinguished by their song, which will be heard most frequently at the onset of the nesting period. If left to their own devices, Java Sparrows may build a bulky, rounded nest in a suitable shrub or elsewhere in the aviary. Sometimes, especially in a relatively small enclosure, only the dominant pair will build a nest.

Pairs of Java Sparrows (especially the white variety) can also be persuaded to breed in a spacious, box-type cage with an attached nest box. Results from birds kept in these surroundings are not likely to be as good as those obtained from birds kept in a flight, however.

Q & A...

● *If I pair a white Java Sparrow with a gray, what is likely to be the color of their chicks?*

The majority of their chicks will be white—although a number will have areas of gray plumage, and there may even be some gray chicks. Normal rules of genetic inheritance do not apply here. Even if you pair pure whites together over a number of generations, offspring revealing the gray ancestry of these birds will appear occasionally.

● *I have some Java Sparrows with entirely black heads. Is this a new mutation?*

Almost certainly not—this is normally the result of a phenomenon known as acquired melanism and can be the result of the birds' seed mix. Too much hemp in the diet is the most likely cause. If this is withdrawn, the feathering is likely to revert to normal at the next molt.

● *At what stage do Java Sparrows molt out into adult plumage?*

This change usually occurs at about three months of age. Until this stage the white plumage on the sides of the face has a decidedly yellowish tinge, with the remainder of the plumage being gray.

Bengalese Finch SPECIES: LONCHURA DOMESTICA

Chocolate and white

Fawn and white

◀ If you are looking for finches which are easy to care for and can generally be relied on to breed without difficulties, then the Bengalese is an ideal choice.

THE BENGALESE IS UNIQUE, SINCE THESE BIRDS do not occur in the wild. They are thought to be descended from crossings involving the Sharp-tailed Munia (*Lonchura striata*), which is widely distributed across Asia. The Bengalese was almost certainly first developed in China, from where these birds were then introduced to Japan during the 1700s—although it was not until 1860 that they were first seen in the West. These versatile birds are ideal for newcomers to the hobby, as well as for more experienced enthusiasts who want to show their birds.

Popular Varieties

A number of distinctive varieties of this finch are now well known, while a few are more localized, being most often seen in Japan.

The common colors include chocolate, which is considered to be closest to the natural form, as well as fawn and chestnut. Pure-colored individuals of this type, showing no white markings, are described as selfs. The patterning of pied variants, such as the fawn and white, tends to be random. This feature has been standardized to an extent, however, with the result being that

Q&A...

● **Can I pair crested Bengalese Finches together?**

The crested mutation in the Bengalese does not appear to have a lethal factor associated with it so, yes, pairings of this type can be carried out safely.

● **Can you tell me about the pearl mutation?**

This is considered to be one of the most attractive color mutations yet documented in the Bengalese. It was spotted by chance in a Japanese pet store during the 1980s. A silvery tone extends over the head, wings, and tail, which display the luster of a pearl. The chest is also spotted with silver, while the coloration of the body is similar to that of a self chestnut. There can be quite wide variations in the depth of coloration, which is proving hard to stabilize to the desired level. Such is the excitement surrounding this mutation that these Bengalese are commanding very high prices.

● **I have two fawn Bengalese, but they are very different in color. Why is this?**

Different strains of fawns vary quite widely in their depth of coloration, ranging from pale orange to a much deeper rust-red. What was probably natural variation at first has been affected by selective breeding to reproduce this deeper coloration in the plumage.

Fact File

Family name:	Estrildidae
Length:	5in (13cm)
Distribution:	Does not occur in the wild.
Color variant availability:	Widely available

Compatibility: Pairs can be mixed with other finches of similar size or kept as a colony, and may even be housed with Cockatiels.

Pet potential: Pairs will breed in cages in the home, although they will not become very tame in them.

Diet: Seed mixture consisting of assorted millets plus a lesser amount of canary seed. Also offer other seeds such as niger. Greenstuff and seeding grasses also important.

Health problems: Over-breeding these finches can lead to egg-binding.

Breeding tips: Restrict breeding to the summer months in temperate areas.

Nesting needs: Nest box needed, or may build their own nest.

Typical clutch size:	5-8 eggs
Incubation:	14 days

Rearing requirements: Eggfood, soaked millet sprays, and greenfood.

Fledging: Young leave the nest when they are about 22 days old.

Lifespan:	Can live for 7–8 years.

▶ *The close relationship between the Bengalese and other members of the mannikin group is clearest in the so-called self varieties—such as this self fawn—which can be distinguished by their lack of white plumage.*

well-matched pairs of these birds can be bred for exhibition purposes.

A dilute factor that causes the dark areas of plumage to be paler than normal has occurred. It can be combined with both the self and the pied variants. Among other forms, albino Bengalese exist but are rare. They are pure white and have red eyes.

A growing range of feather variants has also been created. There is a well-established crested form, with a flattish circular crest on the head which must not obscure the eyes. Although uncommon in the West, frilled forms of the Bengalese have been bred in Japan. In varieties where the breast feathering is affected, such birds are described as *Chiyoda*. It is possible to combine frilled and crested mutations, creating the *Chiyoda Bonten*. The *Dainagon* is even more unusual—this variety is crested, but with a collar of longer feathers around the neck.

Care and Conditions

Because of their social natures, Bengalese are better known in North America as Society Finches. They are very easy birds to care for, and they will settle well either in aviary surroundings or in a large flight cage in the home. Breeding is quite straightforward, although cocks can only

be distinguished by their song. Once identified in this way, breeders often place a split celluloid ring on one of the legs so that the cocks can be identified at any time in the future.

The reliable nature of Bengalese means that they are often used as foster-parents for rearing the young of other estrildids, particularly Australian finches such as Gouldians. Transferring the eggs from the Gouldians to Bengalese at a similar stage in their breeding cycle is the most reliable method, but pairs will accept young chicks alongside their own if necessary.

Asian and African Munias
GENERA: LONCHURA, AMADINA

THESE ESTRILDIDS ARE KNOWN BY A VARIETY OF different names, including nuns and mannikins, as well as munias. This can lead to confusion, because the names are often interchanged. Furthermore, these birds should not be confused with the manakins found in parts of Central and South America. They are members of a totally separate family and are primarily frugivorous.

Popular Varieties

Color mutations are not established in these finches, but individuals may vary considerably in appearance as a result of regional differences.

Silverbill (*Lonchura malabarica*). These munias have a very wide distribution across Asia into Africa, with two distinctive geographical populations being recognized. The Asian form (*L. m. malabarica*) extends from Muscat and Iran eastward to India and Sri Lanka. It can be distinguished easily from the African Silverbill (*L. m. cantans*) by the presence of white, rather than dark, feathering on the rump and uppertail coverts. The beak of the Asian race is also paler, particularly on the lower bill. The plumage coloration in both cases is similar, however, with the upperparts being a darker shade of brown than the remainder of the body, which is fawn.

Pearl-headed Silverbill (*Lonchura griseicapilla*). A gray head with white speckling on the sides of the face characterizes these African estrildids, which are also sometimes known as Gray-headed Silverbills. The wings are brown, as are the underparts, but the plumage here is redder, becoming paler near the vent. Cocks may have darker gray plumage on their chests.

Nutmeg Finch (*Lonchura punctulata*). Also described as the Spice Finch or Spice Bird, there are 12 recognized subspecies of this munia, whose distribution extends eastward to the Philippine Islands. Variations in plumage and size are seen, but these are not indicative of the individual's gender. The head and wings are brown, with a slightly reddish tone on the head. The underparts are whitish with brown or blackish edging to the individual feathers here.

White-headed Nun (*Lonchura maja*). The whitish head coloration helps to distinguish this species, which is also called the Pale-headed Mannikin. Chestnut coloration is present on the back and the breast, becoming black on the abdomen. The white plumage of the hen is sometimes slightly duller than the cock's, but distinguishing pairs visually is almost impossible.

Tri-colored Nun (*Lonchura malacca*). Also

Fact File

Family name:	Estrildidae
Length:	4–5in (10–13cm)
Distribution: Widely distributed across southeast Asia, including islands here, and Africa.	
Color variant availability:	None
Compatibility: Can be housed with other finches of similar size or kept as breeding colony on their own.	
Pet potential: Although they can be kept indoors they will not become very tame.	
Diet: Typical foreign finch seed mix featuring assorted millets plus a lesser amount of canary seed, as well as other seeds such as niger in small amounts. Greenstuff and seeding grasses also important.	
Health problems: Overgrown claws; these will need clipping back carefully.	
Breeding tips: Keeping more than one pair of these finches together usually gives better results.	
Nesting needs: Nest box needed, or may build their own nest.	
Typical clutch size:	4–6 eggs
Incubation:	12–14 days
Rearing requirements: Eggfood, soaked millet sprays, and greenfood.	
Fledging: Young leave the nest when they are about 21 days old.	
Lifespan:	Can live for 6–8 years.

Silverbill
(Asian)

Nutmeg
Finch

Silverbill
(African)

Tri-colored Nun

Pearl-headed
Silverbill

White-headed Nun

▲ *In general, munias are social birds and should be kept in groups with others of their kind, especially for breeding purposes. This will also help to ensure that you have at least one true pair.*

known as the Chestnut Munia, because of the coloration over the wings. The head and lower underparts are black, with cream-colored plumage on the breast separating these two areas. Visual sexing is not possible, in common with most other Asiatic munias.

Magpie Mannikin (*Lonchura fringilloides*). This is one of the larger species, with a proportionately strong bill. Its head and neck are black, as are the rump and uppertail coverts. The plumage over the mantle is browner, with the wings also being this color. The underparts are whitish, with darker areas evident on the flanks. The sexes are alike in appearance.

Bronze-winged Mannikin (*Lonchura cucullata*). The head of these African mannikins is black, sometimes having a greenish sheen, and the

Q&A...

● **Are munias aggressive?**

In general, mannikins are not aggressive birds, but they can sometimes prove disruptive if introduced to an established group of waxbills, for example, simply because they will want to investigate possible nests, whether or not these are occupied.

● *Are some munias more aggressive than others?*

The African species, particularly the Magpie Mannikin and Cut-throat, have a reputation for being more assertive. This may be partly because they are slightly larger and have more powerful bills than their Asiatic relatives. Silverbills can be disruptive because they often attempt to take over a nest that is already occupied.

● *Do any of these finches have an attractive song?*

No. In fact, they are so quiet that it can sometimes be difficult to detect the song of a cock even if you are standing close to the aviary when he is singing. Even so, by watching their behavior (particularly the cock's display), it should soon be possible to recognize pairs—particularly at the start of the breeding period.

Magpie
Mannikin

Bronze-winged
Mannikin

Cut-throat ♂

♀

▲ *African munias, like their Asian counterparts, can be prone to overgrown claws. These will need to be trimmed back carefully, to prevent young chicks from being accidentally pulled out of the nest.*

underparts are whitish. The flanks show traces of brown barring—which is the dominant color across the wings—sometimes with an obvious grayish hue present here. The uppertail coverts are also barred. There is no visual means of distinguishing the sexes.

Cut-throat (*Amadina fasciata*). The cock Cut-throat or Ribbon Finch is very distinctive, thanks to the bright crimson plumage extending in a broad band from below each eye around the throat. There is individual blackish speckling, particularly on the head which is otherwise whitish. The coloration of the body overall is browner, with less speckling and a darker patch on the abdomen. Hens can be distinguished easily by the lack of red plumage on the throat. In Alexander's or the East African Cut-throat (*A. f. alexanderi*), the plumage is darker overall and the speckling is more pronounced over the body.

Red-headed Finch (*Amadina erythrocephala*). Also known as the Paradise Sparrow, sexing is again straightforward in this species since only the cock displays the characteristic red plumage on the head. The overall plumage is grayish-brown on the wings, with speckling apparent over much of the remainder of the body.

Care and Conditions

Munias may be less brightly colored than some finches, but they will make a handsome sight, especially in a planted flight. Compared with waxbills, they are relatively hardy once acclimatized, but it will be beneficial to have a power supply available. Additional lighting will then provide an extra opportunity for the birds to feed during dark winter days in temperate areas.

Munias are also easier to care for during the breeding season, particularly once the chicks have hatched, since they are far less insectivorous than waxbills. Although they will often eat livefood during this period, they are less reliant on invertebrates as a source of protein and can usually be persuaded to take eggfood without difficulty at this stage. Greenfood, especially seeding grasses, should also feature prominently in their diet at this stage.

Large finch wicker nesting baskets may be chosen as nest sites, although some pairs prefer

▲ *The Red-headed Finch is one of the few munias which can be sexed visually, making it easy to select pairs for breeding purposes. In the photograph above the male is on the right.*

to construct their own nests—particularly if there is a dense stand of bamboo in the aviary, which affords excellent cover. Their nests are bulky and domed, being made from a variety of materials gathered in the aviary and lined with softer items such as feathers. By offering a wide range of possible nesting sites, the likelihood of these munias interfering with other aviary occupants during the breeding period will decrease.

It may take a year following a move before the birds settle sufficiently to start breeding in new surroundings but, once settled, they may rear two or three rounds of chicks in succession. It may be useful to ring the young after fledging, if not before, using numbered celluloid rings for identification purposes. Otherwise, it will be impossible to distinguish them from the adult birds later in the year or determine their parentage easily. Using numbered rings will also help you to keep accurate records in a stock register.

Q&A...

● **What is the best way to house munias for breeding purposes?**

Lively, active birds by nature, these finches will not thrive within the confines of a cage, although silverbills may be persuaded to nest in these surroundings. Breeding results are invariably better when a group of the same species is housed in a well-planted flight. Even so, do not assume that individuals that fail to breed are all of the same sex. Within a group, a distinct flock order evolves, and it is likely to be the dominant pair or pairs that breed, rather than all of the birds.

● **Can I keep several types of munia in the same aviary?**

There is usually little quarreling under these circumstances, but there is a risk—especially if you just have two birds of each species—that they could hybridize with the other pairs if they themselves are not a true pair. Their resulting offspring are unlikely to hold any interest for other breeders and are often infertile.

● **Can any of these estrildids be bred successfully in cages?**

Generally, no, with the possible exception of silverbills and, to a lesser extent, the Cut-throat and Red-headed Finch. Cages tend not to offer them sufficient privacy.

Parasitic Whydahs GENUS: VIDUA

THESE AFRICAN BIRDS ARE SOMETIMES CALLED widow birds, due to the way in which the color of cocks is transformed at the start of the breeding season, with black often becoming prominent in their plumage at this stage. They make fascinating aviary occupants, although successful breeding represents a considerable challenge.

Popular Varieties

Despite their small size, these birds rank among the most long-lived of any finches.

Fischer's Whydah (*Vidua fischeri*). As with other related species, the appearance of the cock is transformed at the onset of the breeding season. The crown of the head becomes a pale creamy-buff, as does the abdomen, with the back, wings, and chest becoming a glossy black color. The tail is transformed by the appearance of four long, straw-like plumes—which is why this species is also known as the Straw-tailed Whydah.

Pin-tailed Whydah (*Vidua macroura*). The top of the head and the area around the bill are black. This color extends down over the wings and onto the chest as well, with the four long, central

◀ *A pair of Fischer's Whydahs in breeding condition. Out of color, the sexes are hard to distinguish, being a drab shade of brown with darker wing markings.*

Fact File

Family name:	Viduinae
Length: 5in (13cm); cocks in color may develop tail feathers up to 10in (25cm) long.	
Distribution:	Africa south of the Sahara.
Color variant availability:	None
Compatibility: Pairs can be mixed with waxbills.	
Pet potential:	None
Diet: A typical foreign finch seed mix, comprised mainly of mixed millets and some canary seed. May also eat other seeds such as niger and maw. Will also eat seeding grasses, greenstuff, and invertebrates.	
Health problems: Scaly leg due to mites can afflict	

these birds, creating a whitish, crusty appearance.

Breeding tips: It is important to choose the correct host species.	
Nesting needs: Cocks should be housed with several hens.	
Typical clutch size:	3–4 eggs
Incubation:	12–14 days
Rearing requirements: Small livefood essential for host waxbills. Eggfood, soaked millet sprays, and greenfood may also be eaten.	
Fledging: Young leave the nest at about 21 days old.	
Lifespan:	May live for 20 years.

Pin-tailed Whydah

Senegal Combassou

▲ *When out of breeding condition, cocks of both the Pin-tailed Whydah and the Senegal Combassou closely resemble the hens.*

tail feathers also being black in color. Hens are predominantly sandy-brown, with areas of black streaking—notably on the head.

Senegal Combassou (*Vidua chalybeata*). At the outset of the breeding period the cock assumes a stunning, steel-blue coloration, with ashen-colored wings and tail. Its blue coloration has led to this whydah also being called the Village Indigo-bird, particularly as it is often seen in the vicinity of human settlement in the wild.

Care and Conditions

A large, planted aviary is recommended for these birds, with a clear area that can be seen easily from a distance serving as a display site for the cock. It is generally better to purchase birds when they are in color because, being polygamous, a cock should be housed in the company of three or four hens. If two cocks are housed together in the same aviary they are likely to fight, especially when in breeding condition.

You must also pair the whydah with a suitable waxbill. This is because whydahs lay their eggs in the nests of waxbills rather than attempting to hatch the eggs themselves—hence the name of parasitic whydahs.

While the Pin-tailed Whydah has been recorded as using the nests of over 19 different species, most success in aviary surroundings has been achieved by housing them in the company of Red-eared Waxbills (see page 60). Fischer's Why-dahs are much more specific in their choice of host. They need to be accommodated with the Purple Grenadier (see page 57), whereas the Senegal Combassou uses the Red-billed Firefinch (see page 60) for this purpose.

Q&A...

● **What do the abbreviations "OOC" and "IFC" mean when describing Pin-tailed Whydahs?**

These letters refer to the cock's plumage. "OOC" stands for "Out of Color," indicating that the cocks are not in their nuptial plumage—which will make it harder to distinguish the sexes. "IFC" means "In Full Color," meaning that cocks can be easily identified, although it is no guarantee of perfect feather condition.

● **Do these whydahs ever rear their own chicks?**

There are no recorded cases in the *Vidua* whydahs, although this has been documented on occasions in the Senegal Combassou and related species.

● **How can I get whydahs to rear their own chicks?**

If you want to try persuading Combassous to breed in this way, provide them with a range of nest sites, including wicker nests, nest boxes, and nesting material such as horse hair and dried grass for constructing their own nests. It is still important to house a cock with several hens, and a plentiful supply of livefood will be essential if the Combassous hatch their own chicks.

Sparrows, Whydahs, and Weavers

GENERA: PASSER, EUPLECTES, PLOCEUS, QUELEA

NONE OF THESE BIRDS IS DIFFICULT TO MAINTAIN, but pairs may be reluctant to nest, so breeding results are not especially common. For those prepared to specialize, however, these birds offer considerable scope.

Popular Varieties

Many weavers display nuptial plumage, with cocks being especially colorful at this time.

Golden Song Sparrow (*Passer luteus*). Cocks are easily recognizable by their canary-yellow head and underparts, with the back and wings being chestnut. Hens are predominantly brownish.

White-winged Whydah (*Euplectes albonotatus*). Black plumage predominates in cocks when breeding. There is a yellow patch on the shoulders, and the distinctive white area is evident

▲ *A cock White-winged Whydah. When in eclipse plumage, cocks can be recognized by the darker streaking on their backs.*

◀ *Golden Song Sparrows often prefer to build their own nests, seeking out seclusion in clumps of gorse or similar spiky plants hung up in the aviary to provide a framework for them.*

Fact File

Family name:	Ploceidae
Length:	5in (13cm)

Distribution: Africa south of the Sahara. Some species also found in southern Asia.

Color variant availability:	None

Compatibility: Only mix with birds of similar size, such as Java Sparrows. Golden Song Sparrows should be housed with waxbills.

Pet potential:	None

Diet: Typical foreign finch seed mix, based mainly on millets with a lesser amount of canary seed. Seeding grasses and greenstuff also eaten readily, along with soaked seed.

Health problems: Hens can be vulnerable to egg-binding, especially if allowed to nest when the weather is cold.

Breeding tips: Some species polygamous, and cocks must be housed with several hens.

Nesting needs: Nesting basket needed in some species, although weavers will build their own nests.

Typical clutch size:	2–5 eggs
Incubation:	12–14 days

Rearing requirements: Eggfood, soaked millet sprays, and greenfood. Livefood is often eaten in increased amounts at this stage.

Fledging: Young will leave the nest at about 15 days old.

Lifespan:	Can live for 7–15 years.

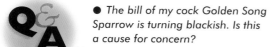

● *The bill of my cock Golden Song Sparrow is turning blackish. Is this a cause for concern?*

No—this is quite usual and is simply a sign that he is coming into breeding condition. The bills of hens remain horn-colored throughout the year.

● *What are the breeding requirements of the White-winged Whydah? Does it lay its eggs in the nest of waxbills?*

No, *Euplectes* whydahs rear their own chicks, but they are polygamous, so a cock must be housed with several hens.

● *Do I need to color feed my Red Bishop to maintain his fiery orange color?*

This is usually recommended, because over the course of several molts this color will fade in intensity. If you do not want to use a commercial coloring agent, see if you can persuade the birds to eat finely grated and chopped carrot. This contains a natural coloring agent. Color feeding is only worthwhile when the cock is coming into color and not when he is going into eclipse plumage.

▶ *A pair of Red Bishops (also known as Orange Bishops) in breeding condition. The cock is the lower bird. Outside the breeding season, hens can be recognized by their more clearly defined markings.*

at the base of the primary feathers on the wings. Out of breeding condition, these birds are mainly brownish buff, paler beneath, with the yellow shoulder patches just visible.

Red Bishop (*Euplectes orix*). The cock of this weaver has fiery orange plumage on the neck, chest, and lower part of the body when in breeding condition. The remainder of the plumage tends to be black, with the wings being brown. Hens look rather like cocks out of color, being predominantly brownish with dark streaking.

Napoleon Weaver (*Euplectes afer*). Also called the Golden Bishop, this bird looks much like the Red Bishop, except yellow replaces orange in the plumage, and the black on the face does not extend above the eyes. Out of color, the yellower coloration of the Napoleon's underparts helps to separate them. The darker coloration on the back of cocks distinguishes them from hens.

Baya Weaver (*Ploceus philippinus*). An Asiatic species, cocks in color have a yellow head and underparts, with the back and wings being blackish-brown. Hens that are out of color have yellowish-white underparts, with streaking on the upperparts, and are paler brown than cocks.

Red-headed Quelea (*Quelea erythrops*). The cock's head is reddish and the wings are streaked, while the underparts are brownish with a red hue on the flanks. Hens have brown heads.

Care and Conditions

The weavers are so called because of their habit of building elaborate nests. They molt into colorful plumage at the start of the breeding period, and must generally be housed in groups comprised of a cock and several hens. Members of this group can be quite destructive in a planted flight if they are not supplied with suitable nesting material for weaving purposes, such as raffia, reeds, sedges, and grasses. Weavers are relatively hardy once acclimatized, although Golden Song Sparrows need frost-free winter housing.

New World Finches

THIS DIVERSE GROUP OF FINCHES ARE NOT especially common in aviculture, but pairs will breed readily and consistently if they are housed under suitable conditions, with their care being straightforward.

Popular Varieties

The following is indicative of the major genera that may be encountered. Species related to those listed will require similar care.

Red-crested Finch (*Coryphospingus cucullatus*). The distinctive crest is carmine-red with black edging, contrasting with the black wings and the deep reddish color of the breast and underparts. Hens are easily distinguished by their predominantly brown coloration and smaller crest.

Ringed Warbling Finch (*Poospiza torquata*). There is a broad black band running through the eyes, with a white stripe above, while the top of

▲ *The male Red-crested Finch will raise his crest to its full height when alert, challenging a rival, or displaying to an intended mate.*

◀ *Ringed Warbling Finches resemble tits in the rather jerky manner in which they move—especially when seeking invertebrates such as spiders in the vegetation.*

Fact File

Family name:	Emberizidae
Length:	4–6in (10–15cm)

Distribution: South America; Cuban Finch occurs only on Cuba.

Color variant availability:	None

Compatibility: Pairs can be kept with other birds of similar size, but signs of aggression may arise during breeding season.

Pet potential:	None

Diet: Seed mixture consisting of assorted millets plus some canary seed. Offer other seeds such as niger as well. Greenstuff and seeding grasses also important, along with livefood. A softbill food can also be beneficial.

Health problems: Overbreeding can lead to egg-binding.

Breeding tips: Seclusion very important for success at this stage.

Nesting needs: Open-fronted nest box or nesting basket needed; some pairs prefer to build their own nest.

Typical clutch size:	5–8 eggs
Incubation:	12–14 days

Rearing requirements: Eggfood, soaked millet sprays, and greenfood. Varied livefood is particularly important at this stage.

Fledging: Young leave the nest at 14–16 days old.

Lifespan:	Can live for 7–8 years.

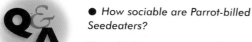

● *How sociable are Parrot-billed Seedeaters?*

... These birds are not especially sociable, and their bills can cause injury. They can even inflict a painful nip if handled carelessly. They should only be housed on the basis of one pair per aviary. It may be possible to mix them with other birds such as mannikins and Diamond Doves, but even so, watch for signs of disagreement—which are most likely during the breeding season.

● *Are Ringed Warbling Finches good songsters?*

No. Rather like the Golden Song Sparrow, their song is very limited. Cocks are most likely to sing at the start of the breeding season, when they will often become less tolerant of the company of others of their own kind.

▲ *The powerful bill of the Parrot-billed Seedeater enables these birds to crack even relatively hard-shelled nuts with little difficulty.*

◄ *A male Saffron Finch. Hens are much duller, with olive-green plumage over the head and streaking extending across the mantle as well as the head.*

the head and back are gray. The underparts are grayish-white, with an area of black across the upper chest. White patches are evident among the black plumage on the wings, while the undertail coverts are reddish-orange. Hens can usually be distinguished by their paler coloration.

Saffron Finch (*Sicalis flaveola*). The top of the head is orangish, becoming yellower on the sides. Olive-green upperparts contrast with the yellow on the chest and abdomen.

Parrot-billed Seedeater (*Sporophila peruviana*). The most obvious feature of these finches is their large beak, with the upper bill being strongly curved like a parrot's. Hens lack the black feathering present on the underparts of the cock.

Cuban Finch (*Tiaris canora*). The head of this species is black, with the mantle being olive-green, becoming brownish-green over the wings and back. Bright yellow plumage extends from just above the eyes, broadening and linking across the chest in a crescent shape. The underparts are olive, becoming grayer near the vent.

The yellow areas of plumage are paler in hens, with their coloration being duller overall.

Care and Conditions
Although these birds differ quite widely in appearance, their care is rather similar in all cases. They can be housed in an outdoor aviary over the summer months in temperate climates, but need to be provided with heat and lighting over the winter.

It is not uncommon for pairs to start nesting in late summer rather than spring, however, so their chicks may fledge quite late in the year, particularly as they tend to be double brooded. Only the Cuban Finch has been consistently bred in box-type breeding cages, although Saffron Finches have also nested successfully in such surroundings. They are fairly undemanding in terms of nesting requirements, adopting a variety of boxes and foreign finch baskets for this purpose, as well as sometimes constructing their own nests in the aviary vegetation.

Mynahs and Starlings

GENERA: GRACULA, ACRIDOTHERES, STURNUS, SPREO, LAMPROTORNIS

THIS LIVELY GROUP OF SOFTBILLS IS EASY TO keep, and pairs will usually breed readily once established in their quarters. They include the only species of soft-bill that is popular as a pet— the Greater Hill Mynah, whose powers of mimicry may even exceed those of parrots.

Spreo Starling

Greater Hill Mynah

Purple Glossy Starling

Popular Varieties

Many starlings, particularly those of African origin, have metallic-sheened plumage, with iridescent hues of purple, green, and blue. Asiatic species generally have more muted coloration, with gray, black, and white colors predominating.

Greater Hill Mynah (*Gracula religiosa*). This species is mainly black, with some irides-cent shades of purple and green visible in bright light, typically from the head down onto the wings. Bare yellow folded patches of skin, known as wattles, extend around the cheeks to the back of the neck. There is a white area of plumage on the flight feathers. Varia-tions in size often occur, depending on the sub-species concerned.

Common Mynah (*Acridotheres tristis*). Some-what similar to the Hill Mynah, but smaller and

▲ *Starlings and mynahs make attractive aviary occupants, with many species having an iridescence to their plumage that can only be appreciated in an outdoor flight when sunlight plays on the plumage.*

Fact File

Family name:	Sturnidae
Length:	8–13in (20–33cm)
Distribution:	Africa and southern Asia.
Color variant availability:	None
Compatibility: Pairs best housed on their own for breeding purposes.	
Pet potential: Hill Mynahs are able mimics if trained from an early age. Other species are far less talented in this respect.	
Diet: Diced fruit, low-iron softbill food, or similar mynah pellets, plus livefood.	

Health problems: Can be vulnerable to gapeworms.	
Breeding tips: Provide plenty of nesting material, such as dried grasses, small twigs, and moss.	
Nesting needs:	Parakeet-type nest box.
Typical clutch size:	2–6 eggs
Incubation:	12–15 days
Rearing requirements: Livefood needed in larger quantities at this stage.	
Fledging: Young leave the nest at around 25–30 days old.	
Lifespan:	May live for 10 years or more.

grayer in color—particularly on the underparts—with more white visible in the wings. The bare area of yellow skin only extends from the sides of the bill to the back of the eyes.

Spreo Starling (*Spreo superbus*). Also known as the Superb Starling, this African species can be distinguished by the chestnut feathering on its underparts, with dark blue, iridescent plumage on the chest and back of the head. The head itself is black, the wings are iridescent green, and the eyes are a very pale shade of yellow.

Purple Glossy Starling (*Lamprotornis purpureus*). The iridescent purple plumage on the underparts contrasts with green plumage on the wings. The tail feathers are short and square, with the eye color being brilliant yellow.

Malabar Mynah (*Sturnus malabaricus*). Characterized by long, narrow, grayish head feathers with white shafts, with the plumage on the back being browner. The throat is whitish, and the underparts are a pinkish-cinnamon shade.

Care and Conditions

None of these starlings can be sexed visually, and so endoscopic or DNA sexing will be necessary to identify pairs with certainty. They do not require a planted aviary, but there should be plenty of perches, since starlings are active birds and will hop readily from branch to branch. All these species are quite hardy once established in their quarters, but they must have adequate protection from the worst of the weather.

Their nest is an untidy structure, and the nest box is stuffed with an assortment of material collected around the aviary. Although omnivorous for much of the year, pairs will become highly insectivorous once their chicks have hatched, and a constant supply of livefood will be necessary during this period to ensure that the young are reared successfully. These must be removed as soon as they are independent, because the adult birds are likely to want to nest again and may attack their previous offspring.

▲ *Chestnut coloring predominates in the tail feathers of the Malabar Mynah, giving rise to the species' alternative name of Chestnut-tailed Starling.*

● **What should I look for when seeking a Hill Mynah as a pet?**

... Start with a genuine youngster of around 8–12 weeks of age, often described as a "gaper." At this stage, young Hill Mynahs are duller in color than adults, lacking the distinctive sheen on their plumage. Their wattles are also much less prominent, not yet having developed into folds of skin.

● **How often should I spray my pet mynah?**

A bath is actually a better option, both to maintain the mynah's plumage in good condition and also to keep its feet clean, which could otherwise become infected. Wash the perches off regularly as well for this reason. A large, heavyweight dogbowl partially filled with tepid water will make an ideal bath.

● **How can I tell if my starlings have gapeworms?**

Symptoms are most apparent in young birds, which breathe rather noisily, with their bills partly open. This is due to the presence of these parasites at the top of the air-pipe (glottis) at the back of the mouth, where they cause an obstruction. Handle the birds very carefully, therefore, to avoid restricting the air supply any further. This condition can be treated by an avian veterinarian.

Blue Magpies GENUS: UROCISSA

THESE MAGNIFICENT MEMBERS OF THE CROW family are not uncommon in aviculture, particularly the red-billed species, and breeding is quite feasible in a large aviary.

Popular Varieties

No color variants have yet been recorded in these species, which are sometimes called blue pies.

Red-billed Blue Magpie (*Urocissa erythrorhyncha*). This species has a prominent black area on the head, with bluish-white feathering extending down over the nape of the neck, merging with dark blue over the back and wings. The lower chest and abdomen are whitish. The long tail feathers, curved at their tips, are bluish above, with black and white markings evident on the shorter feathers in the tail. The bill, legs, and feet are red, with the sexes being alike in appearance.

Yellow-billed Blue Magpie (*Urocissa flavirostris*). The entire head and upper breast in this species are black, apart from a white patch across the nape of the neck. The back and wings are bluish, with white edging to some feathers, while the underparts are yellowish-white. The long tail feathers are blue on their upper surface, and the others are again barred black and white. The bill, legs, and feet are yellowish.

Care and Conditions

These active and lively corvids require spacious surroundings, and a relatively high aviary helps to show their magnificent appearance to best effect. Their calls can be rather raucous, although they are not as noisy as some of the larger parrots. Blue magpies are also capable mimics, and have been taught to whistle on occasions. Although their size and habits preclude them from being kept as pets, a pair may

◀ *A Red-billed Blue Magpie. Both species of blue magpies are intelligent birds and may enjoy having some of the puzzle-type toys made for parrots in their aviary, to help keep them amused.*

Fact File

Family name:	Corvidae
Length:	27in (68.5cm)

Distribution: The Himalayan region of Asia, east to China.

Color variant availability:	None

Compatibility: Keep pairs on their own; predatory and aggressive by nature.

Pet potential:	None

Diet: Omnivorous; diced fruit, softbill food, or mynah pellets, plus livefood such as mealworms, crickets, and waxworms should be offered. Will also eat pinkies.

Health problems: Can be vulnerable to tapeworms acquired from invertebrates that have been eaten.

Breeding tips: Twigs and sticks needed to form the basis for the nest site.

Nesting needs: A suitable platform to provide a secure base for the nest. Sides must be high enough to contain the sticks and twigs used for the nest.

Typical clutch size:	3–6 eggs
Incubation:	17 days

Rearing requirements: Increased amounts of live-food vital.

Fledging: Young leave the nest when they are about 23 days old.

Lifespan:	May live for 15 years or more.

◀ *The stout bill of the Yellow-billed Blue Magpie is designed to cope with a varied diet. They thrive in roomy aviaries.*

become surprisingly tame even in aviary surroundings and will sometimes take food from the hand. Nevertheless, like other members of the crow family, these birds are willful and can also prove aggressive on occasions.

Both species have identical requirements. For breeding purposes, a well-supported platform, preferably one disguised among vegetation, is recommended. This can be made from stout plywood or may even take the form of a very large wicker basket, of the type sold for plants. The magpies will build a fairly loose nest of twigs and similar items here, and incubation usually proceeds without any problems.

The first few days after hatching tend to be critical for the survival of the young, however, and disturbances should be kept to an absolute minimum at this stage due to the risk of the young birds being cannibalized by their parents.

If all goes well, the young blue magpies will grow very quickly. When they first leave the nest, they have distinctly shorter tails than the adults and are duller in coloration. As soon as they are eating independently, transfer them elsewhere because the adult pair may want to nest again.

Q&A

● *How hardy are Red-billed Blue Magpies?*

... They are quite able to winter outdoors in temperate areas without additional heat, although a spacious shelter should be incorporated into their aviary, giving them somewhere to retreat when the weather is bad.

● *One of my Red-billed Blue Magpies caught a mouse in its aviary. Will this harm it?*

Rodents can carry a number of diseases that are harmful to aviary birds, and so contact with rodents should be avoided if possible. There is also the possibility that the mouse may already have been poisoned elsewhere, and it could obviously be dangerous for the bird if it then eats the mouse. Since these corvids are easily able to catch an unwary mouse, the aim should be to eliminate these rodents by means of safe traps.

● *Why is the red-billed species also known as the Occipital Blue Pie?*

This is because of the difference in coloration of the plumage on the top of its head—known technically as the occiput—compared with its yellow-billed relative.

● *Why is it that some blue magpies eat their own young? Is it due to lack of food?*

No, assuming that you have provided sufficient food in the aviary, the most likely cause of this behavior may be boredom. So, rather than providing livefood in a bowl, it may be better to sprinkle this over the aviary floor so that the magpies have to hunt for it here. This should distract the adults sufficiently to prevent cannibalism from occurring.

Touracos and Plantain-eaters

GENERA: TAURACO, MUSOPHAGA, CRINIFER

THESE SOFTBILLS ARE UNUSUAL, IF NOT unique, in a number of ways. Unlike most birds, they are able to alter the position of their feet so that they can either perch with three toes pointing forward and one pointing back, or with two pointing forward and two pointing back. Another feature is the red, copper-based compound present in the flight feathers of touracos. This is not found in any other bird species.

Popular Varieties

There are essentially no color varieties, although a cinnamon form of the White-cheeked Touraco, with a decidedly brownish hue to its plumage, has been recorded. Sexes look alike in all the species described here.

▲ *A White-cheeked Touraco. It is important to keep a close watch on pairs at the beginning of the breeding period, in case cocks start to harass their mates.*

White-cheeked Touraco (*Tauraco leucotis*). Originating from northeast Africa, this species has areas of white plumage on both the hind cheeks and also in front of the eyes. The head crest is dark blue, and the remainder of the body plumage is predominantly dark green in color.

Violaceous Touraco (*Musophaga violacea*). Bluish-black colors predominate in the plumage, with the upperparts being a more glossy shade of violet-blue. The top of the head is reddish.

Gray Plantain-eater (*Crinifer piscator*). Also known as the Gray Go-away Bird on account of the sound of its calls, this west African species is predominantly grayish, with the head and neck being brown. The nape feathers are edged with white, and the underparts are also quite pale.

Care and Conditions

Touracos benefit from being kept in a planted aviary, but they are quite likely to be destructive

◀ *For all types of touracos, make sure that plenty of perching sites are provided in a well-planted aviary. This is a Violaceous Touraco.*

toward growing vegetation—frequently nibbling off buds and shoots in particular. The perches should be arranged so that these lively birds can run along them. It is possible to accommodate touracos satisfactorily with non-aggressive softbills of similar size—fruit pigeons and doves are suitable companions, for example, particularly since their feeding requirements are similar. Although relatively hardy, touracos must have access to a frost-free shelter where they can be confined when the temperature is likely to fall below freezing, because they are very vulnerable to frostbite.

Seasonal produce can be offered in their diet, with some items, such as peas or spinach, being quite easily grown at home if you have a yard.

At the outset of the breeding period, cocks can become very aggressive toward their intended mates, and cover in the aviary at this stage will allow the hen to escape from what can otherwise become almost continuous harassment by her intended partner. A choice of feeding stations in the aviary is also recommended for the same reason. The level of aggression differs among individual pairs, and also from one year to the next. Usually it soon passes, and once egg-laying has commenced, things should then progress smoothly. Remove the young from the aviary once they are feeding on their own, because touracos may lay again soon afterward.

The body plumage of these birds is soft and easily shed, so they need to be handled with particular care to avoid feather loss.

Q&A

● *Do plantain-eaters really need this particular fruit?*

... No, it's certainly not essential to their diet, nor are bananas—which are more widely available. In fact, as with other members of the touraco family, greenstuff should figure more prominently in their diet than fruit.

● *I'm worried because my touracos are only eating greenstuff and fruit. Surely this is not enough to keep them in good condition?*

As you have discovered, touracos and plantain-eaters do not like loose softbill food—possibly because it is difficult for them to eat these small pieces with their large bills. To ensure that your touracos are receiving a more balanced diet with adequate protein, offer them low-iron softbill pellets.

● *What is the best way to provide softbill pellets?*

Texture seems to be important in the feeding habits of these birds, and so it will be better to soak the pellets in a clean bowl, just covering them with cold water. Leave the pellets to stand for about ten minutes, by which time they will have swollen up and softened, appearing more like berries to the birds.

● *Are touracos susceptible to iron storage disease?*

This can be a potential problem with this group of birds, and it is definitely advisable only to provide them with a low-iron softbill food or, better still, equivalent softbill pellets. Do not offer them large quantities of dried fruits, such as raisins and sultanas, because these can add to the birds' iron intake. Nevertheless, small amounts of such fruits, soaked and rinsed beforehand, will increase their calorific intake in cold weather.

Fact File

Family name:	Musophagidae
Length:	16–19in (41–48cm)
Distribution:	Widely distributed across Africa.
Color variant availability:	Virtually unknown
Compatibility: Pairs are best housed on their own for breeding purposes.	
Pet potential:	None
Diet: Chopped greenstuff such as red lettuce, cress, chickweed, dandelion, and similar items. Diced fruit plus a low-iron softbill food and similar mynah pellets also needed.	
Health problems:	Susceptible to frostbite.

Breeding tips: Secluded breeding site among vegetation is preferred.

Nesting needs: Platform-type nesting site should be provided, along with suitable nesting material such as twigs.

Typical clutch size:	2–3 eggs
Incubation:	21–25 days

Rearing requirements: May eat eggfood. Often disinterested in livefood, but it should be offered as an option.

Fledging: Young will leave the nest at around 28 days old.

Lifespan:	May live for 15 years or more.

Sugarbirds and Tanagers

GENERA: CYANERPES, TANGARA, THRAUPIS

THE SOFTBILLS FEATURED HERE ARE ALL POPULAR and are often kept as part of a mixed collection. The larger species, such as Mountain Tanagers, need to be housed with companions of similar size, because they will bully smaller birds.

◄ *A pair of Purple Sugarbirds—the hen is the lower bird. Sugarbirds, also known as honeycreepers, are less hardy than tanagers, partly due to their smaller size.*

Popular Varieties

The following are among the most widely kept species. No mutations are currently known.

Purple Sugarbird (*Cyanerpes caeruleus*). Cocks display stunning purple coloration all year, with a black stripe reaching the eyes and a bib under the throat. The wings and tail are black, and the legs yellow. Hens are greenish, streaked on the underparts, with a blue stripe behind the bill.

Red-legged Sugarbird (*Cyanerpes cyaneus*). Cocks in breeding color resemble the Purple Sugarbird, but have red legs and lack a black bib under the throat. They also have a brighter blue area on their head. Cocks in eclipse plumage resemble hens, which lack the yellowish facial color seen in the Purple Sugarbird.

Paradise Tanager (*Tangara chilensis*). A green head, blue coloration under the throat, and bluish-green underparts are characteristic of this species. The upper back and wings are black, with the lower back and rump being bright red.

Black-eared Golden Tanager (*Tangara arthus*). This species is recognizable by black feathers

Fact File

Family name:	Thraupidae
Length:	16–19in (41–48cm)
Distribution: Widely distributed in Central and South America.	
Color variant availability:	Unknown
Compatibility: Pairs can be mixed with other softbills of similar size, but individuals may become aggressive at the start of the breeding season.	
Pet potential:	None
Diet: Sugarbirds need nectar as a major part of their diet, plus fruit like papaya, and a low-iron softbill food. Nectar less important for tanagers. Berries are eaten readily, as are soaked, low-iron mynah pellets.	
Health problems: Can be susceptible to iron storage disease.	
Breeding tips: Seclusion is essential; planted flight required.	
Nesting needs: Moss, horse hair, even spiders' webs are incorporated to form cup-shaped nest in vegetation.	
Typical clutch size:	2 eggs
Incubation:	12–14 days
Rearing requirements: Plenty of small livefood essential. Eggfood can also be offered.	
Fledging:	Leave the nest at around 14 days old.
Lifespan:	May live for 8 years or more.

forming the ear coverts, with black edging on the wings, and orangish-yellow plumage elsewhere.
Bay-headed Tanager (*Tangara gyrola*). Green plumage, with bluish suffusion on the underparts combined with pale brown feathering on the head, help to characterize these tanagers.
Palm Tanager (*Thraupis palmarum*). Plumage is mainly bluish-green, appearing bluer in some lights than in others. The underparts are grayer.

Care and Conditions

Planning wintertime care for these birds is important, although they can be allowed into a sheltered, outside flight during the summer months in temperate areas. The Palm Tanagers are likely to be the most hardy of the species featured here, but even they cannot be expected to overwinter without heat.

One of the greatest difficulties when breeding tanagers is being sure you have a true pair. Unless you can obtain a proven pair, you will probably need to acquire several of these birds in the hope of having at least one true pair. This can actually prove to be the best solution in the longer term, because it ensures that you have the basis for a breeding colony. It is advisable to allow a pair to nest on their own, however, to avoid possible conflict with other members of the group.

▲ *Sexing tanagers, such as this Black-eared Golden Tanager, is usually very difficult, although the cock will sing with increasing vigor as the time for breeding approaches. Their song is quite appealing.*

● **I just bought a Bay-headed Tanager, but it looks quite different from the one I already have. Does this help sex them?**

Unfortunately not. While some tanagers have a relatively small natural distribution, the Bay-headed is widely distributed from Central America down into South America. As a result, there are nine distinctive races, all of which vary with regard to their plumage.

● **Do tanagers need nectar?**

Unlike sugarbirds, nectar is not an essential part of their diet. However, if supplied, it must be given in a tubular drinker. Otherwise, the birds may try to bathe in it and end up with very sticky feathers. All these birds are avid bathers and should be provided with a container of fresh water for this purpose every day, to maintain their plumage in top condition.

● **How should I offer fruit to these birds?**

This depends on the species concerned. It must be chopped into very small pieces for sugarbirds, but tanagers can use their bills to nibble out chunks of fruit without any difficulty.

Laughing Thrushes

GENUS: GARRULAX

ALTHOUGH THE LAUGHING, OR JAY, THRUSHES do not rank among the more colorful softbills, their care is straightforward, and if you are looking for friendly, hardy birds with an attractive song, then these are an ideal choice.

Popular Varieties

There is plenty of scope for specialization within the group, with three of the most widely kept species being described here.

White-crested Laughing Thrush (*Garrulax leucolophus*). The head and upper breast are white, with the feathers on the head forming a distinctive crest. On each side of the face a broad, black stripe extends from the bill to behind the eyes. The remainder of the plumage is brown, being of a more reddish tone where it meets the white feathering. Hens can sometimes be recognized by their smaller, grayer crests. Other differences in appearance are the result of subspecific variation, with this widely distributed member of the family ranging from India to Indonesia.

Red-tailed Laughing Thrush (*Garrulax milnei*). This colorful species has crimson-red wings and tail feathers, with orangish-brown coloration prominent on the head. There is a blackish area under the throat, also extending to the eyes, with the tail coverts being silvery-gray.

▲ *Like other laughing thrushes, White-crested Laughing Thrushes are bold birds that are easily tamed to take livefood from the hand in the aviary.*

Hoami (*Garrulax canorus*). This species is predominantly brown (paler on the underparts), with a band of whitish feathering extending in a stripe beyond the eyes. The singing ability of this species has led to it also being called the Chinese Nightingale and Melodious Jay Thrush. The sexes are identical, as in most laughing thrushes.

Fact File

Family name:	Timaliidae
Length:	9–12in (23–30cm)
Distribution: Widely distributed across Asia, extending east to China and south to Indonesia.	
Color variant availability:	None
Compatibility: Fairly aggressive, especially toward smaller birds and even their own kind.	
Pet potential:	None
Diet: Omnivorous diet of diced fruit, berries, invertebrates, plus mynah pellets or softbill food suits them well. Will also eat pinkies and even some greenstuff and seed.	

Health problems:	May suffer from gapeworms.
Breeding tips: A well-planted flight is necessary.	
Nesting needs: Require a variety of materials, including small twigs, moss, and coconut fibers, to build cup-shaped nest in the fork of a tree or bush.	
Typical clutch size:	4 eggs
Incubation:	13–14 days
Rearing requirements: Livefood must be offered in increased amounts. Eggfood may also be eaten.	
Fledging: Young will leave the nest when about 21 days old.	
Lifespan:	May live for 10 years or more.

Care and Conditions

A small group of these birds housed together can make a very attractive display and can bring out the playful side of their natures, but you will need to watch for any serious signs of bullying toward the weakest member of the group.

Pairs are definitely best housed on their own for breeding purposes, and even then the cock may prove aggressive toward his intended mate, particularly during the courtship period before eggs are laid. One of the best ways to recognize birds that have paired is to note how they behave at night; couples roosting next to each other are usually true pairs. It may be worthwhile offering them a container of damp mud at this stage, since pairs will sometimes plaster their nest, helping to bind the material here together. The interior is usually lined with softer materials, to create a bed on which the eggs are laid.

Laughing thrushes have a less appealing side to their nature as nest-robbers. They may even eat their own young on occasions—particularly if faced with a shortage of livefood. It may help to distract them from their own chicks if they have to search for the livefood on the floor of the aviary, however, rather than having it provided in a convenient container.

Q&A

● **Where do these birds get their name from?**

... The term "laughing" comes from the sound of the loud calls of many species. Their alternative name of jay thrushes derives from their resemblance to jays in terms of shape, movement, general demeanor, and habitat preference.

● **Can the Hoami mimic the calls of other species?**

Yes, it has been known to copy song passages from other birds housed in close proximity, particularly if a cock is being housed on his own. Hoamis have a wide vocal range and tend to sing mostly in the morning and evening, particularly during the breeding season. They are certainly the most talented songsters of the 43 species comprising the genus *Garrulax*.

● **Is it true that these birds will eat sunflower seeds?**

Some laughing thrushes eat these seeds in small quantities. They have an unusual way of eating them, since they cannot crack them in their bills to extract the kernel in the way that a parrot does. Instead, the bird holds the seed against a perch with its foot, and then breaks the casing open by repeatedly pecking at it.

▼ *The Red-tailed Laughing Thrush is one of the more colorful members of its group. The bird's lively and active nature makes it an interesting aviary occupant.*

Babblers   GENERA: LEIOTHRIX, YUHINA

BABBLERS ARE A LARGE FAMILY COMPRISED of about 280 species, differing widely in size and appearance. Many are relatively hardy when they have become acclimatized, and their care is usually fairly straightforward.

Popular Varieties

A number of babblers are well known in bird-keeping circles—especially those which are of Asiatic origin, like the ones described here.

Pekin Robin (*Leiothrix lutea*). The head, back, and wings are grayish-green, with the area around the eyes being white, while the sides of the head are of a more silvery tone. The bill has a red tip. The breast is yellowish-orange, becoming significantly darker on the underparts. The flight feathers are very colorful, displaying reddish and yellow markings. It is not possible to distinguish pairs reliably by differences in the coloration of their plumage.

Silver-eared Mesia (*Leiothrix argentauris*). Black

▲ *The Pekin Robin can be recommended as a good choice for those new to the hobby of keeping softbills, being very straightforward in its requirements.*

● **Are Pekin Robins talented songsters?**

... Yes; for this reason they are sometimes called the Pekin Nightingale. The bird is not a true robin, nor is it confined only to China, as its name might suggest.

● **What causes the variations in color seen in Pekin Robins?**

These particular babblers occur over a wide area of mainland Asia, extending from India eastward to China. This helps to account for the divergence in coloration that may be seen in their plumage. Although it is often said that hens have a grayer tinge to the white feathering in front of the eyes, this is not an entirely reliable means of distinguishing the sexes.

● **Do yuhinas need nectar?**

A nectar solution should be given as part of their daily diet. They use their narrow bills to probe flowers to obtain nectar, and it is for this reason that members of this group are also sometimes called flowerpeckers.

● **Is it possible to keep these three species together?**

This will not normally cause any problems, with Silver-eared Mesias mixing well with their close relatives, as well as with yuhinas. The only problem may occur during the breeding season, since Pekin Robins are known to steal eggs from other birds' nests.

▲ *The Silver-eared Mesia is a close relative of the Pekin Robin. However, it may not prove to be quite as hardy when acclimatized.*

Fact File

Family name:	Timaliidae
Length:	4–6in (10–15cm)
Distribution: Extensive distribution across Asia, extending into China.	
Color variant availability:	None
Compatibility: Often included in mixed collections of non-aggressive birds, although Pekin Robins have a reputation as egg thieves.	
Pet potential:	None
Diet: Mixture of diced fruit, berries, softbill food, soaked pellets, and livefood. Pekin Robins will sometimes eat seed in small amounts.	
Health problems:	Vulnerable to the cold.

Breeding tips: Provide conifers and similar plants in the flight to give nesting cover, because these birds require secluded surroundings for breeding.

Nesting needs: Open-sided nest box, along with a range of nesting material, such as moss, horse hair, and coconut fibers.

Typical clutch size:	3–4 eggs
Incubation:	13–14 days

Rearing requirements: Livefood needed in greater quantities; eggfood may also be eaten.

Fledging: Young leave the nest when they are about 14 days old.

Lifespan:	May live for 7 years or more.

◀ *The narrow bill of yuhinas, such as the Black-chinned Yuhina shown here, reveal that nectar and insects should feature prominently in their diets.*

Care and Conditions

Even though they may sometimes be in poor feather condition when first obtained, the plumage of these birds will improve quite rapidly—particularly if given the opportunity to bathe on a daily basis. The Pekin Robin is easy to feed, although yuhinas have more specialized needs, requiring nectar and a higher proportion of livefood in their diet. Microcrickets are ideal as a source of livefood, while in a planted aviary the birds will forage for themselves, seeking out invertebrates such as small spiders and aphids.

Once they are fully established in their quarters, all these birds are quite hardy, although they should be housed in frost-free accommodation. A flight that forms part of a birdroom is ideal for this purpose. The birds can be kept in here when the weather is at its coldest, without having to catch and then transfer them to separate accommodation for the winter. As a result, they will not need to settle back in their quarters during the following spring, and this increases the chances of successful breeding. It is not unusual for pairs to rear two rounds of chicks in aviary surroundings during the warmer months of the year. Breeding is particularly likely if there are dense conifers or stands of bamboo to provide the birds with cover for their nests at this stage.

plumage covers the head, apart from the silver feathering forming the ear coverts. The breast feathering is orangish-yellow, with a band of this color also encircling the neck. The remainder of the body and wings is predominantly gray, apart from the chestnut coloration visible on the flight feathers and the red plumage of the rump. Again, the sexes are alike.

Black-chinned Yuhina (*Yuhina nigrimentum*). A black crest, black areas between the eyes and the bill, gray upperparts, and whiter underparts distinguish these small birds. The crest feathers are raised when the bird is alert, but they are folded flat when it is resting.

Bulbuls

GENERA: SPIZIXOS, PYCNONOTUS

IT IS THE ASIATIC SPECIES OF BULBUL THAT ARE well known in aviculture, with those originating from Africa being rare—although their care is similar. Members of this family are, in general, easy to cater to, and can be recommended for those with no previous experience of keeping softbills.

Popular Varieties

Bulbuls are not noted for their coloration, but in a number of species their rather dainty appearance is enhanced by the presence of crests. The sexes are alike in coloration.

Collared Finchbill (*Spizixos semitorques*). This species is predominantly olive-green, with a black head and white streaking on the sides of the face, and a white band dividing the black and olive areas on the throat. There is a gray area on the nape of the neck.

Red-whiskered Bulbul (*Pycnonotus jocosus*). A black vertical crest, with red patches beneath the eyes linked with white areas of plumage here,

◀ *The Collared Finchbill has a shorter, stockier bill than most bulbuls, and it may sometimes eat a little seed in addition to a typical softbill diet.*

Fact File

Family name:	Pycnonotidae
Length:	4–6in (10–15cm)
Distribution: Representatives of the family occur in Africa and Asia.	
Color variant availability:	None
Compatibility: Ideal for a mixed collection in the company of non-aggressive softbills of similar size. Can also live in groups.	
Pet potential:	None
Diet: Mixture of diced fruit and berries, sprinkled with a low-iron softbill food, is recommended. Livefood and soaked mynah pellets should also be provided.	
Health problems:	Vulnerable to gapeworms.

Breeding tips: A well-planted flight gives the best hope of success.

Nesting needs: Offer an open-sided nest box, although a pair may prefer to build their own nest in vegetation. Provide suitable nesting materials, such as moss, horse hair, and coconut fibers.

Typical clutch size:	2–5 eggs
Incubation:	13 days

Rearing requirements: Small invertebrates should be offered in greater quantities, while eggfood may also be eaten.

Fledging: Young leave the nest when they are about 13 days old.

Lifespan:	May live for 8 years or more.

● *Do bulbuls have an attractive song?*

... Although their name actually comes from the Turkish word for nightingale, bulbuls are not especially talented songsters compared with other softbills, such as the Hoami.

● *The feathering on one of the bulbuls I have bought is in poor condition. Is this a sign of old age?*

This is unlikely, and is more often a reflection of how the bird was kept previously. The feathering of bulbuls is generally quite soft compared with other birds and can be damaged easily by careless handling. Lack of bathing facilities will worsen the situation. In most cases, with good care, the feathering will soon regrow—particularly once the bird is transferred to an outside aviary when the weather is warmer. Although estimating the age of these birds is difficult, heavily scaled legs are often an indicator of advancing years.

● *Is it possible to tame bulbuls?*

Yes, once these birds are established in their quarters, they can become quite confiding in an aviary, particularly if you offer them livefood, such as mealworms, on a regular basis. Bulbuls are certainly not shy birds that skulk away into the vegetation when you approach the flight.

Red-vented
Bulbul

Red-whiskered
Bulbul

▲ *Muted colors typify most bulbuls, with the appeal of these birds stemming more from their bold and amusing personalities. Some, such as the Red-whiskered Bulbul, can be quarrelsome, however.*

help distinguish these bulbuls. The underparts are whitish, apart from the undertail coverts, which are red. The wings and back are brown. They are also known as Red-eared Bulbuls.

Red-vented Bulbul (*Pycnonotus cafer*). Much darker in color, but retaining red plumage on the undertail coverts, these crested bulbuls have brown ear patches, with the remainder of the head and chest being blackish. The plumage on the lower breast and abdomen is scalloped, with whitish edges to the individual feathers here, and a paler area in front of the vent. The tips of the tail feathers are white.

Care and Conditions

The best way of obtaining a true pair of bulbuls is to select a small group and allow them to pair up. Cocks can be recognized at the start of the breeding season not only by their song but also by their display—the red markings under the tail

being used at this stage, with the tail feathers themselves being held open. A hen will respond by lowering her crest and wings. Bulbuls will usually nest quite readily in a planted flight, building a cup-shaped nest in these surroundings. A pair will usually choose a bush for this purpose, so that the nest can be well concealed. It will be made from material gathered around the aviary and usually lined with feathers.

They are not destructive birds, although they may pluck some leaves to form a nest lining at this stage. If you offer an open-sided nest box, then it is important also to position this in a secluded part of the flight. Bulbuls can be mixed with a variety of other birds, including both softbills and finches of similar size. They will be quite hardy once established in their aviary, although they must have adequate protection from the elements, in the form of access to a well-lit shelter or birdroom.

Aracaris and Toucans

GENERA: PTEROGLOSSUS, RAMPHASTOS

Banded Aracari

Toco Toucan

▲ ▶ *Aracaris can be distinguished from most toucans by their narrower, less colorful bills. They are also more inclined to live in groups without fighting.*

WITH THEIR LARGE, OFTEN COLORFUL BILLS and relatively short tails, these birds are unmistakable in appearance. Breeding successes have become far more common over recent years, thanks in part to a much clearer understanding of the dietary needs of aracaris and toucans.

Popular Varieties

These active, lively birds need to be housed in spacious flights rather than cages. Toucans can utter loud, harsh calls, but those of aracaris are less disturbing.

Banded Aracari (*Pteroglossus torquatus*). This species shows the typical patterning seen in most aracaris. The color of the head, throat, wings, and tail plumage is dark—usually green and black—with a browner area around the nape. The underparts are yellowish, with a dark band in the vicinity of the lower chest, edged with red. A marking of similar color, shaped rather like a triangle, is present in the center of the chest. There is also red on the rump. The bare patch of skin encircling the eye is mainly bluish. Although there is some individual variation, the sides of the upper bill tend to be fairly pale, with a dark

area running along the top, while the lower bill is black. The edges of the upper bill are clearly serrated. The sexes look identical.

Toco Toucan (*Ramphastos toco*). Undoubtedly the most recognizable of all toucans, with a predominantly glossy black body, a white region covering the throat and chest, and crimson-red plumage under the tail. The area around the eyes is yellow, with a circle of deep blue skin highlighting the eyes. The broad bill is an orangish-yellow color, with black at the base, particularly on the lower bill and also at the tip of the upper bill. Visual sexing is very difficult, but it is often said that the bills of cocks are broader, and they may also be slightly larger overall.

Care and Conditions

The feeding habits of aracaris and toucans involve holding food items that cannot be swallowed whole against a branch with one of their feet and then tearing off pieces of suitable size. These are then grasped at the end of the bill and tossed up into the air, being caught and swallowed in virtually one movement. As far as food preparation is concerned, therefore, while these

● **How social are aracaris?**

Studies suggest that they may live in family groups, with related birds assisting the breeding pair in the rearing of their chicks. Although they can be housed in groups in a large aviary, it may be better to keep pairs in adjoining flights. This can provide a social stimulus while lessening the possibility of fighting.

● **What is the best way to handle these birds?**

The first step, as always, is to restrain the wings with the palm of your hand. Next, place the first two fingers of your hand on either side of the neck, to steady the head. Toucans can jab with their bills, so do not place your face within range when you are trying to restrain one of these birds. They may also try to bite your finger—again, a painful experience.

● **Why do these birds have such large bills?**

It seems likely that the long bill enables these birds to reach fruits or other food items that would otherwise be out of reach in their tree-top homes. The bill is only suitable for taking hold of objects, however. Toucans are not able to gnaw food with their bills.

birds can swallow grapes and cherries whole, it is advisable to dice up large fruits, such as apple, into smaller pieces, since this should ensure the perches stay cleaner.

Once established in their quarters these birds are relatively hardy. Their plumage is quite thin, however, so they must have a heated shelter to give them protection from the elements. Toucans must be kept in individual pairs. Even then, aggression toward the female by her intended partner is not uncommon prior to egg-laying. It may be necessary to separate them for a time to ensure the hen's safety. The bills of chicks are small at first, and the young develop relatively slowly compared with many other softbills.

▶ *The large entrance hole to the nest box can be seen behind this Toco Toucan. A deep nest box or suitable hollow log should be provided both for roosting and for breeding purposes.*

Fact File

Family name:	Ramphastidae
Length:	16–22in (41–56cm)
Distribution: The family occurs in Central and South America.	
Color variant availability:	None
Compatibility: Toucans must be housed in individual pairs on their own. Aracaris may also live harmoniously in larger groups in a spacious aviary.	
Pet potential:	None
Diet: Mixture of diced fruit and berries, sprinkled with a low-iron softbill food. Livefood is also necessary, along with low-iron mynah pellets. Will also eat pinkies.	

Health problems: Very vulnerable to iron storage disease.

Breeding tips: Ensure cock does not attack the hen at the start of the breeding period.

Nesting needs: Parakeet-type nest box or adapted hollow log should be provided, lined with a thick layer of wood shavings.

Typical clutch size:	2–4 eggs
Incubation:	16–19 days

Rearing requirements: Pinkies (for larger species); also provide invertebrates in greater quantities.

Fledging: Takes place at around 40–60 days old.

Lifespan: May live for 12 years or more.

Barbets   GENERA: PSILOPOGON, LYBIUS, MEGALAIMA

LIVELY AND ACTIVE, THESE SOFTBILLS RESEMBLE small toucans, although their beaks are neither as long nor as colorful. But beware—they may use their beaks against other birds or owners!

Popular Varieties

Although there may be slight variances in plumage coloration between individuals, no color mutations have yet been recorded in this group of softbills.

Fire-tufted Barbet (*Psilopogon pyrolophus*). An attractive species, these Asiatic barbets are mainly green, being slightly darker on the back and wings. Black feathering is evident on the head, with a grayish area on the face, and there is a yellow band on the upper chest, edged with a black band below. The sexes look similar.

Bearded Barbet (*Lybius dubius*). Glossy black plumage covers the head and back of this African species, with a black band also dividing the chest and abdomen. The underparts are reddish, with the thighs being black. The flanks are pale yellowish-white, and a series of tiny black dots here is indicative of a hen bird.

Great Barbet (*Megalaima virens*). Sometimes called the Giant Barbet, this is the largest of the barbets. It has a bluish-green head, with brown coloration on the top of the wings—which are otherwise green. The upper chest is also a shade of bluish-green. The streaked underparts are yellowish-green, and the undertail coverts are bright red. The sexes look similar, although the cock may sometimes be slightly larger.

◄ *A Fire-tufted Barbet. The fine, hair-like structures visible around the base of the bill are a characteristic feature of this group of birds. Provide a nest box for roosting purposes.*

Fact File

Family name:	Capitonidae
Length:	9–12in (23–30cm)
Distribution: Africa and Asia. Other species also occur in the New World.	
Color variant availability:	None
Compatibility: Barbets can be aggressive and need to be housed in pairs on their own.	
Pet potential:	None
Diet: A mixture of diced fruit, berries, and low-iron mynah pellets or softfood. Livefood necessary and may also eat pinkies.	
Health problems: Vulnerable to iron storage disease.	

Breeding tips: Avoid the cock attacking the hen at the beginning of the breeding period. Two separate feeding sites may help prevent bullying.

Nesting needs: Parakeet-type nest box or adapted hollow log should be provided, lined with a thick layer of wood shavings.

Typical clutch size:	2–4 eggs
Incubation:	16–19 days
Rearing requirements: Invertebrates should be provided in greater quantities.	
Fledging:	Takes place around 40–60 days old.
Lifespan:	May live for 12 years or more.

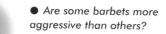

● *Are some barbets more aggressive than others?*

... This seems to be the case, with the Great Barbet being particularly pugnacious, both toward other birds and its own kind. Others may be more tolerant—at least outside the breeding period. Never be tempted to place a single barbet in a flight and then add another later, since this will almost certainly lead to fighting.

● *Are barbets noisy?*

Barbets generally have louder calls than many softbills, but these are usually only uttered when the birds are excited or alarmed—perhaps by the presence of a cat nearby.

● *I've just acquired a pair of Bearded Barbets, and they are not in the best of feather condition. Any suggestions?*

Their plumage is naturally quite soft, like that of toucans, and can easily be disturbed by handling. It may be that your birds have been unable to bathe regularly, particularly if they have been housed indoors. Provide a large, heavyweight dogbowl of tepid water for this purpose. Many barbets will bathe daily if they can, and this helps to maintain a good gloss on their feathering.

▲ *The Bearded Barbet gets its name because of the feathering under the bill. Note the dark spots on the flank, indicating that this is a hen bird. Like other barbets, these birds are entertaining aviary occupants.*

Care and Conditions

Barbets can be broadly divided into two groups. Those with predominantly green plumage—such as the Fire-tufted—are birds of the forest. They tend to be more frugivorous in their feeding habits compared with many African species, which require a more insectivorous diet. In either case, however, it is important to provide a low-iron softfood or similar mynah pellets, because these birds are highly susceptible to iron storage disease—a progressive condition that is likely to be fatal.

Since barbets may attack the timber supports of an aviary, they will need secure quarters. A well-planted flight is recommended, to provide cover. This lessens the likelihood of aggression between the birds, particularly if there is more than one feeding site in the aviary. It is also worth including a large log if possible, so that the barbets can attack this with their stout bills. You can also provide a hollow log on one of the vertical uprights in the aviary as a potential nest site, allowing a pair to construct their own nesting chamber within. This can lead to difficulties in terms of inspecting the nest site, however, and so it may be better to offer an ordinary, stoutly constructed plywood nest box, covering the area around the entrance with cork bark to mimic the effect of a natural tree trunk.

As a result of their soft feathering, barbets are not especially hardy, and they are likely to need heated winter quarters. It therefore helps if their aviary forms part of a birdroom, in which they can be confined over the winter as necessary.

It is not recommended that you house barbets in flight cages because of their active and potentially aggressive natures. Some species tend to be more quarrelsome than others, and the Great Barbet has a bad reputation in this respect. It may be necessary to house these birds individually, since even true pairs may disagree at times, particularly at the start of the breeding season.

Hornbills GENUS: TOCKUS

EVEN THOUGH THEY ARE NOT ESPECIALLY ACTIVE, these unusual-looking softbills make fascinating aviary occupants, particularly in the breeding period. None of the hornbills is brightly colored, and no color variants are known.

Popular Varieties

The majority of hornbills are too large to accommodate in a typical garden aviary and tend to be seen only in zoos and bird parks. These two African species can be kept and bred with relative ease in backyard surroundings, however.

Red-billed Hornbill (*Tockus erythrorhynchus*). The head is dark brown, with a white area beneath. The upperparts are brownish-black, with prominent white spots evident on the wings here. The underparts are primarily whitish. The bill is slightly curved and blood-red in color, being generally larger in the case of the cock.

Yellow-billed Hornbill (*Tockus flavirostris*). Similar in coloration but slightly larger overall than the Red-billed and easily distinguished by the yellow color of the bill. Cocks of this species display a slightly raised area, called the casque, along the top of the upper bill close to its base.

Care and Conditions

Hornbills are relatively hardy once acclimatized, but they must have frost-free accommodation where they can be encouraged to roost when the temperature drops below freezing, because these birds are especially vulnerable to frostbite.

Hornbills' food needs to be diced into small

▼ *Hornbills' eyelashes are actually specialized feathers. They help to protect the eyes against injury, and may also prevent flies from becoming a nuisance. A Red-billed is seen left and a Yellow-billed below.*

Fact File

Family name:	Bucerotidae
Length:	19–21in (48–53cm)
Distribution: Africa. Other species also occur in Asia.	
Color variant availability:	None
Compatibility: Pairs best housed on their own for breeding purposes, or in the company of bigger, non-aggressive softbills.	
Pet potential:	None
Diet: Mixture of diced fruit, berries, and low-iron mynah pellets or softfood. Daily supplies of livefood are important. May also eat pinkies.	
Health problems:	Very susceptible to frostbite.

Breeding tips: Remove the young when they are feeding on their own, since they are vulnerable to attack by the adults.

Nesting needs: Parakeet-type nest box or adapted hollow log should be provided, lined with a thick layer of wood shavings. Damp mud or clay also needed to wall over entrance hole.

Typical clutch size:	4–5 eggs
Incubation:	30 days
Rearing requirements: Invertebrates should be provided in greater quantities. Also extra pinkies.	
Fledging:	Takes place when 60–66 days old.
Lifespan:	May live for 15 years or more.

pieces so that it can be swallowed easily, because although their bills are dexterous, they are not designed for chewing off portions. Hornbills are very alert, however, and are able to grab passing invertebrates with ease.

They are normally quite quiet birds, although the gurgling call of the cock will be heard with increasingly frequency at the start of breeding. For breeding purposes, a pair should be provided with either a hollow natural log or a nest box which has cork bark fixed around the entrance hole. This will create more natural conditions for the birds and may also make it easier for them to construct their own covering here.

Once the nest hole has been excavated by the birds, the female retreats inside and is walled in with a mixture of mud or clay and droppings by her partner, who feeds her throughout the breeding period. The hen, and for a while the chicks as well, are fed through a hole in the plastered-over entrance to the nest. In the wild, this strategy keeps the nest safe from predators. Toward the end of the rearing period, when the chicks are growing fast and they need increasing amounts of food, the hen may break out and assist in rearing their offspring. While incarcerated, it is quite usual for the hen to molt. Even after being shut into such a small space for weeks, the hen can still fly as strongly as ever.

The cock is likely to become increasingly insectivorous once the chicks have hatched, therefore be prepared to provide livefood in increasing quantities at this time.

Q & A ...

● *How should I provide the birds with material for walling up the hen?*

The best way to do this is to put some mud or clay in a heavy, earthenware dish and place it on the aviary floor. Ensure that the mud or clay does not dry out, because it will be of no value to the birds if it does. (It should be moist, rather than flooded.) The hornbills may often choose to mix this with their own droppings.

● *I have just acquired a pair of Red-billed Hornbills, and am rather worried by their hunched-up perching position. What is the problem?*

Almost certainly, nothing at all! These birds do sit in a very peculiar way, just as you describe, with their heads resting right back on their necks.

● *My Red-billed Hornbills catch and eat snails in the aviary. Can I collect these from the yard for them?*

Appealing though this may be in terms of biological pest control, it is not to be recommended. There are several potential dangers. First, the snail may have been poisoned. Second, there is a very real danger that the snail could be carrying gapeworms which will be transmitted to the birds if they eat an infected snail. This can be a life-threatening condition, with young birds being especially vulnerable.

Sunbirds   GENUS: NECTARINIA

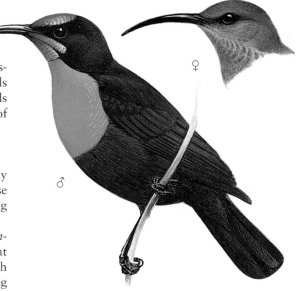

THESE SMALL SOFTBILLS ARE OFTEN regarded as the Old World equivalent of hummingbirds. They are rather similar in appearance, displaying iridescence in their plumage and possessing long bills with which to probe flowers for nectar. Sunbirds cannot feed on the wing by hovering in front of flowers in the way that hummingbirds can.

Popular Varieties

In many species, cocks are much more brightly colored than hens. Some cocks display eclipse plumage, however, so that outside the breeding period the sexes are identical in appearance.

Scarlet-chested Sunbird (*Nectarinia senegalensis*). The crown, sides of the face, and throat region are a dark, iridescent shade of green, with the characteristic scarlet feathering extending over the the lower throat onto the breast. The remainder of the plumage is glossy black and dark brown. Hens have brown upperparts and grayish-white underparts with dark streaks.

Copper Sunbird (*Nectarinia cuprea*). In breeding condition, the cock often looks black from a distance in some lights, but at close quarters his true coppery and purple shades become apparent. The cock resembles the hen throughout the remainder of the year, being olive-brown on the upperparts, with dark brown wings and tail. The plumage on the underparts is yellowish-olive.

Care and Conditions

Sunbirds are surprisingly pugnacious toward each other despite their small size, but they can be kept safely in the company of birds such as white-eyes and small tanagers. A fresh solution of nectar should be supplied for them at least once a day, and it is important that the drinker itself is cleaned thoroughly. A bottle-brush is the best tool for this purpose.

During the summer months, once they are acclimatized, these sunbirds can be allowed out into a sheltered, planted aviary in temperate

▲ *Cock sunbirds such as this Scarlet-chested Sunbird are invariably much more brightly colored than hens. Sexing can be complicated by the fact that immature sunbirds of both sexes resemble hens, however.*

areas, and they are most likely to breed in such surroundings. The hen will construct a hanging, purse-shaped nest in the vegetation or may sometimes be persuaded to use an open-fronted nest box for support. Ensure sufficient livefood will be available once the chicks have hatched, because tiny invertebrates such as fruit flies and microcrickets are needed in large quantities throughout the rearing period. Spiders are also a popular rearing food. Remove the young as soon as they are feeding independently, because the adult pair may then be ready to nest again.

When sunbirds are brought indoors for the winter, it is important to provide adequate cover in their flight here so that the hen is not bullied. A choice of feeding sites is also recommended, because some cocks become very territorial about a particular nectar drinker. Food deprivation is very dangerous for these small birds.

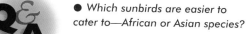

● *Which sunbirds are easier to cater to—African or Asian species?*

...Generally, those from Africa are easier to look after because, in dietary terms, they tend to be less insectivorous outside the breeding period. They are also considered to be slightly hardier, although some members of both groups are found in mountainous areas where the temperature can fall very low at night. Originating from the tropics, sunbirds are conditioned to a fairly standard day length through the year, and so in temperate areas the use of artificial lighting to extend the feeding period is recommended.

● *Hen sunbirds all seem rather similar in appearance. How can I be sure I have a hen of a particular species?*

Yes, they can be hard to distinguish, but you can usually check on an individual's identity by consulting a specialist field guide containing comprehensive illustrations and descriptions.

● *My cock Scarlet-chested Sunbird keeps chasing the hen, and I'm worried that this will put her off breeding. Is there anything I can do?*

Try removing the cock for a brief period—although the situation could become worse again when you reintroduce them. Providing an extra drinker may allow the hen to feed without being unduly harassed, and including some trellis work in the aviary can also be helpful—providing a screen behind which she can retreat out of sight on occasions. Once breeding starts in earnest, this aggressive behavior on the part of the cock should pass.

▲ *The iridescent plumage of cock Copper Sunbirds is most apparent in outdoor flights, when sunlight is falling on their feathering.*

Fact File

Family name:	Nectariniidae
Length:	5in (13cm)
Distribution: Africa. Other species also occur in Asia.	
Color variant availability:	None
Compatibility: Can be kept in pairs as part of a mixed collection of small softbills but should not be mixed with others of their own kind.	
Pet potential:	None
Diet: Nectar solution must be provided fresh at least once a day, along with a mixture of finely diced fruit, sprinkled with low-iron grade softfood. Livefood such as small crickets should also be provided on a regular basis.	

Health problems: Can be at risk of developing candidiasis.

Breeding tips: Ensure cock does not attack the hen at the start of the breeding period.

Nesting needs: Provide a variety of materials such as horsehair, moss, and even spiders' webs if it is possible, which will be used to construct the nest.

Typical clutch size:	1–2 eggs
Incubation:	13 days

Rearing requirements: Tiny invertebrates vital at this stage.

Fledging: Young leave the nest when they are about 17 days old.

Lifespan: May live for 7–10 years.

White-eyes GENUS: ZOSTEROPS

Chestnut-flanked
White-eye

Oriental
White-eye

▲ *White-eyes are generally of similar appearance and prove to be among the easiest of nectar feeders to maintain and breed in aviary surroundings, although they are not hardy and must have snug winter quarters.*

ALTHOUGH THERE ARE ABOUT EIGHTY-FIVE different species of white-eyes (or zosterops as they are also known), most species are quite similar in appearance, and in some cases it can be very hard to distinguish between them. White-eyes are lively, attractive birds, and they are considered the easiest of all nectivores to keep, living well in groups. The feature that makes these small birds instantly recognizable is the circle of white plumage around the eyes.

Popular Varieties

The width of the white eye feathering may vary from species to species. African white-eyes tend to have more yellowish-green body plumage.

Chestnut-flanked White-eye (*Zosterops erythropleura*). This eastern Asian species is instantly recognizable thanks to the chestnut markings on the flanks. The upperparts are gray-green, with the underparts being yellower. Visual sexing is not really practical, although picking those individuals with the darkest, and also the lightest, chestnut coloration is said to give the greatest

Fact File

Family name:	Zosteropidae
Length:	5in (13cm)
Distribution:	Asia. Other species also occur in Africa.
Color variant availability:	None
Compatibility: White-eyes are social and can be kept in groups or in the company of other smaller softbills.	
Pet potential:	None
Diet: Fresh solution of nectar needs to be provided daily, plus diced fruit sprinkled with low-iron grade softfood. Soaked mynah pellets and sponge cake soaked in nectar (rather than water) can also be offered. Livefood such as small crickets should also be offered to these birds daily to maintain good	
health. Limit nectar if necessary to avoid addiction.	
Health problems: Poor feathering can lead to chilling and hypothermia.	
Breeding tips: Keeping a group together should ensure that you have at least one pair.	
Nesting needs: Various materials including horse hair, moss, and spiders' webs will be used to construct the nest. May use an open-fronted nest box for their nest.	
Typical clutch size:	1–2 eggs
Incubation:	12 days
Rearing requirements: Small invertebrates vital once the chicks have hatched.	
Fledging:	Takes place around 12 days old.
Lifespan:	May live for 7 years.

▶ *The sleek appearance of this Chestnut-flanked White-eye shows that it has been bathing regularly. Always provide bathing facilities for white-eyes to keep plumage healthy.*

likelihood of obtaining a true pair. **Oriental White-eye** (*Zosterops palpebrosa*). Various races of this species exist. They range in color from a green to a more yellowish shade. The most popular variety has dull green upperparts, showing a more yellowish shade on the throat and breast and becoming grayer on the lower underparts. There is a bright eye ring of white feathers. The sexes look similar, but cock birds can sometimes be distinguished by the slightly brighter yellow feathering on their underparts.

Care and Conditions

Among the appealing features of white-eyes are their lively natures and incessant curiosity. These characteristics make them easy to feed, and they are valued for persuading other softbills sharing their accommodation to sample unfamiliar food. Even so, never be tempted to switch their nectar food suddenly, because (as is the case with other nectar-feeding birds) this can give rise to serious, or even fatal, digestive upsets.

In spite of the difficulty in sexing white-eyes visually, cocks can be distinguished by their quiet, attractive song. If possible, provide the birds with spiders' webs which they can incorporate into their nests, along with other material. Although they may adopt an open-fronted nest box, pairs prefer to build in the vegetation planted in the flight. The cup-shaped nest itself is often very well hidden here. This is partly because of its relatively small size and also because its sides are deep enough to conceal the sitting bird. Often the birds will choose a site with leaves directly above, making the nest even more difficult to see. The breeding cycle is short, with both members of the pair sharing the incubation duties. Having reared one brood successfully, the pair is likely to nest again.

Q & A

● **Are white-eyes hardy in temperate areas?**

Like other small birds, they are not well-equipped to survive the rigors of a temperate winter without extra heat in their quarters. Extra lighting is also advantageous. If necessary, the birds can be brought indoors and housed in a flight cage, but their diet means that the perches will need to be washed or replaced regularly since they are likely to become sticky.

● **I think my white-eyes are nesting, but I can't be sure. Should I investigate?**

No, do not disturb them unless you suspect that something is wrong, because the pair may desert their nest, abandoning any eggs or chicks within. Confirmation that chicks have hatched will be provided by the presence of bluish eggshells on the floor of the flight, dropped well away from the location of the nest by one of the adults. As the chicks grow and their food demands increase, you should be able to locate the nest by watching the adults flying back and forth.

● **If the pair nest again, will they use the same nest?**

Almost certainly not, even though it is empty. Pairs will normally build a new nest in another part of the aviary. It is important to provide them with fresh nesting material for this purpose. A new nest reduces the likelihood of parasites being passed to the new chicks.

Fruitsuckers and Fairy Bluebirds

GENERA: CHLOROPSIS, IRENA

FRUITSUCKERS ARE ALSO SOMETIMES DESCRIBED as leafbirds, due to the predominantly green coloration of their plumage. The term "fruitsucker" comes from the way they push their bills into soft fruit before sucking up the juice.

Popular Varieties

Whereas the fruitsuckers are highly attractive songsters, the Fairy Bluebird is sought after mainly due to the cock's stunning coloration.

Hardwick's Fruitsucker (*Chloropsis hardwickei*). Green plumage extends from the area above the bill over the top of the head and over the back and wings. A prominent black bib extends from the eyes down onto the upper breast, with blue patches on the sides of the throat area here. The underparts are orangish. Hens lack blue feathering on the wings. They also have less black plumage on the throat, and yellower underparts.

Golden-fronted Fruitsucker (*Chloropsis aurifrons*). In this species the blue coloration extends across the throat, with the black feathering being edged by a bright yellow band. The underparts are entirely green. Hens have a reduced area of

◀ *A pair of Hardwick's Fruitsuckers. The hen is the lower bird. The cock's orangish underparts mean this species is also known as the Orange-bellied Fruitsucker.*

Fact File

Family name:	Irenidae	**Health problems:**	Infections of the feet.
Length:	8–10in (20–25cm)	**Breeding tips:** Aviary must be densely planted, with the nest usually being built in a bush.	
Distribution:	Asia		
Color variant availability:	None	**Nesting needs:** Materials such as twigs, moss, and coconut fiber required for constructing the nest.	
Compatibility: Pairs should be kept apart from each other, but can be mixed with other softbills of similar size such as bulbuls.		**Typical clutch size:**	2 eggs
		Incubation:	13 days
Pet potential:	None	**Rearing requirements:** Eggfood and small invertebrates needed when the chicks have hatched.	
Diet: Mixture of diced fruit and a low-iron softbill food or mynah pellets, plus some livefood. A fresh solution of nectar (or sponge cake soaked in nectar) can be provided daily, but beware of addiction.		**Fledging:** Young leave the nest when they are about 14 days old.	
		Lifespan:	May live for 8–10 years.

● *Where should I place feeding pots and drinkers for these birds?*

... These birds spend most of the time off the ground and in the treetops, so it is not recommended that you place them on the ground because they will be reluctant to fly down to feed. Instead, provide them with a feeding table. This need not be an elaborate structure, but it must be held firmly in place and should be easy to wipe clean on a daily basis.

● *The song of my Golden-fronted Fruitsucker seems to have changed to that of a Shama sharing its aviary. Is this possible?*

Fruitsuckers have a very varied range of notes in their repertoire. But as you've discovered, they can also prove to be quite talented mimics of other birds sharing their quarters with them.

● *What is the best way to breed fruitsuckers?*

The most likely way to achieve success is to house a pair in adjoining aviaries with a removable panel between them. The cock will sing more frequently at the start of the breeding season, and then you must watch the behavior of the birds closely. Once the hen starts to respond to these overtures, remove the partition—still being alert to the possibility that they may quarrel. It will then be a matter of separating them in due course, and hopefully removing their chicks as well once they are feeding independently.

Golden-fronted Fruitsucker

Fairy Bluebird

▲ *Although they may differ widely in coloration, fruitsuckers and Fairy Bluebirds have identical needs. Breeding results are more easily accomplished with Fairy Bluebirds, since members of a pair are usually more readily compatible with each other.*

black feathering, and have green, rather than orangish-yellow, plumage above the bill.

Fairy Bluebird (*Irena puella*). The cock has glossy blue plumage extending over the top of the head and across the shoulders and back. The sides of the face, and all of the remaining plumage, is black, with the irises being bright red. Hens are easily distinguished, being a greenish-blue shade over the entire body.

Care and Conditions

A high standard of cleanliness is vital with all softbills; Fairy Bluebirds are especially vulnerable to foot problems if kept on dirty perches. Fresh-cut branches are recommended if the birds are not kept in planted aviaries—although such surroundings will be vital for breeding these birds. Fruitsuckers represent a particular challenge, because they are very territorial, and cocks should be housed separately from each other to prevent serious fighting.

Compatibility for breeding purposes is also very difficult to achieve with these birds, since the cock will often turn on his intended mate, harassing her so much that the pair have to be separated. In contrast, Fairy Bluebirds usually live quite harmoniously in pairs, and with other softbills of similar size, so that breeding is more likely to be successfully accomplished with this species than with fruitsuckers.

Thrushes GENERA: COPSYCHUS, ZOOTHERA

THRUSHES ARE AMONG THE MOST ATTRACTIVE of all songsters. They are quite easy to maintain, although they are often rather territorial.

▲ You can easily win the confidence of Shamas by providing them with livefood on a regular basis. Before long, they will be eating out of your hand.

Popular Varieties

It is not unusual for these fine songsters to pick up the songs of other birds housed in the aviary. **Shama** (*Copsychus malabaricus*). The head and upperparts of the cock are glossy black, as are the longest tail feathers. There is a prominent area of white plumage on the rump and upper-tail coverts, which is why this species is some-times called the White-rumped Shama. Black plumage also extends across the chest, with the abdomen being a shiny shade of chestnut. Sexing is straightforward, with hens being primarily dull brown—although gray is evident on their

upperparts. The size of this species varies slightly throughout its wide, southeast Asian range. Age also affects appearance, with the tail feathers of young cocks being as up to 3in (7.5cm) shorter than those of adults.

Orange-headed Ground Thrush (*Zoothera citrina*). Originating from a similar area to the Shama, the head and most of the underparts of this species are rusty-orange. The wings, back, and tail are slaty-gray, with white barring on the wings. Hens have duller orange coloration with brownish, rather than gray, feathering on the wings. There is some subspecific variation across

Fact File

Family name:	Turdidae
Length:	8–10in (20–25cm)
Distribution:	Asia
Color variant availability:	None
Compatibility:	Can be quarrelsome.
Pet potential:	None

Diet: Mixture of diced fruit sprinkled with softbill food, low-iron mynah pellets, and invertebrates such as mealworms and waxworms.

Health problems: Can suffer from gapeworms.

Breeding tips: Aviary planted with plenty of vegetation affords the greatest likelihood of success.

Nesting needs: Twigs, leaves, dried grass, and moss may all be incorporated in the construction of the cup-shaped nest.

Typical clutch size:	3–4 eggs
Incubation:	13 days

Rearing requirements: Small invertebrates vital once the chicks have hatched.

Fledging: Young leave the nest when they are about 17 days old.

Lifespan:	May be 8–10 years.

● *Which species are suitable companions for Shamas?*

It is usually better to house a pair on their own for breeding purposes, but you can choose other robust softbills—such as bigger bulbuls and fruitsuckers— as companions at other times. Do not keep more than one pair of Shamas together, however, because this is likely to result in serious fighting.

● *Do Orange-headed Ground Thrushes feed and breed on the ground as well?*

These birds should be provided with food and water bowls on a part of the floor that can easily be cleaned on a regular basis. It is usual for the nest to be built some distance off the ground—for instance, in the fork of a tree. It is constructed from twigs, leaves, and other materials and may have damp mud smeared on the outside.

▲ *A cock Orange-headed Ground Thrush. These birds enjoy bathing, and a suitable container of water should be provided daily for this purpose.*

their wide range; the Indian form known as the White-throated Ground Thrush (*Z. c. cyanotus*) is the most distinctive with white, rather than orange, areas on its face, also extending onto the throat.

Care and Conditions

Once established in their quarters, these birds are relatively hardy, but they must have a dry shelter with heating available to offset the worst of the winter weather in temperate areas. The arrangement of the perches in a flight for Shamas is especially important. They must not be placed too close to the ends of the flight, to avoid the birds catching their long tails there. (The tails are flicked upward when the birds are excited or at any hint of danger, and the feathers could be easily damaged as a result.) Shamas are very active, and they should only be housed in flights and never in cages.

Care should be taken when planting out the aviary for the Orange-headed Ground Thrush, to ensure the birds feel secure there. There should also be a covering over the entire aviary roof, because it is vital that the floor of the aviary does not become flooded with water when it rains. Coarse bark chippings on the floor of the flight will not be as harsh on the feet of these birds as concrete or paving slabs. A grassy area is also appreciated, since they will often probe here for worms and other invertebrates with which they can supplement their regular diet.

Do not mix these particular thrushes with other ground-dwelling birds such as Chinese Painted Quails, since they are quite aggressive.

Budgerigar SPECIES: MELOPSITTACUS UNDULATUS

BUDGERIGARS RANGE WIDELY OVER THE ARID interior of Australia, although they are absent from the southwest, as well as from the eastern seaboard and Tasmania. When the explorer and naturalist John Gould returned to England from Australia in 1840 with a pair of these birds, he could not have imagined the huge popularity that this delightful parakeet would achieve.

Gould's brother-in-law bred from the pair, and before long the Budgerigar was a firm favorite with the Victorian middle classes, who were enchanted by its powers of mimicry. Once it was clear that Budgerigars could be persuaded to nest without difficulty, huge commercial breeding collections—numbering up to 100,000 birds—were established in France to meet European demand. Such extensive breeding programs soon produced color mutations, beginning with the light yellow in 1872. This stimulated even greater interest, and the first blues to be bred caused a sensation when exhibited in 1912.

Today, Budgerigars are bred in a wide range of colors and color combinations. New varieties such as the spangle and the clearbody are still emerging (although less frequently than in the past), while a few of the older color varieties have sadly died out but could re-emerge in the future. One mutation that is possible in theory, but has not yet arisen, is a black Budgerigar.

Variations in the markings have also become widespread, and in many cases these can be combined with different colors, creating potentially many thousands of possible combinations.

Colors

Generally speaking, Budgerigar colors can be divided into green or blue series, based on the presence or absence of pigments in their plumage. These pigments have a direct impact on the color of a Budgerigar, as can be seen from the chart on page 119. Budgerigars do not have a true blue color pigment; rather, the blue color is a result of light reflecting off the so-called "blue layer" in their feathers—just as it does in other parrots with areas of blue plumage.

The coloration of the Budgerigar may also be influenced by the presence of a gene called the dark factor. This has resulted in the development

---

Fact File

Family name:	Psittacidae
Length:	7in (18cm)
Distribution:	Australia

Color variant availability: Very many varieties available.

Compatibility: Usually get along well if introduced outside the breeding period. Likely to harass smaller birds. Typically kept in flocks of their own kind.

Pet potential: Talented talkers; vocabulary can exceed 500 words.

Diet: A typical Budgerigar seed mix, comprised of millets and plain canary seed. Greenstuff such as chickweed. Also carrot and apple.

Health problems: Susceptible to tumors. Overgrown bills common in pet birds, and scaly face common in aviary stock.

Breeding tips: Should be kept in a colony or within sight and sound of each other. These birds still retain strong colonial nesting instincts, and a single pair in isolation may fail to breed.

Nesting needs: Nest box lined with concave.

Typical clutch size: 4–6 eggs

Incubation: Hen usually sits alone. Eggs should hatch after 18 days—sometimes later for first eggs, since hen may not start incubating at once.

Rearing requirements: Provide softfood for breeding birds to raise protein intake. Also soaked seed.

Fledging: Young birds will leave the nest at about 5 weeks old, and will be independent by 6 weeks.

Lifespan: Exhibition birds often live for no more than 5 years; pet birds can live for 7–10 years or more.

Cere of the hen is brown and that of the cock blue or purple

♂

♀

♂

Opaline cobalt

Opaline sky blue

♂

● **Will my Budgerigar's color affect its ability to talk?**

... All Budgerigars are effective mimics. The main influence on their ability to talk is the way in which they are taught, and so it is vital to have a regular daily session with your bird. Although certain individuals seem to be more talented than others, this is not affected by the color of plumage.

● **Is it a good idea to let my Budgerigar out of its cage to fly around the room?**

Yes—Budgerigars are naturally active birds that need exercise. It is no coincidence that pet Budgies are more prone to obesity than those kept in aviaries and are at greater risk from fatty tumors (lipomas). Regular room flying will keep them fitter and tone their flight muscles.

● **Do Budgerigars have any homing instincts?**

Flocks of homing Budgerigars do exist, but such birds are specially trained to return to their aviary in groups. A single Budgerigar that escapes will probably not be able to find its way back, because it will have no knowledge of the area. You will therefore need to find your pet quickly, because a Budgerigar is unlikely to survive for more than two or three days outside.

▲ *It is easy to understand the popularity of Budgerigars. They are hardy, easy to breed, and are available in an almost countless variety of colors and markings. They are also active and sociable and are talented talkers.*

Color Pigmentation

		Melanin (black)	Psittacin (yellow)
GREEN SERIES	Light green	+	+
	Lutino	—	+
	Yellow & Green pied	—/+	+
BLUE SERIES	Sky blue	+	—
	Albino	—	—
	White & Blue pied	—/+	—

of three possible shades within both the green and blue series. In the green series, the natural color in the absence of the dark factor is called light green. A single dark factor in the bird's genetic makeup causes it to be dark green. The deepest shade of green—known as olive—occurs when there are two dark factors in its makeup. The three equivalent colors in blue series birds are sky blue, cobalt, and mauve respectively.

Gray. There used to be two forms of the gray Budgerigar, but the recessive form, developed in the 1930s, disappeared in the next decade. This is probably because the dominant form—which is indistinguishable in appearance—could be bred more easily. Combining gray and green coloration on the same bird has in turn led to the creation of gray-greens that are relatively dark in color, although not as dark as an olive. Gray-greens are the green series equivalent of the gray itself, which due to its lack of yellow pigment belongs to the blue series.

Yellow-faced. Until the 1930s, yellow coloration could not occur on blue series birds, but this changed with the advent of the yellow-faced mutations. There are two distinct forms, the deepest-colored being known as yellow-faced type 2, or golden-faced. This characteristic can also be transferred to grays, making yellow-faced grays, although yellow-faced violets are the most popular combination of this type.

Fallow. One of the principal characteristics that helps distinguish the fallows from other varieties is their red eyes. Several distinctive strains have been reported during the domestication of the Budgerigar, with the first fallows emerging in the United States during 1931 (although this particular variety was not established). Today, it is the German variety which is most widely kept. It can be distinguished easily from the English form by the presence of an iris around its pupils. Green series fallows have a striking yellowish—rather than green—body coloration with brownish markings. Blue fallows also have paler coloration than normal.

Violet. One of the most highly prized modern varieties is the visual violet, which is actually a separate dominant mutation. To create this requires a combination of blue coloration and the dark factor. The violet mutation can also be

bred in conjunction with dark green, making violet-dark greens (though these have a more yellowish tone to the plumage rather than being pure dark green). Such birds are much sought after to improve the quality of visual violet strains. The violet characteristic can also be introduced to pied bloodlines.

Lutino and Albino. Lutino Budgerigars are a rich buttercup shade of yellow—with their red eyes also resulting from the lack of melanin pigment—while the albino has no color pigment at all in its feathering. It may have a very faint blue tinge in good light, however, again resulting from the blue layer, but without the melanin pigment to support this color.

Pied Patterning

Pied is a combination of contrasting light and dark shades. The pattern of markings in pieds is random in nature, with some Budgerigars being

▲ *A group of young Budgerigars, reflecting some of the different varieties now available. Note that their eyes lack a white iris encircling the pupil at this stage. The barring on the head may also extend down to the cere.*

▶ *A Danish recessive pied. This is one of two pied mutations in existence. This mutation has solid, dark plum-colored eyes. The distribution of the pied markings varies between individuals.*

more lightly variegated than others depending on the distribution of the relevant color pigments through their plumage. These remain consistent throughout the bird's life. The two different types of pied mutation can be distinguished easily on the basis of their visual appearance.

The Australian dominant pied, which was first recorded in 1935 from an aviary near Sydney, is larger than the Danish recessive pied and has a distinctive iris around the dark pupils in its eyes. Danish recessive pieds were first exhibited in

Light green (wild)

Dark green

♂

♀

♂

♂

Olive-green

Gray-green

▲ *The basic color range within the green grouping—caused by the dark factor mutation—is shown here. Light green is the natural color, but occasional dark-factor birds are seen in wild flocks, too.*

● *Why do hen birds tear up sand sheets more often than cocks?*

... This is an indication that they are ready to breed. This can also be confirmed by the state of the cere; it will be a richer, deeper, brown than usual at this stage.

● *Can I be certain which are the parents of Budgerigar chicks hatched in my aviary?*

There can be no guarantee in this respect, because cock Budgerigars are not averse to mating with other hens, particularly when their own partners are incubating eggs. This can give strange results in terms of the color varieties that are produced. As a consequence, exhibition breeders in particular house individual pairs of Budgerigars on their own, to be certain of the progeny.

● *What is the best way of arranging the perches in an aviary of Budgerigars?*

Provide at least two, running across each end of the flight. In addition, you could cut off the crown of a suitable tree or bush and set it into a large tub. This will give the birds a range of alternative perching sites. Never place food or water containers under perches, since their contents will soon become soiled.

Copenhagen in 1932. When seen in a good light, their eyes are actually a deep plum color. Other characteristics include less distinctive black spots on the cheeks, while the cere of cock birds stays purplish like that of a young Budgerigar, rather than taking on the more usual blue coloration.

Wing Markings

Changes to the patterning of the Budgerigar's wings have greatly increased the number of possible color variants. These changes did not occur until quite late in the bird's domestication, and arose in locations as far apart as Scotland, Australia, and Belgium. The opaline is now one of the most common variants. It first emerged during the 1930s and is characterized by light barring on the head and neck, with the usual darker markings on the wings. Unfortunately, in some

cases the melanin appears on the forehead as distinct black areas of "flecking." The opaline characteristic can be teamed with most other colors and patterns, including pieds, although in this case there may be clear areas breaking up the opaline patterning—a feature of pieds.

Changes to the melanin granules in the wings can also affect the coloration of the markings. The cinnamon mutation occurs when the melanin coloration is modified to a chocolate shade. In the case of the graywing, the melanin dilutes to gray, while in whitewings, it is even paler. The corresponding mutation in green series birds is described as the yellow-wing, where the markings are again much paler than usual.

The spangle is one of the newer varieties, first recorded in 1978 from an Australian aviary. In this variety, there are changes in the distribution of the melanin granules, which have resulted in

▶ *In the case of the lacewing light yellow, the color mutation affects not only the color but also the delicate wing patterning. This variety is currently quite scarce.*

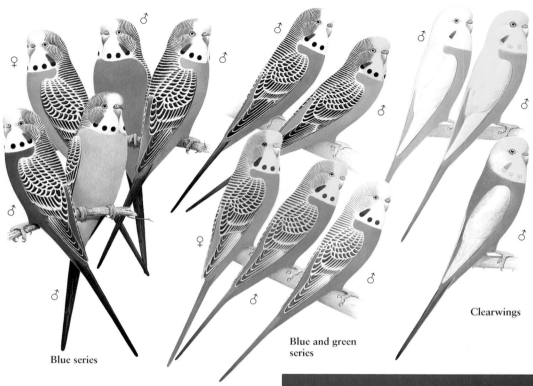

Blue series

Blue and green series

Clearwings

the dark areas being confined to the edges of the individual feathers, while the centers are much lighter. This not only affects the back and wings, but also the throat spots. There is a visual difference between single and double factor spangles, which can also be separated on the basis of their genetic makeup, because double factor birds have much paler overall markings.

Crested Budgerigars

Alterations to the length of the plumage have resulted in the creation of crested Budgerigars. This feature occurs irrespective of color. Crested Budgerigars are never paired together, however, because of a lethal factor in the genetic makeup. Instead, they are paired to non-crested birds. There are three types—full-circular crest, half-circular crest, and tufted crest.

▶ *Thanks to its dominant mode of inheritance, the striking spangle has grown quickly in availability. For instance, pairing a spangle with a normal light green Budgerigar is likely to produce further spangles.*

Pieds and
clear-flighted

Opalines

Red-eyed

▲ *The phenomenal success of the Budgerigar is due in no small measure to the huge number of varieties that breeding has produced. This is just a selection of the different combinations of body coloration and wing patterning available.*

Care and Conditions

Because Budgerigars are prone to digestive problems, hygiene is especially important. Such disorders are usually grouped under the general heading "enteritis," but may have a variety of causes. Often bacteria are to blame, and especially when starting out you may encounter a high incidence of enteritis, particularly if you buy stock from several different sources. A particular eating habit of these parakeets aggravates the problem; Budgerigars often nibble at their droppings once they have dried. They may do this to gain the benefit of vitamins that have been produced by bacteria in the large intestine. Since the vitamins cannot be absorbed there, the birds must eat the food again after excretion. In doing this, however, they risk picking up harmful bac-

teria, especially if an individual Budgerigar has had no previous exposure to them. Over time, the colony as a group will gain a greater immunity to such potentially harmful microbes, but initially a higher than expected level of illness may result.

There are some steps you can take to reduce the likelihood of birds falling ill during this critical early period after setting up the aviary. Using a vitamin B supplement may help lessen the urge to eat their droppings, while a probiotic added regularly to the drinking water will protect against infections of the intestinal tract.

Cleanliness also plays a vital role in health care, particularly where food and water containers are concerned. Hoppers are much better than open food bowls. They will also make it easier to take care of the Budgerigars by ensuring that you can see just how much seed they have available. In a bowl, this can be very difficult because of a covering of husks on the surface. There is also no risk of the seed hopper being fouled with droppings, and the aviary itself will be much easier to keep clean since the husks will fall through into the base of the hopper drawer instead of being scattered around the aviary.

Closed bottles are also more hygienic, especially those that fit through the aviary mesh. The birds should be provided with fresh drinking water every day, and the bottles should be washed out thoroughly at least once a week—or more frequently if they become soiled with droppings. Should you need to disinfect them, be sure to use one of the specialist avian products now available for this purpose. These are entirely safe when used as instructed.

Good housekeeping in the aviary is a key factor in ensuring that your birds remain healthy. The paper lining on the floor of the shelter should be changed every week and the outside flight cleaned at the same time. A concrete base is an essential requirement for Budgerigar aviaries, where a number of birds are being housed together instead of just an individual pair. This type of flooring is much easier to clean thoroughly—the best tool for the job is a power-jet attachment on a hose, which will blast off any dirt. Any tenacious areas can be scrubbed clean later. A disinfectant can also be used effectively on this type of surface.

The floor area must have a built-in slope, and you should also provide a drainage hole at the corner to allow the water to drain away quickly. But keep this hole quite small to prevent rats and mice from gaining access to the aviary. During the molting period you may need to make sure that the hole does not become blocked up by feathers.

The perches in the outside part of the flight are likely to be washed off regularly by the rain, but you will need to scrub or replace those in the shelter and covered area of the flight on a regular basis. This applies particularly in the case of an outbreak of scaly face, where the mites may be deposited on the perches by the birds rubbing their bills and sides of their faces as they try to relieve the irritation caused by these parasites. The mites could then be picked up by other birds.

It is especially important to remove from a

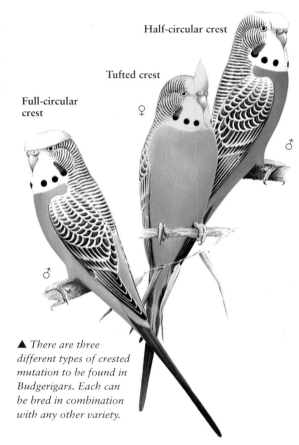

Half-circular crest

Tufted crest

Full-circular crest

♀

♂

♂

▲ *There are three different types of crested mutation to be found in Budgerigars. Each can be bred in combination with any other variety.*

flight any Budgerigar that appears to be ill, to safeguard the health of the others. Also, do not try to introduce a new arrival to the aviary immediately. Instead, you should keep the bird in isolation for at least two weeks. Start by spraying it with a special avian aerosol that kills mites, so there will be no chance of introducing these parasites or lice to other birds. The treatment will need to be repeated after two weeks, just before the bird is released into the communal flight. This also provides an opportunity for the newcomer to settle down. It will then be under less stress when it joins its new companions, so reducing the possibility that it could fall ill.

The Budgerigar as a Pet

When looking for a pet, you should always try to obtain a recently fledged Budgerigar, since young birds settle much more readily into the home. A bird aged between six and nine weeks old is an ideal choice. Older Budgerigars are

Q & A...

● *Why have there been spiky feathers on my Budgerigar's head for weeks?*

The bird may be suffering from a deficiency in the output of hormones from the thyroid glands in the neck. Check that there is sufficient iodine available in the diet, for this could be a contributory factor. An iodine nibble can be recommended for this purpose, but choose a white, rather than pink, block for exhibition Budgerigars, to prevent their facial feathering from becoming stained prior to a show.

● *My Budgerigar's leg has swollen up beneath its ring. What causes this, and what should I do?*

The problem seems to be more common in Budgerigars than in other birds, and requires urgent veterinarian intervention if the bird is not to lose its leg. There is no obvious reason why this problem occurs, but it could be that the leg is being compressed by the band. It is much harder to remove an aluminum rather than a celluloid ring. On no account should you try to do this yourself with a pair of pliers, for you are very likely to injure the bird in the process and could end up worsening the situation. Aluminum is a soft metal, and if it becomes bent this will increase the pressure on the leg. Your vet will have the right tools for cutting the band off. Once it has been removed the swelling should gradually subside, but some indication of this problem is likely to remain for the rest of the bird's life.

● *My young Budgerigars leave the nest and then seem unable to fly. What is the problem?*

They are likely to be afflicted by French molt, which is a viral infection that causes the flight feathers to break off—soon after fledging in most cases. It is possible for these to regrow in mild cases, but sometimes such birds may be permanently handicapped. Find homes for the youngsters as pets, and disinfect the breeding cages—and especially nest boxes—thoroughly, and remember that tools used for cleaning the nest box, like brushes, may also be contaminated by the virus.

● *Can I leave the young Budgerigars in with their parents once they are out of the nest and feeding themselves?*

The young Budgerigars may make a nuisance of themselves by going back into the nest box and possibly damaging the eggs if the hen has laid again, so it is best to remove them, with minimum disturbance, when they are roughly six weeks old.

▲ *Budgerigars are naturally sociable, and pet birds kept on their own often benefit from the sense of companionship provided by a mirror. Other toys can also be beneficial to their well-being.*

◄ *The dark-eyed clear white is an uncommon variety. It is similar to the more widely kept albino, which can be recognized by its red eyes. Dark-eyed clears retain some melanin pigment, giving the black eye color.*

Budgerigar

likely to be much more reluctant to allow themselves to be handled, and they will also prove less talented as mimics.

Most people prefer to keep a cock bird as a pet, although it is a myth that male Budgerigars learn to talk more easily than hens. Male birds will certainly chatter more than hens, and are also likely to be less destructive. It is quite common for adult hens to attempt to nibble wooden ornaments and furniture, and even strip small pieces of wallpaper when they come into breeding condition, if left unsupervised when out of their quarters. They may also lay eggs on the floor of their quarters.

It is not easy to tell the difference between cocks and hens soon after they have left the nest, especially if no individuals of the opposite sex are present. Try looking closely at the cere—the fleshy area around the nostrils and directly above the bill. In a young cock, the cere tends to be a shade of blue or purple and also appears more prominent compared with a hen's of similar age.

Hens will only start to get their distinctive brownish cere at about 12 weeks of age, when the characteristic barring on the forehead is also lost in those color varieties where it was present. This is also the stage when the white iris starts to develop, although in a few varieties (for example, some fallows) this adult characteristic is never present.

Allow a young Budgerigar to settle down in its new quarters for a day or two after its arrival. This is essentially the same procedure as for other members of the parrot family. You can then begin the training process. At first, you may find it hard to persuade Budgerigars to return to their quarters. Their speed in flight makes them difficult to catch, and they often perch on the highest vantage point in a room. The best strategy is to draw the curtains or turn off the lights, after carefully noting your pet's whereabouts. Then, using a small flashlight, you should be able to easily

▶ *Even though it is only 18 days old, this Budgerigar chick clearly displays the pattern of distinctive markings in its feathering.*

● *My hen Budgerigar is laying eggs on the floor of her cage. What should I do?*

Leave her with the eggs as she lays them. By taking them away you are encouraging her to lay more, and this will tax her body reserves of calcium and other constituents, making it more likely that she will suffer from egg-binding. These eggs will not have been fertilized, and so having completed her clutch, she will soon lose interest in them. Once she is no longer sitting on the eggs you can remove them safely.

● *I am breeding my Budgerigars on a colony system. Unfortunately, there seems to be a lot of fighting taking place. What can I do about this?*

Ensure that all the nest boxes are positioned at the same height, to eliminate any fighting over the upper boxes, and provide at least twice as many boxes as pairs so that the birds have an adequate choice.

● *My Budgerigars seem to be producing a lot of infertile eggs. What is the reason for this?*

This may be because you are pairing up your birds and transferring them to the nest boxes too late. The hens are ready to lay immediately, and so retreat within the nest box almost at once, which means that mating does not take place. So, try blocking off the nest box for a week or so after transferring the birds to their breeding cages. Also, check that perches are fixed firmly in place.

▲ *Offering a variety of suitable foods will contribute to the health and happiness of your Budgerigars. These birds have been provided with parsley and a watermelon.*

locate and then gently recapture the Budgerigar, because it will not fly in the dark.

Budgerigars as Aviary Birds

A group of these lively birds makes an attractive sight in a garden aviary. Unlike many other parrots, they can be kept and bred quite easily under these conditions, although the birds will pair randomly. As a result, you are likely to find that an ever-increasing number of the offspring produced each year will be light green—the natural coloration of these birds.

By breeding Budgerigars in cages, however, you can devise pairings that are likely to give you the maximum number of chicks of a particular color. This is why many breeders, especially those with exhibition stock, prefer to house their birds in a large aviary and then pair them up individually in cages in a birdroom, even though this means more work during the breeding period.

Budgerigars are naturally hardy birds and do not require additional heating or lighting over the winter months, unless they are breeding during this period. If the birds are nesting on a colony system rather than in breeding cages in a birdroom, the breeding period should be restricted to the summer months only. Otherwise, the risk of problems such as egg-binding and chilling of eggs will be significantly increased.

Although Budgerigars are not very destructive compared with some parakeets, they may whittle away exposed areas of wood in the aviary, and eventually weaken the structure. It therefore pays to design the aviary in such a way that no loose edges are accessible to the birds. Equipping the aviary with a plentiful supply of fresh perches will provide them with wood that can be nibbled easily to keep their bills in trim.

Grass Parakeets GENUS: NEOPHEMA

THERE ARE SEVEN SPECIES OF GRASS PARAKEET. They get their name from their habit of feeding on grass seeds on the ground. Grass parakeets have been popular with birdkeepers for over a century, with all of today's birds being captive-bred for generations. In size and shape they are similar to the Budgerigar, although they are not closely related.

Grass parakeets tend to be rather nervous birds and will not settle well within the home. This is a pity, since many varieties have striking coloration. They are, however, ideal subjects for the aviary and will breed readily in such surroundings.

Popular Varieties

The emergence of a number of color mutations over recent years has further heightened interest in the group.

Turquoisine Grass Parakeet (*Neophema pulchella*). This species can be sexed easily, since cock birds have an obvious red wing bar and much

◀ *The red-bellied mutation of the Turquoisine Grass Parakeet. The cock, on the left, is more colorful. Like other grass parakeets, these birds are an excellent choice for a garden aviary in urban surroundings.*

Fact File

Family name:	Psittacidae
Length:	8–9in (20–23cm)
Distribution: Australia, including Tasmania and other offshore islands.	
Color variant availability:	Wide choice
Compatibility: Best kept apart from other members of the genus.	
Pet potential: None. Only suitable as aviary birds.	
Diet: Plain canary seed and mixed millets, with the addition of some sunflower seed and groats. Seeding grasses, chickweed, and apple.	
Health problems:	Susceptible to roundworms.
Breeding tips: Usually easy to sex visually, and	

pairs will nest reliably—often for 10 years or more.

Nesting needs: Nest box measuring about 8in (20cm) square x 12in (30cm) deep.

Typical clutch size: 4–6 eggs

Incubation: Eggs should begin to hatch after 18–19 days; this period may be longer for the first eggs since they may not start incubating immediately.

Rearing requirements: Provide softfood for the breeding birds, to raise their protein intake. Soaked seed is also valuable.

Fledging: Will leave the nest when aged about 1 month old.

Lifespan: Can live for 15 years or more.

more blue coloration on the face compared with hens. Unfortunately, these parakeets tend to be more aggressive than others of their kind, so you should avoid housing them in adjoining flights because they are likely to quarrel with their neighbors through the mesh. Double-wiring is essential for keeping them apart. Turquoisine Grass Parakeets (especially young birds) are also more susceptible to nervousness than other grass parakeets, but are just as prolific when it comes to breeding, with pairs usually producing double broods.

Color mutations have been developed extensively in this species over recent years. The most striking is probably the yellow. In this variety the blue areas are paler than usual—while the red plumage of the cock bird is unchanged in intensity—and the green feathering has acquired a distinctly yellowish hue.

The red-fronted color form is seen at its most dramatic in cocks, where the color extends up the abdomen and chest. (This reddish color is confined to the belly in hens.) It can be teamed with other mutations, for example the yellow, creating in this instance red-fronted yellows. Less striking are dark factor birds; jades are a lighter shade than olives. Pieds have also been bred (though they have not proved especially popular) as has a rare cinnamon form.

Splendid Grass Parakeet (*(Neophema splendida)*. This species is also known as the Scarlet-chested Parakeet, because of the stunning chest coloration of adult cocks. Hens resemble female Turquoisines, but can be distinguished from them because their lores (the feathers close to the bill) are blue rather than whitish. Because they inhabit only very remote areas of Australia and are rarely seen, these beautiful parakeets were once thought to be extinct. However, two pairs that were captured and brought to Britain in the 1930s (one of which was presented to King George V) later nested successfully there, confirming the avicultural potential of the species. Since then, it has become one of the most widely bred parakeets in the world.

Various blue mutations have been recorded, most notably a sea-green form, which retains a greenish hue to its plumage. The breast of the cock bird is reduced to a pale, salmon-pink color.

● *Are grass parakeets noisy?*

No, these birds are not especially noisy. In fact, their calls have a rather attractive musical quality, making them an ideal choice for a suburban aviary, where they are unlikely to cause offense to neighbors.

● *Why are roundworms such a problem in grass parakeets?*

These birds are particularly vulnerable to roundworms because they spend much more time on the aviary floor than, say, South American parrots, which rarely come down to the ground in search of food.

● *Can I design my aviary so as to lessen the risk of a build-up of roundworms?*

Yes, having a solid floor to the aviary—rather than a grass or gravel base—will help, because it is much easier to clean this type of surface thoroughly. In a clean environment, the parasitic worm eggs will not be able to build up and cause a hazard to the birds when they are combing the floor for food scraps.

▲ *Splendid Grass Parakeets are now a familiar sight in aviaries around the world, but in the 1930s the species was thought to be virtually extinct in the wild. A number of color varieties, especially blues, are widely kept, with pairs usually nesting very readily.*

A genuine white-fronted blue has emerged as well, along with a red-bellied form equivalent to that seen in the Turquoisine. Pieds are also known in this species, along with a rare cinnamon form.

Bourke's Grass Parakeet (*Neophema bourkii*). The coloration of these birds is unique among the parrot family; they exhibit a pinkish tone, particularly on the belly. Cocks can be recognized quite easily by the blue area above the bill and extending over the eyes, whereas this area is whitish in hens. Subtle shades of brown are also visible in the plumage of these particular parakeets, making them unlike any other member of the genus.

The desirable pink coloration has been emphasized still further in the rosa mutation, which is caused by a sex-linked recessive gene. Sadly, however, this gene also removes the blue coloration that serves to tell the sexes apart easily—although cocks in this form tend to have grayer brows than hens.

Among the other established mutations is the yellow, often also known as the cream, which is

basically a paler, red-eyed form of the normal coloration. Traces of blue remain on the plumage but are less conspicuous and are usually confined to the shoulder region. The cinnamon or Isabella mutation also has red eyes, but with a pronounced brownish color, especially over the wings, which are much darker in the normal form. Cross-breeding involving cinnamon and rosa Bourke's Grass Parakeets has seen the emergence of the pink color form, an extremely striking red-eyed variant.

Elegant Grass Parakeet (*Neophema elegans*). This species is less popular than the Bourke's, probably because it is less colorful. Cock birds can usually be distinguished by the broader blue banding across the forehead and the deeper yellow facial coloration, although the differences between the sexes are less marked than in other grass parakeets. Care of these birds is much the same as it is for other related species. Pairs will usually nest readily and produce double broods.

Color variants of Elegant Grass Parakeets are few in number and scarce. The attractive lutino variety—a red-eyed yellow form, with white

◄ *The rosa form of Bourke's Grass Parakeet has a distinctly pinker hue to its plumage than the normal form. Like other grass parakeets, they are generally most active in the early morning and at dusk.*

Splendid Grass Parakeet

Bourke's Grass Parakeet

Turquoisine Grass Parakeet

Blue-winged Grass Parakeet

▶ *A selection of grass parakeets. Unlike some of its close relatives, the Blue-winged species breeds better when kept in a colony rather than as individual pairs.*

Q&A...

● **Can grass parakeets be kept in colonies?**

No, pairs should generally be kept on their own, although it is possible to house them in the company of other, unrelated birds, such as doves or some of the larger finches like Java Sparrows.

● **Do these parakeets need heated winter quarters?**

Grass parakeets are quite hardy and so are not unduly affected by low temperatures. But coming mainly from arid areas, they are prone to respiratory illnesses in long spells of damp, foggy weather. This is when it is vital to persuade them to roost in the aviary shelter under cover.

● **What is the safest way to introduce grass parakeets to a new aviary?**

It helps when introducing a pair to an aviary for the first time to keep them confined in the shelter for several days. This not only means that they will be able to find their food and water without difficulty, but they will also come to regard this as a safe place once they have the free run of the whole aviary. So, if a cat jumps on top of the aviary, they will seek refuge in the shelter rather than flying around wildly, risking injury or even death.

replacing blue plumage—remains a rarity. It was first bred in Belgium in 1972. There is also a sex-linked cinnamon.

Blue-winged Grass Parakeet (*Neophema chrysostoma*). One of the most peaceful members of the group, this species has proved to be very reliable when breeding, and the young are less nervous that other grass parakeets. The frontal band again provides a way of distinguishing the sexes, being larger in the case of cocks. Unlike the Elegant, there is only one band visible, although these two species are somewhat similar in appearance. No color mutations of the Blue-winged have yet been recorded.

Other species. The other two members of this genus—the Rock Grass Parakeet (*Neophema petrophila*) and the even rarer Orange-bellied Grass Parakeet (*Neophema chrysogaster*)—are virtually unknown in the birdkeeping hobby.

Care and Conditions

A flight measuring 9–12ft (2.7–3.6m) in length attached to a shelter measuring 3ft (0.9m) square will be required for a pair of grass parakeets.

Because of the very active nature of these birds, perches should be positioned at either end of the flight so that the birds can fly back and forth easily. Place the crown of a tree in a pot and position this in the aviary, too; it will add variety to the birds' environment and will provide them with a range of extra perching sites.

It is especially important that the aviary shelter is well lit, to attract the parakeets to roost under cover when the weather is bad. You must cover any exposed glass or perspex here with a wire-mesh frame; this will prevent the parakeets from attempting to fly through the barrier, which they would otherwise be unlikely to see. Their thin skulls are especially at risk from fractures, and the brain is susceptible to cerebral hemorrhages—both of which may well prove fatal. The risk is greatest when transferring newly acquired birds to a new aviary. Young birds that have recently left the nest can also be very nervous at first, panicking and flying around at the slightest sign of danger.

The choice of floor covering is a major consideration in an aviary housing these parakeets, because they are particularly vulnerable to roundworm infestations. It is worth having a fecal sample from newly acquired birds checked by your vet for the presence of these parasites. Alternatively, you can simply have the birds dewormed prior to releasing them into their permanent quarters. This should prevent the infestation from becoming established in the aviary, where it will be much harder to eliminate.

Feeding these parakeets is very straightforward; indeed, this is one of the reasons for their long-standing popularity. A seed mixture consisting of plain canary seed and millets is ideal, supplemented with a little sunflower seed and groats. The use of a general-purpose vitamin and mineral supplement is also a good idea, and as always, a constant supply of cuttlebone and grit should be available as well. Daily portions of greenstuff such as chickweed (*Stellaria media*), seeding grasses, and similar items should be offered, with green vegetables, such as spinach, a valuable dietary supplement during the winter period in temperate areas. In general, grass parakeets do not like fruit, but they will eat apple and carrot regularly.

▶ *The Elegant is not as colorful as some grass parakeets, although a small area of orange plumage is found on the lower abdomen of some individuals. Cocks of this species have a reputation for being rather aggressive.*

During the rearing period a pair will consume large quantities of soaked seed, with millet sprays a particular favorite. They may also be persuaded to take an eggfood or some other form of softfood at this stage, and this will be beneficial because its higher protein content will help the chicks' growth.

The nesting period of these parakeets should be restricted to spring through late summer in temperate areas, otherwise there is an increased risk of hens becoming egg-bound. In addition, both eggs and chicks will become chilled if the birds are allowed to nest during the colder months. Out-of-season nesting can usually be prevented by removing the nest box during this period.

Unlike many birds of the parrot family, grass parakeets only use a nest box when breeding and not for roosting. They are also not disinclined to choose a nest box placed in the flight, since they tend to breed naturally in isolated tree holes where these can be found, rather than in dense woodland. Even so, if you have a particularly nervous pair it may be worth fixing a nest box in the shelter as well, to provide an alternative site for them.

The cock bird will signal the start of the nesting period by singing more determinedly and displaying to his intended mate. He may start to chase her up and down the flight if she does not respond immediately to his overtures, although these particular parakeets are not markedly aggressive at this stage. She will start to spend more time around the nest box. It may help if this is fixed in such a way that the birds are able to rest on top of it, as well as on the entry perch. This allows them to become accustomed to the location of the nest box, and may also help to prevent the hen from being harassed too intensively by the cock during the preliminary stages of courtship.

Once the hen has laid, the cock remains in the vicinity of the nest, spending periods inside with

● *What should I use to line my grass parakeets' nest box?*

... Provide wooden chips for this purpose, because the bills of these parakeets are not especially strong. They will encounter difficulties in whittling away larger blocks of timber to create a nest lining.

● *How will I know when the eggs have hatched?*

You are most likely to hear the calls coming from inside the nest box or see the egg shells on the floor of the flight, confirming that newly hatched chicks are present.

● *Is there anything that I can do to prevent newly fledged Turquoisine chicks from injuring themselves?*

Plant climbing nasturtiums up the far end of the aviary in the early spring, so that by the time the chicks leave the nest there will be an obvious barrier of dense green leaves trailing up the mesh.

his mate as well, although he does not take an active part in the incubation process. Try to avoid any unnecessary disturbance near the flight during this period, since there is a possibility that the eggs may be scattered and damaged if the birds dash out of the entrance hole. Under normal circumstances, the incubation period will pass peacefully.

The major danger period occurs about one month later, when the chicks leave the nest for the first time. Not only will they be extremely nervous, but they may also be harassed by the cock, particularly if he is eager to breed again. The young parakeets should therefore be removed to a nursery flight as soon as you are absolutely sure that they are eating on their own. Otherwise—especially in the case of young cock birds—there is a real risk that they could be attacked and fatally wounded by their father.

Rosellas GENUS: PLATYCERCUS

► *Though rarer than other rosellas, the Green Rosella needs similar care. A spacious flight is needed to prevent these birds from growing obese.*

ROSELLAS ARE ANOTHER GROUP OF PARAKEETS that are very popular with birdkeepers around the world. There are eight species in this genus, varying in coloration from the showy to the more conservative. However, all can be recognized quite readily by the scalloped patterning over their wings, their distinctive cheek patches, and the broad tips to their tails. Although visual sexing is, unfortunately, difficult in many cases— and in some species impossible—this does not seriously compromise breeding success.

Popular Varieties

Especially in recent years, an ever-increasing range of color mutations has been developed within this group of birds. The most popular of these are described below.

Green Rosella (*Platycercus caledonicus***).** This species is the largest member of the genus and is also known as the Tasmanian Rosella (it is not found on mainland Australia). It is not the most popular of the rosellas in birdkeeping circles, partly because of its relatively dull coloration. At first glance it resembles the Yellow Rosella, but it is significantly darker in color than this species, particularly over the wings. Hens may be recognized by the presence of small areas of orangish-red plumage in the vicinity of the throat.

Crimson Rosella (*Platycercus elegans***).** It is not surprising that this species, which is native to the eastern seaboard of Australia, has become one of the most widely kept of all parakeet species. Its beautiful crimson-red coloration makes an unusual and striking contrast with its areas of black and blue feathering. Young birds differ very significantly in appearance from adults, however, with green predominating in their plumage.

In terms of color mutations, the blue form of this rosella (which is also known as Pennant's Parakeet) is the most commonly available today. In this variety, the characteristic crimson feathering is replaced by white plumage; other colors

Q&A...

● **I'm thinking about acquiring an Adelaide Rosella. Can you tell me something about this bird?**

In the wild, this bird is restricted to a relatively small area around Adelaide in southern Australia. The coloration of Adelaide Rosellas is extremely variable, with some displaying much more orange on their underparts than others. Some bird experts take the view that this population is the result of natural hybridization between the Crimson and Yellow Rosellas. Whether true or not, fertile offspring of similar appearance have certainly been produced by hybridization in aviaries.

● **Are rosellas hardy?**

Yes, these birds are usually capable of overwintering outside without artificial heat, and aviary strains have been raised in temperate areas for many generations. There is one particular exception to this general rule— Brown's Rosella may need special care during the winter, since this is the time when it most commonly prefers to breed in northern latitudes.

Fact File

Family name:	Psittacidae	**Nesting needs:** Nest box about 10in (25cm) square x 24in (60cm) deep.	
Length:	10–14.5in (25–37cm)		
Distribution:	Australia, including Tasmania.	**Typical clutch size:**	4–6 eggs
Color variant availability:	Wide choice	**Incubation:** 18–22 days; Green Rosellas usually incubate their eggs the longest.	
Compatibility: Pairs should be kept on their own.			
Pet potential: None; only suitable as aviary birds.		**Rearing requirements:** Provide soaked millet and plain canary seed, as well as greenfood and egg-food.	
Diet: Millets, canary seed, and sunflower seeds.			
Health problems: Susceptible to roundworms.			
Breeding tips: Pairs will breed reliably over long periods and can be prolific. Visual sexing is very difficult. Signs of aggression indicate incompatibility.		**Fledging:** The young are ready to leave the nest at about 5 weeks old.	
		Lifespan: Can live for 25 years or more.	

are essentially unaffected. There are also dilute yellow and lutino variants now being bred for the aviculture trade.

Eastern Rosella (*Platycercus eximius*). This is another species that has vivid red plumage, extending over the entire head and down over the upper chest. The remainder of the chest and upper abdomen are bright yellow, becoming green toward the vent. The cheek patches are pure white in cocks but may have more of an off-white tone in hens—although visual sexing is again difficult. The most vivid coloration is displayed by the subspecies described as the Golden-mantled Rosella (*P. e. cecilae*); this is often abbreviated simply to "GMR." The distribution of these parakeets extends right across the southeast of the continent, with the Golden-mantled population occurring in the northern part of the species' range.

Among the color mutations now being bred the most striking is probably the red form, which has an interesting history. It was first recorded in the wild in 1837 by John Gould, who regarded it as a separate species and named it the Fiery Parakeet (*P. ignatus*). As this description suggests, these birds have far more red on their underparts than others of the species, with this coloration extending right down to the undertail coverts. The red coloration also features prominently among the scalloped plumage covering the wings.

Undoubtedly the most unusual mutation, however, is the black form; the undersides are predominantly black, although cock birds of this mutation can be easily sexed by their red bib.

▲ *A Crimson Rosella, also known as Pennant's Parakeet. These birds are sometimes prone to plucking the feathers of their offspring in the nest. Once the young fledge, however, the feathers should regrow.*

This color variant first arose in the aviaries of breeders in New South Wales, Australia.

Mealy Rosella (*Platycercus adscitus*). Although it is less immediately striking than some other rosellas, the Mealy has an attractive combination of colors in its plumage. The name "Mealy" refers to the color of its head (as do its alternative common names, the Pale-headed Rosella, and the Blue-cheeked Rosella). It has yellow edging to the black feathers on the back and wings, with the underparts having a bluish tone. Young birds may show occasional red feathers when they fledge, but these soon disappear. Visual sexing is difficult, although mature hens often have a stripe on the underside of their wings.

Western Rosella (*Platycercus icterotis*). Also known as the Stanley Parakeet, this is the smallest member of the genus and is often regarded as being the most docile. It is surprising that these rosellas are not more widely kept. One reason for this may simply be that they are less common than the Mealy species—possibly because they often only produce one, and not two, clutches of eggs in a season. Not only is their coloration attractive, but they can also be sexed visually; the hens have green mottling on their chests among the red plumage here. The natural distribution of the Western Rosella is the southwestern corner of the continent.

There is a naturally occurring subspecies (*P. i. xanthogenys*), in which the scalloping over the wings is reddish rather than green. A blue color mutation is also currently being developed, along with a lutino variant.

Yellow Rosella (*Platycercus flaveolus*). The simple color scheme of these parakeets, with yellow plumage predominating, makes identification easy. The cheek patches are bluish, and there is a narrow red band above the cere. The coloration of the sexes is almost identical, though the hen may have a wing stripe. A dilute yellow mutation, which has resulted in a lessening of the blue and melanin in the plumage, has also been recorded but is not commonly seen. The natural distribution of Yellow Rosellas is the inland part of southeastern Australia, away from the coast.

Brown's Rosella (*Platycercus venustus*). This bird, which is also known as the Northern Rosella, is an avicultural rarity, particularly outside

● *I understand that my rosellas were dewormed recently by their previous owner. Should I repeat this treatment?*

Yes, playing safe and deworming them again will probably be the safest course of action before you transfer the birds to their permanent quarters. It is much easier to prevent roundworms gaining access to an aviary by this means, rather than trying to eliminate these parasites once they have become established in such surroundings.

● *Is it possible to keep rosellas on a colony basis in a large aviary?*

No, this is not recommended because they can become very aggressive, particularly during the breeding period. Brown's Rosella is one of the worst offenders in this regard. Confine yourself to one pair per aviary; even then, you should watch the birds carefully to ensure that the hen is not being badly harassed by her would-be mate.

● *I have just lost my hen Crimson Rosella midway through the breeding season. Can I pair my cock with a nine-month old hen?*

Definitely not; this can be a recipe for disaster, because an adult cock is likely to attack a young, immature hen in his frustrated desire to go to nest. Even providing the cock bird with an older hen may result in aggression on his part, since she may be reluctant to breed immediately in unfamiliar surroundings. It is therefore better to wait until after the breeding season to introduce the birds, since the risk of aggressive behavior by the cock will then be significantly reduced.

Australia. It can be identified by its black head, white cheeks, and yellowish-cream underparts.

Care and Conditions
Rosellas are active birds, but some species such as the Green Rosella are prone to obesity, so it is important that they are housed in an aviary that provides them with plenty of flying space. The flight should therefore be at least 12ft (3.6m) in length, with the shelter being a minimum of 3ft (0.9m) square. In order to encourage the birds to fly as frequently as possible, the aviary must not be cluttered with perches. There should be two main perches, located at either end of the flight. Moreover, to help you in cleaning out the

Golden-mantled
Rosella

♂

Western
Rosella

♂

Yellow
Rosella

Mealy Rosella

◀ *The characteristic cheek patches and scalloping over the wings that distinguish the rosellas from other Australian parakeets can be seen clearly in this group of four species. Because the tail feathers do not taper along their length, the rosellas are also described as broadtails. They are hardy birds and can be prolific when breeding. Pairs often produce two clutches of chicks in succession.*

and mineral supplement should also be used regularly, with grit and cuttlebone being made constantly available. Soaked seed is especially popular, and this should be provided in increasing quantities during the breeding season. Green foodstuffs such as chickweed and sweet apples must also feature regularly in the diet of these parakeets.

Rosellas should be at least 18 months old before being expected to breed, although they may attempt to do so at an earlier age before they are fully mature. This is not to be recommended, however, since it increases the likelihood of problems such as egg-binding. These birds prefer a reasonably deep nest box, which should be lined with a couple of inches or so (about 5cm) of wood chips. It needs to be positioned in a reasonably secluded part of the flight and should always be sited under cover so that there is no risk of the interior becoming flooded during a heavy downpour.

Some pairs of birds, particularly Crimson and Eastern Rosellas, will often lay eight or nine eggs in a clutch. Provided that they are supplied with adequate rearing foods, such as eggfood and soaked seed, they can cater to this number of chicks successfully.

As soon as the young rosellas are feeding on their own, which will be within two weeks of leaving the nest box, they should be transferred to alternative accommodation. Otherwise, they are at particular risk of being attacked by the cock bird, who is likely to be keen to breed again without the distraction of his older offspring around him.

aviary, it is a good idea to lay paving slabs on the floor beneath these perches, since this is where most of the rosellas' droppings will accumulate. If you are able to remove these droppings effectively, and to disinfect the surrounding area regularly, this will help minimize the risk of these parakeets succumbing to intestinal roundworms.

Rosellas are very easy birds to cater to, particularly as regards their diet. A combination of cereal seeds such as millets and plain canary should form the basis of a seed mixture for them, with other items such as a little sunflower seed, safflower, and possibly small pine nuts added for variety whenever they are available. A vitamin

Barnard's and Port Lincoln Parakeets
GENUS: BARNARDIUS

THESE RELATIVELY LARGE PARAKEETS OCCUR IN a number of localized forms throughout their range, which extends across much of southern Australia. The genus consists of two species, but over seven different races are recognized. In many respects they resemble rosellas (see pages 136–139) and require similar care, although they differ significantly in terms of coloration, with green being the predominant color in their plumage.

Popular Varieties
Both these species of parakeets have a long avicultural history—being first bred in Europe in the 1870s—and make spectacular and colorful aviary occupants.

Barnard's Parakeet (*Barnardius barnardi*). This species occurs on the eastern side of the continent. The forehead is red, and a yellow band extends across the lower breast. The mantle over the back is dark blue in cocks but greener in hens—whose overall coloration may be duller. The rest of the plumage is mainly bluish-green.

The most distinctive of the four races is the Cloncurry (*B. b. macgillivrayi*). It occurs in the eastern part of Northern Territory and the adjacent area of Queensland. It is an attractive pale green, with its plumage having more pastel hues than the standard Barnard's. Adult birds lack the red frontal band seen in Barnard's Parakeet, and the abdomen is bright yellow.

Port Lincoln Parakeet (*Barnardius zonarius*). This species commonly occurs in western and central parts. It has a black head, showing some blue feathers here as well, with a yellow neck collar and abdomen. The chest and wings are green. Hens' heads are usually brownish-black.

The distinctive race known as the Twenty-eight (*B. z. semitorquatus*) has an entirely green abdomen and a band of red plumage above the cere. This is the biggest Australian parakeet and is found in the southwest corner of the continent.

Care and Conditions
These parakeets need spacious surroundings, and their flight should be at least 12ft (3.6m) in length—preferably longer—with perches located at either end. A plentiful supply of softer branches should also be provided for the parakeets to exercise their bills on, rather than trying to gnaw the wooden framework of the aviary.

A rosella-type diet will suit these birds well. They often prefer to feed on the ground, and a food bowl can be placed on the floor of the birds'

◄ *The rare blue form of Barnard's Parakeet. It still retains the neck band, giving rise to the species' alternative name of Mallee Ringneck Parakeet. (Not to be confused with ringnecks of the genus* Psittacula.)

Barnard's
Parakeet

Port Lincoln
Parakeet

▲ *Because of the relative difficulty in sexing young individuals of these species, it is advisable to check by means of DNA testing that you actually have a true pair.*

● *Do many color mutations exist in these parakeets?*

Q&A... There are several, but none is common. There is a blue form of Barnard's Parakeet, and lutinos were reported from the wild in 1927. Occasional blue Port Lincolns have been bred in Europe and Australia, and blue and lutino mutations of the Twenty-eight also exist. In these blues, the collar around the neck is white, rather than yellow, with the underparts having a whitish hue where yellow plumage is normally seen in the Port Lincoln.

● *What gauge mesh should I use in an aviary containing Barnard's Parakeets?*

These are large parakeets with robust bills, and this means that they are likely to damage the aviary woodwork if they gain access to it. The woodwork should therefore be adequately screened. It is recommended that 16-gauge mesh is used on the flight panels, rather than lighter 19-gauge mesh.

● *Does the scarcity of these parakeets mean they are difficult to breed?*

There is no real reason to explain their relative scarcity, and neither is there anything about their care that is likely to present any particular problems. Once established, pairs usually continue breeding regularly for many years. You may, however, need to be patient when trying to obtain stock—especially of Barnard's.

● *How can I tell if the cock is displaying to the hen?*

The broad tail of these parakeets figures prominently in their display, with the cock fanning the feathers and moving the tail rapidly from side to side. As the breeding season approaches cocks usually become more active, flying repeatedly up and down the flight.

shelter for this purpose, although they are likely to scatter seed as they feed. When introducing birds to an aviary, provide seed bowls adjacent to a perch, since they may be reluctant to descend to the ground at this stage.

A stout nesting site should be provided to withstand their bills; some breeders offer hollow logs. Pairs will adapt quite readily to nest boxes, however. An enclosed entrance may encourage a reluctant pair to take an interest in a nest box.

Fact File

Family name:	Psittacidae
Length:	13–16in (33–41cm)
Distribution:	Australia
Color variant availability:	Extremely rare
Compatibility: Fairly aggressive, so pairs should be housed on their own.	
Pet potential: None; only suitable as aviary birds.	
Diet: Typical Australian parakeet mix consisting mainly of plain canary seed and mixed millets, with some groats and sunflower seed. Greenfood and sweet apple should also be provided.	

Health problems: Highly susceptible to roundworms.	
Breeding tips: Compatibility is important for success. Can be double brooded.	
Nesting needs: Nest box measuring about 10in (25cm) square x 2ft 6in (75cm) deep.	
Typical clutch size:	4 eggs
Incubation:	21 days
Rearing requirements: Soaked seed and green-stuff. Some pairs may eat softfoods.	
Fledging: Will leave the nest at just over 5 weeks old.	
Lifespan:	Can live for 20 years or more.

Red-rumped Parakeet and Related Species   GENUS: PSEPHOTUS

THESE BIRDS ARE SIMILAR IN APPEARANCE TO grass parakeets (see pages 130–135) but have proportionately longer tail feathers. They are all colorful birds, with considerable variation in plumage between the four species of the genus.

Popular Varieties

This group includes some of the most attractively colored of all the Australian parakeets.

Red-rumped Parakeet (*Psephotus haematonotus*). Originating from southeast Australia, this is one of the most attractive and widely kept of all Australian parakeets. They will nest readily in aviaries, and the sexes can be distinguished easily. The cock is considerably brighter in color than the hen, being bluish-green over the head, chest, and wings, while the underparts are yellowish. Hens are grayish-green and lack the characteristic area of red feathering associated with cocks. It is possible to sex these parakeets from the time they begin to feather up in the nest, although it will take at least four months for them to acquire full adult plumage.

The yellow variety of the Red-rumped has been widely kept for many years. It is not pure yellow, but a dilute form of the normal Red-rumped; hens have a yellower hue to their plumage. More recently, a true lutino mutation

▲ *A blue mutation of the Red-rumped Parakeet. This color is due to an autosomal recessive gene mutation. This variety has become more common in recent years.*

has been developed, with the cock retaining the red area of plumage on the rump. In this variety the area over the wings is a paler, lemon-white shade when compared with the yellow coloration on the rest of the body. Hens have paler feathering than cocks.

Fact File

Family name:	Psittacidae
Length:	10–12in (25–30cm)
Distribution:	Australia
Color variant availability: Common in Red-rumpeds.	
Compatibility: Can be aggressive, so pairs should be housed on their own.	
Pet potential: None; only suitable as aviary birds.	
Diet: Good-quality mix of plain canary seed and assorted millets, with some sunflower seed. Greenfood such as chickweed and fresh sweet apple can also be offered.	
Health problems: Susceptible to roundworms.	

Breeding tips: Generally reliable breeders, with pairs easy to identify. Mature by 1 year old.

Nesting needs: Nest box measuring about 2ft (60cm) deep.

Typical clutch size:	4–6 eggs
Incubation:	18–20 days

Rearing requirements: Softfood of various types, such as eggfood or softbill food, may be eaten. Soaked seed such as millet sprays also recommended.

Fledging: The young leave the nest between 4 and 5 weeks old.

Lifespan: Can live for 15 years or more.

In the blue mutation of the Red-rumped, the rump of the cock is white but blue in hens. Their wings are a silvery shade, compared with those of cocks of this color. A number of other mutations are being developed, including pied and opaline varieties—the latter named after the Budgerigar mutation of the same name.

Many-colored Parakeet (*Psephotus varius*). Only recently has the Many-colored started to become more widely available. It is also known as the Mulga Parakeet, since it frequents the interior of southern Australia where mulga grass often grows. Cocks have a yellow area above the cere and an orangish area on the belly. There may be considerable variation in patterning between individuals, with the more brightly colored individuals being preferred. Hens can be recognized by their orangish-red wing bars.

Care and Conditions

The Red-rumped is an ideal choice for beginners, for it is hardy, keen to breed, and not destructive. Red-rumpeds are not noisy, with cocks having attractive, musical calls that are unlikely to cause offense to near neighbors. The Many-colored is less hardy and tends to be a less prolific breeder. The one drawback of the *Psephotus* parakeets overall, however, is their aggressive nature. Pairs should be housed alone, and even then harmony may not prevail all year. Cocks are often very aggressive toward their own young, sometimes killing them before they have fledged. It may therefore be better to start breeding with young birds, rather than an adult pair in which the cock may previously have harmed his offspring.

A typical parakeet diet will suit these birds well. It needs to be augmented regularly with greenfood—particularly when there are chicks in the nest. Some sunflower can be provided in limited quantities as well.

▶ *The Red-rumped and the Many-colored are very similar in their habits, but young Many-coloreds are usually slower to fledge, spending about a week longer in the nest box on average.*

Q&A...

● *What are the other members of this genus called?*

The other two members are the Blue-bonnet (*P. haematogaster*) and the Golden-shouldered Parakeet (*P. chrysopterygius*). The Blue-bonnet has blue feathering around the face and wings. The Golden-shouldered Parakeet, and the subspecies called the Hooded Parakeet (*P. c. dissimilis*), are scarce in aviculture—although numbers of the Hooded have increased recently. The plumage is mainly turquoise-blue, with yellow on the wings.

● *Are there any differences in the breeding requirements of members of this genus?*

The Red-rumped will nest very readily, often proving to be double brooded and more prolific than others of the genus. At the other extreme, the Hooded often prefers to nest in northern climates during the winter, and so it may need to be kept indoors in heated accommodation, with additional heating provided for this purpose.

Red-rumped Parakeet

♂

♀

♂

Many-colored Parakeet

♀

Princess of Wales' Parakeet and Related Species

GENUS: POLYTELIS

THE THREE SPECIES COMPRISING THIS GENUS are widely distributed across Australia. They are well represented in aviculture, mainly due to their distinctive coloration and sleek appearance.

Popular Varieties

Unlike most Australian parakeets, *Polytelis* species can become very tame in aviary surroundings, further enhancing their appeal.

Princess of Wales' Parakeet (*Polytelis alexandrae*). This parakeet is also known as Queen Alexandra's Parakeet, the Rose-throated Parakeet, and the Spinifex Parakeet—the last name derived from a grass found in the parts of arid central Australia where these birds live. They have a pale blue crown, a pinkish throat, greenish wings, and pale bluish-gray underparts; hens generally have a duller and more grayish crown. Immatures resemble hens but with shorter tails, although cocks will soon be identified when they raise the feathers on their crown as they sing.

Color mutations are established in this species, but they are virtually unknown in other *Polytelis* parakeets. Blue Princess of Wales' Parakeets were first recorded in Australia in 1951, and this mutation has now appeared elsewhere. They are attractive birds with sky-blue wing patches, a

Q & A

● *At what age can I sex my young Barraband Parakeets?*

... It can take up to three years for young cocks to molt into adult plumage, although the visual distinctions between the sexes usually become apparent in their second year.

● *How should these parakeets be housed?*

These parakeets will be displayed to best effect in a long flight. If you house more than one pair together, introduce the birds to the same aviary at the same time to minimize the risk of territorial disputes. Their accommodation must include a dry, snug shelter. Although relatively unaffected by the cold, this species dislikes prolonged wet, foggy weather and may succumb to respiratory diseases in such conditions.

● *Will these parakeets nest every year?*

Pairs will often nest reliably over many years, with cocks engaging in a pronounced display—bowing and twisting their heads around in front of the hens before mating. Having selected a nesting site in the aviary, the birds will return here to breed over successive years, although they will normally only roost inside the box in the breeding season. The young are usually very restless when they first leave the nest box. Try to avoid unnecessary disturbances near the aviary at this stage so the fledglings can settle down. This should happen over the course of a week or two.

Fact File

Family name:	Psittacidae
Length:	16–18in (41–46cm)
Distribution:	Australia
Color variant availability: Presently restricted to Princess of Wales' Parakeet.	
Compatibility: Pairs can be social and may mix safely with Cockatiels as well.	
Pet potential: Will become tame in aviary surroundings but not suitable as household pets.	
Diet: Smaller cereal seeds such as plain canary seed and millets, with sunflower seed and groats. Often take sweet apple readily as well as assorted greenstuff, including chickweed.	
Health problems: Most vulnerable to eye infections and roundworms.	
Breeding tips: Egg eating—usually by the cock—sometimes a problem. Remove cock from the nest until eggs have hatched.	
Nesting needs: Nest box measuring about 2ft (60cm) from top to base.	
Typical clutch size:	4–6 eggs
Incubation:	20–21 days
Rearing requirements: Eggfood may be eaten by some pairs. Also offer soaked seed and greenfood.	
Fledging: Will leave the nest at about 5 weeks old.	
Lifespan:	Can live for 20 years or more.

pale violet rump, and silver-blue feathers over the rest of the body. The coral-red bill color is unchanged. A lutino mutation occurred in East Germany in the 1970s and was introduced to the West. Pink and yellow plumage predominate.

Barraband Parakeet (*Polytelis swainsonii*). Also known as the Superb Parakeet. Adult birds are very easy to sex: the elegant-looking cocks are primarily bright green, with a red band under the throat and yellow on the face. Hens are grayish-green, with some blue on the head. Young birds are virtually impossible to sex visually, since they resemble hens. Both sexes have a scattering of red feathers at the top of the legs. Barraband Parakeets can have a long reproductive life, with pairs continuing to breed for 20 years.

Rock Peplar (*Polytelis anthopeplus*). There are two populations of these parakeets, one in eastern South Australia and the other (with more greenish plumage) in the west of the country. This species has many different names including Rock Pebbler, Smoker, and Regent Parrot. Cocks are mainly yellow in color. Hens are olive-green, with red feathering on the lower part of the wings near the flight feathers. Young males have more yellow in their underparts and do not obtain full adult coloration until 18 months old.

Care and Conditions

The natural grace of these parakeets is enhanced by housing them in a long flight. They may even breed successfully on a colony system if housed in suitably spacious aviaries.

The diet of these birds does not differ significantly from that required by other Australian parakeets. Plenty of greenfood should be given regularly, with soaked millet sprays also being favored—particularly when there are chicks in the nest.

These parakeets are very keen rain-bathers, although they will not generally bathe in a water bowl provided for this purpose. Birds housed in an indoor flight for long periods should be sprayed regularly with water to maintain their plumage in good condition.

◀ *A male Princess of Wales' Parakeet. They can easily be tamed in aviary surroundings and will take greenfood readily from the hand.*

Crimson-winged and King Parakeets

GENERA: APROSMICTUS, ALISTERUS

THESE TWO GENERA ARE REPRESENTED BOTH within Australia and further north in New Guinea and on neighboring islands. King Parakeets in particular are very striking birds, and captive strains of the Australian species are well established. Crimson-winged are also popular and are bred regularly in aviaries.

Popular Varieties

Red is a predominant color in these birds. They are among the most expensive parakeets to buy but often breed well once established.

Crimson-winged Parakeet (*Aprosmictus erythropterus*). The combination of the crimson markings on the wings set against the black feathering of the mantle seen in cocks of this species is unique among parakeets. Hens are far less strikingly colored, lacking the black mantle and displaying far less red plumage on the wings. Young birds resemble hens but can be identified by their brown, rather than reddish, eyes.

Australian King Parakeet (*Alisterus scapularis*). This species is found along the eastern seaboard of Australia. Only the cocks show the magnificent, crimson-red coloration that extends over the entire head and most of the body apart from the wings, which are dark green with contrasting pale green wing coverts. Hens have a green head

Australian King Parakeet

♂

Crimson-winged Parakeet

♂

▲ *Cock Crimson-winged and Australian King Parakeets are both more highly colored than hens. Careful supervision is recommended at the start of the breeding period, because both species may be aggressive toward their intended mates.*

Fact File

Family name:	Psittacidae
Length:	14–18in (36–46cm)
Distribution: Australia, New Guinea, and neighboring Indonesian islands.	
Color variant availability:	Very restricted
Compatibility: Pairs should be housed on their own.	
Pet potential: None; only suitable as aviary birds.	
Diet: Cereal seeds such as plain canary seed and millets, plus paddy rice for Kings from New Guinea. Also sunflower seed, pine nuts, greenfood, and fruit.	
Health problems: Vulnerable to intestinal worms, including tapeworms.	

Breeding tips: Patience may be required, but pairs have a long reproductive life that can extend well over a decade.	
Nesting needs: Nest box at least 10in (25cm) square x 3ft (90cm) deep.	
Typical clutch size:	3–6 eggs
Incubation:	21 days
Rearing requirements: Soaked seed, greenstuff, and softfoods.	
Fledging: Young will leave the nest between 6 and 8 weeks old.	
Lifespan:	Can live for 25 years or more.

▲ *The crimson feathers by which the Crimson-winged Parakeet gets its name are clearly seen in this cock. It can take up to three years for the full coloration of the adult cock to develop.*

and chest, with red confined to the abdomen. Sexing the young is relatively easy, because although both sexes resemble hens on fledging, the darker bill of the hen soon becomes apparent.

Care and Conditions

It can take several years for these parakeets to settle down sufficiently in order to start nesting. They must have a long flight—with some cover here as well—because, unlike other Australian parakeets, these are birds of woodland. Adequate wintertime protection is also important, particularly in the case of recently imported stock, which will need very careful acclimatization and heated winter quarters at first.

A typical Australian parakeet mix is suitable for feeding. Pairs can rear chicks on little more than oats and buckwheat added to a standard seed mix, but better results are likely if a more varied diet is provided. Try offering softfood at this stage, as well as greenfood on a regular basis.

● My cock King Parakeet seems intent on chasing his mate constantly, and I'm worried that she may not be feeding. What should I do?

Offering several feeding sites in the aviary at this stage can be helpful if the cock starts to dominate one area, preventing his would-be mate from feeding there. Try placing food and water bowls on the ground as well, since the hen is less likely to be chased here by the cock.

● What should I do to ensure breeding success with these parakeets?

Cocks can be savage when they come into breeding condition, and if their partners do not respond to their advances it may be best to clip the wing of a cock in order to prevent harassment of the hen. It will greatly reduce the likelihood of breeding success if she loses condition. Once egg-laying starts, however, the danger is passed. Remove the chicks as soon as they are feeding independently, since these parakeets are sometimes double brooded. If the chicks are left, not only may they interfere with the nesting activities of the adult birds, but they may also be attacked by the cock.

Kakarikis GENUS: CYANORAMPHUS

Red-fronted
Kakariki

Yellow-fronted
Kakariki

These unusual parakeets originate from New Zealand, being found in more temperate latitudes than many parrots. Their name is derived from a Maori word meaning "little parrot." Kakarikis are very lively and quite unlike other parakeets in the way they scamper over the mesh of their enclosure. They will also detect any gaps through which they can escape, so particular attention needs to be paid to aviary security.

Popular Varieties

There are four species in this genus, but only two are well represented in aviculture. Color variants are now established in the Red-fronted Kakariki, which is the more commonly kept form.

Red-fronted Kakariki (*Cyanoramphus novaezelandiae*). Red-fronted Kakarikis were first bred in Britain in 1891, but it was not until the 1970s that this species became well known in Europe and North America. The birds are unmistakable, thanks to the crimson-red markings above the

◀ *Both the Red-fronted Kakariki and the Yellow-fronted Kakariki occur on North Island and South Island, New Zealand, as well as on neighboring islands. Twice-yearly worming is recommended for these birds.*

Fact File

Family name:	Psittacidae
Length:	8–12in (20–30cm)
Distribution: New Zealand and smaller neighboring islands.	
Color variant availability: Only recorded in the Red-fronted Kakariki.	
Compatibility: Quarrelsome, so pairs should be housed on their own.	
Pet potential:	Can settle in the home.
Diet: A mixture of millets, plain canary seed, and sunflower, plus greenstuff, fruit, and some mealworms.	
Health problems: At risk from roundworms and scaly face.	

Breeding tips: Remove nest box so pairs do not attempt to breed during the winter in temperate areas, to reduce the risk of egg-binding. Position nest box in cool place in hot climates.

Nesting needs: Nest box about 9in (23cm) square x 12in (30cm) deep.	
Typical clutch size:	7–8 eggs
Incubation:	19–21 days
Rearing requirements: Softfood and livefood are usually taken readily and help to meet the growth requirements of the chicks.	
Fledging:	Will leave the nest around 5 weeks old.
Lifespan: Can live for up to 16 years, but this is exceptional.	

cere and the corresponding red patches behind each eye. The rest of the plumage is primarily dark green, although there are red patches on each side of the rump, with the flight feathers being bluish. The bill is a steely-blue shade with a black tip. Visual sexing can only be carried out on the basis of size, with cocks being larger.

The most striking and widely kept mutation is the lutino, in which bright yellow plumage replaces green, making a striking contrast with the crimson-red markings. There is also a green-and-yellow pied form—in which the patterning can be very variable—and a dull cinnamon.

Yellow-fronted Kakariki (*Cyanoramphus auriceps*). This species is easily distinguished from the more common Red-fronted Kakariki by virtue of the extensive area of yellow on the crown, with red coloration here being restricted to a narrow band above the cere. There are no red patches behind the eyes, and the Yellow-fronted is also smaller. Young birds have brown, rather than red, eyes and shorter tails.

Care and Conditions

Try to obtain young birds at the outset, because kakarikis are a relatively short-lived species. Since these birds are not noisy or destructive, they are an ideal choice for suburban aviaries. They will spend long periods on the floor of the aviary, and if they are to be kept in aviaries with concrete floors they should be provided with

fresh-dug tussocks of untreated grass placed in seed trays, which they will dig at avidly.

If possible, restrict breeding pairs to rearing no more than two rounds of chicks in succession. Young kakarikis develop rapidly, sometimes being able to breed by four or five months of age. However, it is advisable to wait until they are a year old before allowing them to nest for the first time, for they will then be fully mature.

▼ *The pied mutation of the Red-fronted Kakariki has no set pattern of coloration. The markings are entirely random between different individuals.*

● **Do kakarikis make good pets?**

A young bird can develop into a very lively companion in the home, but these birds are highly active. If you are seeking a quiet companion to sit on your shoulder for long periods, then a Cockatiel will be a better choice. Kakarikis need spacious enclosures, but make sure the spacing of the bars in large cages does not allow the birds to become caught in them, with fatal consequences.

● **My kakariki sometimes appears to have difficulty perching. What's wrong?**

Kakarikis can be very vulnerable to stress, and this condition often results in them being unable to perch properly. If the bird is transferred to a quiet, darkened place for an hour or so it will usually recover, however.

This type of seizure might also be linked to a low blood calcium level, so a liquid calcium supplement given afterward for a period may be useful in preventing a recurrence of the problem.

● **Are kakarikis fussy feeders?**

No, kakarikis are very adaptable in terms of their feeding requirements, although individual birds may develop preferences. Fruit and vegetables should be offered on a daily basis, with broccoli and celery being useful wintertime choices. Pomegranates and strawberries are relished, as are some milder peppers—the seeds especially are consumed readily.

● **Is breeding straightforward with these birds?**

Yes, it is usually straightforward, with pairs eager to nest. They should be kept on their own, however, as they can be aggressive at this stage.

Lories GENERA: PSEUDEOS, CHALCOPSITTA, LORIUS, EOS

LORIES ARE DISTINGUISHABLE FROM LORIKEETS by their short, square tails. There are a number of different genera represented in aviculture, with many brightly colored species. There are also many localized forms. In most lory species DNA sexing is necessary, with differences in plumage often being linked only to a particular geographical distribution. Lories are unusual among parrots because nectar, rather than seed, forms the basis of their diet.

Popular Varieties

The following are species drawn from the genera that are commonly represented in aviculture.

Dusky Lory (*Pseudeos fuscata*). These lories have highly individual coloration, with some birds having fiery orange plumage whereas other birds have plumage of a yellowish shade. While orange-colored individuals only produce similar-colored offspring, yellow-colored birds can have both yellow and orange chicks in the same nest. It may be possible to recognize pairs of this species, because cocks generally have a more yellowish-white rump compared with hens. Young birds have dark, brownish bills, while those of adults are orangish in color.

Duivenbode's Lory (*Chalcopsitta duivenbodei*). These large lories make spectacular aviary occupants, showing to best effect in a relatively large aviary. Unfortunately, their noisiness may prevent them being kept in built-up areas. Visual sexing is not possible, but young birds are easily recognized by having white, rather than black, skin around their eyes.

Chattering Lory (*Lorius garrulus*). These lories are predominantly scarlet, with green wings, yellow shoulder patches, and green thighs. Young birds have brown bills. The more colorful subspecies known as the Yellow-backed Lory (*L. g. flavopalliatus*) is restricted to some of the Moluccan islands. Like many other lories, the Chattering Lory can become very tame, even in aviary surroundings.

Red Lory (*Eos bornea*). *Eos* lories are smaller and can be identified by their predominantly red plumage, offset with areas of blue, black, and purple. Minor differences in the plumage may indicate subspecies, but even in these it is impossible to distinguish visually between the sexes. Young birds have dark bills and brown irises. Red Lories are found on some of the Indonesian islands such as Amboina and the Kai Islands.

◄ *The Dusky Lory is a popular species, being hardy, colorful, and lively, with pairs generally nesting readily in aviaries.*

Fact File

Family name:	Psittacidae
Length:	10–12in (25–30cm)
Distribution: Australia, New Guinea, Indonesia, and other Pacific islands.	
Color variant availability:	Virtually unknown
Compatibility: Pairs should be housed on their own.	
Pet potential: Can become tame and will talk if obtained when young.	
Diet: Offer a nectar mixture, and fruit such as apples, grapes, and pomegranates provided fresh each day.	
Health problems: Can be vulnerable to candidiasis.	

Breeding tips: Nest box needs to be located in a relatively secluded part of the aviary.	
Nesting needs: Nest box about 10–12in (25–30cm) square x at least 12in (30cm) deep, well lined with coarse shavings.	
Typical clutch size:	2 eggs
Incubation:	24 days
Rearing requirements: Softfood may be eaten when there are chicks in the nest.	
Fledging: Will leave the nest between 10 and 11 weeks old.	
Lifespan:	Can live for over 20 years.

▲ *The brown-and-yellow coloration of Duivenbode's Lory is unmistakable. These large, noisy birds originate from northern New Guinea.*

Care and Conditions

Care is quite straightforward, but the birds' diet means that special attention should be paid to cleanliness.

A typical parrot nest box is needed for breeding, but it will prove very useful to have a side inspection hatch through which you can top up, or even replace, soiled nest litter after the chicks have hatched. Keep the nest in position all year so it can also be used by the birds for roosting.

Q&A

● *Should I keep a lory as a pet?*

Although lories can be kept as pets and may prove to be talented mimics, their messy droppings make it hard to care for them satisfactorily in the confines of the home. Their quarters, including their perches, will need to be washed regularly to prevent a build-up of the sticky droppings characteristic of these birds.

● *How should lories be housed?*

The accommodation needs to be designed so that it can be cleaned easily. A solid concrete floor that can be hosed down is recommended. This is important, since lories produce copious sticky, liquid droppings. Some breeders prefer suspended or hanging cages which can be hosed down daily to clean the droppings. Lories also have relatively powerful bills, so the flight frame should be constructed using 16-gauge mesh. Wipe-clean surfaces are also recommended in the shelter area to ensure proper cleaning and the prevention of mold caused by droppings. Pairs are generally hardy once acclimatized, so heating is not usually required during the winter in temperate areas.

● *How do I feed these birds?*

Commercially prepared diets are widely available and are very straightforward to use, containing all the necessary ingredients to keep these birds in good health. Simply measure out the required amount of water and stir the powder in thoroughly. Make sure you wash the drinkers out thoroughly between feeds. You can also purchase dry diets, intended for use straight from the packet. They can be sprinkled over fruit or offered to the birds in a separate container. Some diets contain more solids and result in less messy droppings.

Lorikeets Genera: Trichoglossus, Charmosyna

The long tails of lorikeets, shown most dramatically in the Papuan Lorikeet *(Charmosyna papou)* help to distinguish these nectar-feeding parrots from the square-tailed lories. They feed in an identical way to lories, with their tongues again being adapted with brushlike structures called papillae that allow them to collect microscopic pollen grains from flowers. Lorikeets also need similar care to lories.

Popular Varieties

Color mutations are rare in these parrots, but they do occur in the Rainbow Lorikeet. Many species have a localized distribution, occurring on just a few islands, and are rare in aviculture.
Rainbow Lorikeet (*Trichoglossus haematodus*). There are more subspecies of this lorikeet than any other member of the parrot family. Twenty-one are recognized, although the general pattern of markings is the same in all cases. The head coloration is dark—often bluish—with colorful patches at the corners of the neck. The wings and back are green, while the breast plumage tends to be yellow, orange, or red, with the feathers here often being edged with darker markings.

The Green-naped subspecies (*T. h. haematodus*), which is found on New Guinea and other islands, is most widely kept in Europe and North America. As its name suggests, the color of its nape has a decidedly greenish hue. In Australia, Swainson's Lorikeet (*T. h. moluccanus*) is common in collections. It is very colorful, usually with a scarlet breast and more vivid blue plumage on the head than is seen in the Green-naped race.

Other forms that are represented in collections include Edwards' Lorikeet (*T. h. capistratus*), confined to the Indonesian island of Timor,

◀ *Swainson's Lorikeet. It is not unknown for these lorikeets to tunnel into the floor of their aviary to nest if they cannot get access to a suitable nest box. Nesting on the floor is unlikely to be successful, however, because the nest will probably be flooded when it rains.*

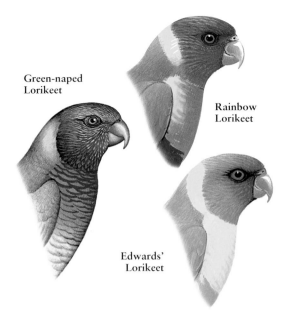

Green-naped
Lorikeet

Rainbow
Lorikeet

Edwards'
Lorikeet

◀ *Differences in the coloration of the head and chest help to distinguish the subspecies of the Green-naped Lorikeet. The Rainbow Lorikeet is one the most colorful races compared with Edwards' Lorikeet, in which the breast feathering is yellow. The Green-naped has greenish-yellow plumage on the sides of the neck.*

Q&A...

● **Why is bill color important in Stella's Lorikeets?**

This characteristic indicates whether or not the birds are in good health. The bill should have a decidedly red tone. Birds with pale bills are likely to be suffering from a degeneration of the liver that cannot be reversed, although they may still be able to live for some time with this condition.

● *Should I use a melanistic or red Stella's for breeding purposes?*

Melanistic birds tend to less expensive to purchase because of their duller plumage, but you may want to bear in mind that, although melanistic individuals paired together, or paired with reds, can produce both melanistic and red offspring, only red offspring will result from pairings of red Stella's.

● *Are lorikeets hardy?*

Yes, most lorikeets are very hardy once they become acclimatized, although there are some variations in this respect. Smaller species are less likely to be able to withstand the rigors of a winter in temperate climates without artificial heat and light being supplied for them. Lorikeets that are kept outside through this period should be encouraged to roost in the aviary shelter, where a nest box should be provided for this purpose.

Massena's Lorikeet (*T. h. massena*), distributed widely on islands to the east of New Guinea, and Mitchell's Lorikeet (*T. h. mitchelli*), found on Lombok and Bali. Although in some races there may be slight variations in color between the sexes, with the breast feathers of cocks often being brighter, DNA sexing is recommended to ensure that you have a pair. Alternatively, it is possible to keep and breed these lorikeets on a colony basis, provided that all individuals are introduced to the aviary at the same time, and there are more nesting sites than pairs.

Goldie's Lorikeet (*Trichoglossus goldiei*). This species is found in New Guinea and has only been available to birdkeepers since 1977. Pairs

Fact File

Family name:	Psittacidae
Length:	7–11in (18–28cm)
Distribution: Australia, New Guinea, and other Pacific islands.	
Color variant availability:	Virtually unknown
Compatibility: Pairs can sometimes be kept in colonies together.	
Pet potential: Their messy feeding habits usually preclude these birds being kept as pets, although they are naturally tame and inquisitive.	
Diet: A nectar food and fruit, such as apples, grapes, or pomegranates, will be required.	
Health problems: Can be vulnerable to candidiasis.	

Breeding tips: Nest box needs to be located in a relatively secluded part of the aviary.	
Nesting needs: Nest box approximately 10–12in (25–30cm) square x at least 11in (28cm) deep, well-lined with coarse shavings.	
Typical clutch size:	2–3 eggs
Incubation:	22–26 days
Rearing requirements: Softfood as well as mealworms may be eaten when there are chicks present in the nest.	
Fledging: Young will leave the nest around 9–11 weeks old.	
Lifespan:	Can live for over 15 years.

◀ The plumage on the head of Goldie's Lorikeet is plum-colored in young birds. However, the bill is lighter in color, being brownish rather than black. The bird shown here has adult plumage. The streaky markings are unique among individuals and can help in identification.

▶ Color feeding is not necessary in order to maintain the brilliant, crimson-red coloration of Stella's Lorikeet, or indeed, any other parrot. Stella's move around their perches with a characteristic hopping action.

have proved to be prolific, however, and these small lorikeets are a delightful acquisition for a relatively small garden aviary, particularly as they will prove to be much quieter than their larger relatives. Their coloration is unmistakable, with a red forehead and crown, becoming mauve on the sides of the face. The underparts are streaked with dark green markings on a lighter yellowish background. Goldie's Lorikeets cannot be sexed visually, but young birds can be identified by their overall duller coloration. Although they will eat some small seeds, such as millets, nectar and fruit are the mainstay of their diet.

Papuan Lorikeet (*Charmosyna papou*). This is one of the most beautiful of all lorikeets, with the subspecies known as Stella's (*C. p. stellae*) being the most widely kept form. There are two quite distinct forms that occur in the wild. The red variety is a striking shade of crimson, with green wings and darker markings across the abdomen and behind the eyes. In this case, hens can be identified easily by the yellow markings on the rump. The melanistic phase, which tends to occur at higher altitudes in the mountainous region of New Guinea where these lorikeets originate, is almost entirely glossy black apart from the dark blue area on the crown, which is retained. In this case, cocks have red patches on the sides of the rump, whereas this area is black in hens. These are quiet, non-destructive birds that show to best effect in a wide flight where their playful natures can be fully appreciated.

Care and Conditions

Cleanliness is vital in an aviary housing these birds. A thick layer of newspaper on the floor of the shelter will allow their droppings to be cleaned up easily. All the species listed here are relatively hardy, but some of the other smaller lorikeets may benefit from some heat in their quarters through the winter.

A proprietary nectar mix should be fed to these birds. Stella's Lorikeet and other members of the *Charmosyna* genus may benefit from a slightly different concentration of the mix—check with the manufacturer or an experienced breeder if in doubt. Nectar must only be provided in sealed drinkers with spouts, rather than open bowls, to prevent the lorikeets bathing in their food with disastrous consequences. Instead, provide a large bowl of water for bathing purposes.

Fruit and items such as sponge cake soaked in nectar should also be offered fresh every day. Lorikeets will also eat greenstuff and vegetables such as pieces of carrot. It is important to provide a range of such foodstuffs, partly to ensure an adequate level of fiber in the diet. Drinking water is also essential, in spite of their liquid diet.

The nesting requirements of these birds are very similar to those of lories, although the nest box size will vary according to the species concerned. Rainbow lorikeets are more destructive when nesting and need a relatively stout nest box. They also tend to feather pluck their young before fledging, although the plumage regrows within a few weeks after the chicks leave the nest.

Cockatoos GENERA: EOLOPHUS, CACATUA

COCKATOOS ARE EASILY IDENTIFIED BY THEIR long crest feathers—which they will raise if excited or alarmed. They are active, noisy birds and can be destructive. They require a spacious, robust aviary sited away from near neighbors who are likely to be disturbed by their raucous calls. Hand-reared cockatoos can make excellent pets but often become spiteful after they mature at four or five years old. Cockatoos lack the "blue layer" in their plumage, resulting in the rather monotone coloration seen in most species.

Popular Varieties

Indonesian, rather than Australian, cockatoos are more widely seen in collections. Color variants are only documented for the Galah species.
Galah Cockatoo (*Eolophus roseicapillus*). Commonly kept in Australia, these cockatoos are scarce elsewhere. The export of Australian birds was banned in 1960, but the prolific breeding habits of Galahs exported before the ban has maintained numbers in the United States and Europe. Individuals showing white, rather than gray, areas of plumage are now being bred. It is not uncommon for the pink body coloration of these cockatoos, which are also called Roseates, to vary in depth.

Lesser Sulphur-crested Cockatoo (*Cacatua sulphurea*). The Timor race (*C. s. parvula*) is the smallest, while the Citron-crested (*C. s. citrinocristata*), which is found on the island of Sumba, can be identified by its orange, rather than yellow, crest feathers.

Umbrella Cockatoo (*Cacatua alba*). These are impressive, snow-white cockatoos. Umbrella Cockatoos should be housed in accommodation built from brick or blocks rather than timber.

Galah Cockatoo

Umbrella Cockatoo

Fact File

Family name: Cacatuidae

Length: 12–18in (30–46cm)

Distribution: Australia, New Guinea, and other Pacific islands including the Moluccas.

Color variant availability: Virtually unknown

Compatibility: Cocks can be aggressive as they come into breeding condition.

Pet potential: Can be very tame. Not especially talented mimics. Noisy and unpredictable as they mature.

Diet: Offer a good-quality parrot mix, with supplements, and a regular supply of greenstuff and fruit such as apples, grapes, and pomegranates.

Health problems: Vulnerable to feather disorders, especially PBFD. Galahs prone to lipomas.

Breeding tips: Allow constant access to the nest box, providing offcuts to gnaw and produce a nest lining. This may help to reduce aggression.

Nesting needs: A nest box, barrel, or large, hollow tree trunk can be provided; as a guide, it should be at least 16in (40cm) square x 20in (51cm) deep. It may be necessary to reinforce the entry hole.

Typical clutch size: 2 eggs, but Galahs known to lay as many as 5 eggs in a single clutch.

Incubation: 25–30 days

Rearing requirements: Soaked seed may be eaten readily when there are chicks in the nest.

Fledging: Young will leave the nest around 10–11 weeks old.

Lifespan: With exercise and proper diet can live for over 70 years.

▲ *The yellow plumage of the Lesser Sulphur-crested Cockatoo is most clearly seen on its head. Distribution of this species is centered on Sulawesi, Indonesia.*

◀ *Crest shape in cockatoos varies widely. That of the Umbrella Cockatoo is perhaps the most impressive, being broad and sweeping in shape.*

Care and Conditions

Compatibility can be a problem in cockatoos, so try to start with a proven pair if possible. It is best to purchase immature birds of known gender and keep them together until they mature, since pair bonding will be more likely. It appears that cockatoos pair for life, so it can be very difficult to pair up an individual that has lost its mate.

Cockatoos may refuse to eat anything other than sunflower seed. It is important to persuade them to eat a wider range of foods, however. This will be easier with chicks, which can be transferred from their rearing food to a complete diet at this stage. Restrict the fat intake of Galahs, to reduce the risk of lipomas. These benign fatty tumors will affect the birds' flying ability.

Q & A ...

● **What is PBFD, and how does it affect cockatoos?**

This is a virus that was first discovered in this group of birds. Testing is now recommended when buying cockatoos, since PBFD is a chronic disease that will ultimately prove to be fatal. Feather condition is vital. Never be tempted to buy birds that have semibald areas, because even if this is not PBFD, the cockatoo is likely to be plucking its own feathers, and this is a difficult condition to treat successfully.

● *Can you give me some more tips on breeding cockatoos successfully?*

A stout nest box should be provided in an easily accessible position, because cockatoos often tend to neglect their youngest chick. As a result, it becomes progressively weaker while its stronger sibling thrives. However, by hand-feeding to top up its food intake, its life can be saved. In some cases, it may be better to remove it entirely from the aviary for hand-rearing, particularly if the adult birds are nervous and resent your repeated inspections of the nest box. Galahs often like to line their nest site with leaves, twigs, and similar material collected in the aviary.

Cockatiel SPECIES: NYMPHICUS HOLLANDICUS

COCKATIELS RANGE WIDELY ACROSS MUCH OF Australia, being absent only from coastal areas. Although the Cockatiel resembles a cockatoo, it is more streamlined, with a long, rather than square, tail. It uses its crest feathers in a similar way to cockatoos, raising or lowering them depending on its mood. Cockatiels also lack the "blue layer" in the plumage, so their appearance depends on their pigmentation. Cockatiels are far easier to cater to than their larger relatives, however, both as pets and aviary birds.

For many years the Cockatiel has been in the shadow of the Budgerigar—with whom it shares a similar avicultural history. Since the emergence of color varieties, this species has become far more popular with birdkeepers, however.

Cockatiels are far less destructive than cockatoos, so they can be housed in an ordinary timber-framed aviary, covered with 19-gauge mesh. It is also possible to house them in a colony, or even in the company of Budgerigars.

The Cockatiel's call consists of a series of whistles; cocks have an attractive, warbling song that is unlikely to offend nearby neighbors. Young Cockatiels settle well as household pets and are long-lived. They will also remain kindly disposed toward their owners at all times—which may not always be the case with their larger relatives!

Popular Varieties

The number of color varieties is more limited than in other parrots, owing to color restrictions imposed by the structure of the plumage. Show standardization has already occurred in some countries, such as the United States. There is no difference between the varieties in terms of their potential talking skills or tameness.

Cockatiels are easy to sex, with males being instantly recognizable by their lemon-yellow heads and circular, orange ear coverts. The remainder of the plumage is predominantly gray, with white in the wing, while the undersides of the tail feathers are blackish. Hens have grayer

▲ *Cockatiels are exceptionally gentle— even when breeding—to the extent that they can be kept quite satisfactorily in an aviary housing finches, smaller softbills, or doves without any risk of aggression.*

feathering over their heads, with yellow barring on the underside of the tail feathers. Young birds resemble hens but have a pinkish, rather than gray, cere and shorter tail feathers. You should be able to distinguish young cocks before they molt into adult plumage at about six months old, since they will start warbling before this stage.

Pied. This was the first mutation to emerge, during 1949 in California. Pieds can be very variable in appearance, with the areas of gray plumage broken by pale yellowish feathering. In a few instances, the feet may be most affected, with the lack of melanin being responsible for pinkish areas here, extending to the nails also. Breeders prefer birds with well-balanced, symmetrical markings, but there are no guarantees of the appearance of the offspring—even if a well-marked pair of birds is bred together.

Lutino. This was developed at the end of the 1950s. It is easily possible to sex birds at close quarters, when the darker yellow barring on the underside of the tails of hens can be seen in good light. This is a sex-linked mutation, rather than an autosomal recessive mutation like the pied.

Cinnamon. Cockatiels showing this warm brown, rather than gray, coloration were first recorded in a New Zealand aviary during 1950, although birds of this color have also been seen among wild flocks in Australia. The melanin pigment is modified to a brown shade. The cinnamon characteristic is sex-linked, with cocks usually being darker than hens as they mature.

Pearl. This mutation affects the distribution of the pigment within the plumage. The center of the feathers is pale, with melanin around the edges, creating a scalloped appearance. In the case of cocks, however, this effect is lost on maturity, because the increased melanin deposition that occurs at this stage cancels out the light pearl markings. More recently, a strain of pearl Cockatiels, in which cocks do not change color, has been developed in the United States. It has proved possible to combine this characteristic with both light and dark colors—giving rise to pearl cinnamons and pearl lutinos, for example.

▲ *The lutino was the mutation that captured the imagination of breeders and was initially responsible for the tremendous growth of interest in the Cockatiel that has been seen in recent years.*

White-faced. These Cockatiels have lost their yellow and orange markings. Hens, therefore, have grayish heads and characteristic white barring on their tails, whereas cocks have pure white facial coloring, with their gray coloration usually appearing to be quite dark. This characteristic has now been linked with other mutations,

Fact File

Family name:	Cacatuidae
Length:	12in (30cm)
Distribution:	Most of Australia.
Color variant availability:	Good choice available.
Compatibility:	Social by nature.

Pet potential: Excellent. Young birds develop into long-lived, tame, talkative companions.

Diet: A seed mix of millets, plain canary seed, groats, sunflower, and a little hemp can be offered, along with greenstuff and sweet apple.

Health problems: Chicks vulnerable to candidiasis. Adults susceptible to roundworms.

Breeding tips: Pairs likely to breed most satisfactorily if housed individually rather than in colonies.

Nesting needs: Nest box measuring about 9in (23cm) square x 12in (30cm) deep, with a generous lining of coarse wood shavings on the base.

Typical clutch size:	5–6 eggs
Incubation:	19 days

Rearing requirements: Provide both softfood and soaked seed such as millet sprays when there are chicks in the nest.

Fledging:	Occurs around 5 weeks of age.

Lifespan: Individuals have lived for up to 30 years.

including both the pied and pearl. It has also been possible to create a snow-white albino, by mating white-faced and lutino mutations.

Dominant Silver. In this British mutation there is a distinctive difference in appearance between single and double factor individuals, with double factor birds being of a significantly lighter shade. When the dominant silver is combined with the white-faced, the platinum variety is created.

Other Colors. There is a rarer, recessive silver mutation in these birds, distinguishable by its red eyes, that originally appeared in the 1960s. A fallow form, which looks like the cinnamon mutation, has also been developed, but it is not yet widely bred. The yellow-face is a more recent addition to the list of Cockatiel mutations; these birds have golden-yellow, rather than orange, cheek patches.

◀ *The yellow-faced pearl cinnamon is one of the most recent additions to the list of mutations. Color combinations of this type are now common in Cockatiels, linking all three types of mutation—facial feathering, markings, and basic body color.*

Care and Conditions

When seeking breeding stock it may be better to start out with young Cockatiels, so that you can be certain of the age of your stock. Deworm the birds to ensure that they are free from these parasites and cannot spread them to other aviary occupants. If you are intending to set up a colony, it is best to introduce all the Cockatiels at the same time, because this minimizes the likelihood of disturbances. Do not introduce new birds to a group during the breeding period, since this could result in eggs and chicks being abandoned. For color breeding purposes, pairs should be housed individually so that you can be certain of the parentage of the chicks. When seeking a pet Cockatiel, you will find that chicks are most plentiful during late spring through to early winter.

A Budgerigar seed mix plus sunflower seed diet was traditionally used for these birds. Nowadays, breeders often offer a high-quality pellet diet, since this avoids relying on a vitamin and mineral supplement to compensate for the low vitamin A level and other shortcomings in seed.

Success is more likely if pairs are housed individually, because if kept on a colony system Cockatiels often decide to cohabit in nest boxes, and adults are unable to incubate all the eggs laid here. These inevitably become chilled during the incubation period, and the overall rate of hatching is reduced. Although Cockatiels are prolific and hens will lay through most of the year, it is better to restrict the breeding period to the warmer months in temperate areas, providing nest boxes in the spring. Newly hatched chicks are covered in thick down. As they grow and their eyes open, they will sway back and forth, hissing menacingly in the nest box if disturbed.

▶ *A primrose pearl pied Cockatiel. The term "primrose" does not describe a separate mutation, but relates to the depth of yellow coloration being used to identify birds having deeper yellowish-white feathering.*

● *Why am I losing Cockatiel chicks soon after hatching?*

... There could be various reasons, ranging from disturbances that cause the adults to leave the nest uncovered through to a genetic weakness, but the most likely explanation is candidiasis, triggered in part by a shortage of vitamin A. Modifying a seed diet with a supplement should assist in overcoming this problem.

● *One of my Cockatiel chicks has white, rather than yellow, down. Is this a sign of ill-health?*

Not at all—Cockatiels soon develop a relatively thick covering of down feathers. These are usually yellow, but in color varieties in which this pigment is missing, such as the white-faced and albino forms, the down is white. You should be able to distinguish albinos at this early stage by their red, rather than black, eyes.

● *Will breeding results be better if I keep my Cockatiels as a group in a large aviary?*

Probably not, because the adults tend to share a nest box and will then be unable to incubate the 12 or more eggs that will be produced. Some may be fatally chilled, while the range in ages of the hatching chicks may mean that the youngest will not survive. You will also be unable to determine pairings—which is very important when seeking to breed a particular variety.

Dwarf Macaws GENUS: ARA

MACAWS RANGE WIDELY THROUGHOUT THE New World, from Mexico southward. The main features distinguishing them from other parrots are an area on their cheeks that lacks facial feathering and their long tails.

Housing macaws can be a costly undertaking, so for many people one of the dwarf species will be more suitable—even though they can be rather noisy on occasions. While hand-reared birds will develop into affectionate companions,

they are not likely to prove especially talented as talkers, rarely mastering a vocabulary of more than 20–30 words.

Popular Varieties

All the macaws featured below are available in North America and Europe, with established pairs usually breeding consistently in suitable aviary surroundings.

Yellow-collared Macaw (*Ara auricollis*). These macaws have a bright yellow collar around the back of the neck. There are brownish-black areas on the head, with the rest of the body being primarily green. The tail feathers are bluish at the base, becoming reddish toward the tips. Like other macaws, they can only be sexed reliably by DNA, although it may be possible to identify cocks because of their bolder head shape.

Red-bellied Macaw (*Ara manilata*). Originating in Guyana and neighboring countries, this species has yellowish facial skin color (that of other dwarf macaws is whitish). Green predominates in its plumage, with some areas of bluish feathering on the head and breast together with a prominent area of maroon-red feathering that extends over the abdomen and between the legs. This species is very susceptible to obesity. This can account for sudden deaths—particularly if birds are stressed due to a move or by cats climbing over the aviary. Provide a quality pellet diet, rather than one based on sunflower seed, and give them plenty of fruit. Red-bellied Macaws benefit from heated wintertime accommodation.

Hahn's Macaw (*Ara nobilis*). The smallest of all the macaws, this species is often described as a mini macaw. Hahn's Macaw ranges widely over northeastern South America. The species is also known as the Red-shouldered Macaw. Apart from their small size, these macaws are identified

◄ *Yellow-collared Macaws originate from the southern part of South America, being found in parts of Brazil, Paraguay, Bolivia, and northern Argentina.*

Fact File

Family name:	Psittacidae
Length:	12–18in (30–46cm)
Distribution:	Most of South America.
Color variant availability:	None recorded
Compatibility: Pairs may be kept on colony basis.	
Pet potential: Can become tame and talkative if obtained when young.	
Diet: Complete diet or good-quality parrot food mix with daily addition of fruit and/or greenstuff.	
Health problems: Dwarf macaws may suffer from feather plucking.	
Breeding tips: Nest box should be positioned in a	

secluded part of the aviary to avoid disturbance.

Nesting needs: Depending on the size of the macaws, nest box measuring approximately 9–12in (23–30cm) square x at least 24in (60cm) deep, well-lined with coarse shavings.	
Typical clutch size:	2–3 eggs
Incubation:	25–27 days
Rearing requirements: Softfood may be eaten when there are chicks in the nest.	
Fledging: Young will leave the nest at 8–12 weeks of age.	
Lifespan:	Can live for over 30 years.

by their green plumage and red feathering on the leading edge of each wing. They also have a white area of bald skin on the face, rather than around the eye as is seen in conures (see pages 166–169). There is also a subspecies known as the Noble Macaw (*A. n. cumanensis*), which has a pale horn-colored, rather than gray, upper bill. This variety is rarely seen in aviculture.

Care and Conditions

These macaws need a stout aviary constructed using timber at least 2in (5cm) square for the frame, covered with 16-gauge wire mesh. Reinforce any weak points that the birds might be able to gnaw. A generous supply of perches, replaced as necessary, will help to divert their attention away from the aviary structure.

A good-quality parrot mixture augmented with a suitable supplement or a complete diet should be offered, along with a selection of fruit and greenstuff. Some individuals often enjoy gnawing at the thick stems of spinach beet, and pomegranates are also very popular with them.

A stout nest box should be provided throughout the year for roosting purposes. As nesting time approaches, the hen in particular will remain in the nest box for periods during the day. The birds may become noisier and, almost certainly, they will become more destructive, gnawing away at their perches and cuttlebone. Provide wood offcuts in the box that the hen can whittle away to form a nest lining. After egg-laying, the hen will incubate the eggs on her own, although the cock may spend some time with her,

● *Can I house more than one pair of dwarf macaws together?*

... This depends on the size of your aviary. Hahn's Macaws have been kept very satisfactorily in this way, and will usually nest without problems if there is a choice of nest sites at roughly the same height. Do not introduce newcomers to an existing group, however. But the young of breeding pairs will be accepted after fledging.

● *My Yellow-collared Macaw has some orange feathers in his collar. Can this be used as a way of telling cocks from hens?*

No, it simply indicates that the coloration of these feathers can differ slightly according to the individual—which may in turn reflect where they originated from. It is not possible to influence this feature by diet nor is it of any significance with respect to identifying true pairs.

● *Is it possible to distinguish young Yellow-collared Macaws from adults?*

Although their plumage is similar, you can recognize youngsters easily because their legs and feet are grayish, rather than pink, when they leave the nest.

● *Will dwarf macaws prove to be double brooded?*

This is most likely in Hahn's Macaws, whereas larger species are less likely to lay again immediately after rearing one round of chicks. It is possible to induce such behavior, however, by taking away their eggs soon after laying and incubating them artificially.

● *Which dwarf macaw makes the best pet?*

Probably Hahn's Macaw—by virtue of its smaller, more manageable size in the home, and also because its calls are not as loud as those of its bigger relatives.

Multicolored Large Macaws GENUS: ARA

Blue and Gold Macaw

Red and Gold Macaw

Green-winged Macaw

THE MULTICOLORED LARGE MACAWS ARE more commonly seen in zoos and bird gardens, because their size means they require spacious accommodation that must also be able to resist their powerful bills. Furthermore, these are noisy birds whose loud calls carry over long distances.

Popular Varieties

All three well-known species have a wide distribution in the wild, and there are variations in size between populations from different areas. **Blue and Gold Macaw** (*Ara ararauna*). Ranging over almost the entire northern half of South America, these macaws can be recognized instantly by their golden-yellow underparts and blue feathering that extends down over the top of the head, the wings, the back, and the upper side of the tail feathers. There is also a very similar but localized and endangered species of macaw known as the Blue-throated or Caninde Macaw (*A. glaucogularis*), from Bolivia.

Fact File

Family name:	Psittacidae
Length:	34–36in (86–91cm)
Distribution: From Central America southward over much of South America.	
Color variant availability:	Rare
Compatibility: Pairs best kept on their own for breeding purposes.	
Pet potential: Can be difficult to cater to adequately in the average home.	
Diet: Complete diet or a good mixture of nuts and seeds, with fruit and greenstuff being provided.	
Health problems: At risk from macaw wasting disease and cloacal papillomas.	

Breeding tips: Be sure to provide adequate support for the nesting site.

Nesting requirements: Nest box approximately 18in (46cm) square x at least 36in (91cm) from top to bottom, well-lined with coarse shavings. A well-secured internal access ladder will be needed.

Typical clutch size:	2–3 eggs
Incubation:	26–28 days
Rearing requirements: Softfood may be eaten when there are chicks in the nest.	
Fledging: Young will leave the nest between 12 and 14 weeks of age.	
Lifespan:	Can live for over 50 years.

▶ *The bare facial skin area of these macaws can indicate the bird's mood, with blushing occurring when they are excited. The pattern of feather tracts is also unique, enabling individual birds to be recognized.*

◀ *Sexing the multicolored macaws with certainty is impossible, although cocks often appear to have slightly bigger heads. The differences in size that are seen throughout their huge range in the wild can be reflected in captive-bred stock, too.*

Green-winged Macaw (*Ara chloroptera*). A rich shade of crimson, with green plumage across the wings merging into blue, distinguishes these macaws. They are sometimes called Red and Green Macaws. Their distribution extends from Central America to northern Argentina. Young birds have tracts of slightly brownish, rather than crimson, feathering running across their otherwise bald facial area, as well as dark eyes—a feature of all young macaws.

Red and Gold Macaw (*Ara macao*). Also called the Scarlet Macaw, this species is instantly distinguishable from the Red and Green Macaw thanks to its redder coloration and the golden-yellow plumage on the wings. It is found from Central America to northern Brazil, but due to a population decline in the north of its range, it is listed as endangered on CITES Appendix 1.

Care and Conditions

A complete food can be recommended or alternatively a diet based on large nuts, such as Brazils, hazel nuts, and walnuts in their shells. They will eat sunflower seeds and peanuts readily, but these should not form the major part of their diet, since this may promote feather-plucking. A general supplement is recommended if nuts are fed and can be sprinkled over the fruit or greenstuff that should be offered every day.

For breeding, a very strong nest site is required to withstand the birds' bills. Wooden barrels are often used for this purpose, supported on a platform under cover in the quarters. Macaws can become aggressive during nesting—especially hand-reared individuals—so be cautious when approaching the nest site at this stage.

Q & A ...

● **Have there been any recorded color mutations in multicolored macaws?**

There is a mutation affecting the Blue and Gold resulting in the loss of the yellow plumage, creating blue and white individuals. One such bird was displayed at the 1974 National Exhibition of Cage and Aviary Birds held in London, England, and others were seen at the 1999 show.

● *What is the reason for my macaws' distinctive smell?*

Macaws can give off a very musky odor, especially when they are in top condition, although as you have discovered, this is not unpleasant or overwhelming. It may come from the oil of the feather gland, but the significance of the odor is unclear—particularly as birds do not usually rely on a sense of smell.

● *How can I help ensure my macaws will breed?*

The best option is to invest in a proven pair, because compatibility is important. Pairing up mature individuals must be carried out cautiously, because they may fight. This risk can be reduced by introducing them on neutral territory, however. An established pair may breed reliably for decades, but it may take five years or more for young birds to mature. Many of the larger macaws will hybridize freely. Although the resulting color combinations can be attractive, the hybrid breeding of these birds is generally frowned upon.

Aratinga Conures

GENERA: ARATINGA, NANDAYUS

NINETEEN DIFFERENT SPECIES FORM THE GENUS *Aratinga*, with the closely related Nanday Conure often being included as well. Green predominates in the plumage of many species, although there are exceptions—such as the attractive Sun Conure. None of the *Aratinga* species can be sexed visually, with differences in markings being of no general significance in determining the gender of these birds.

Popular Varieties

Not surprisingly, the more colorful species are the ones most commonly seen in aviculture.

Sun Conure (*Aratinga solstitialis*). Individuals show variation in their depth of coloration. Orange areas are most pronounced on the sides of the head and the underparts. There is variable green feathering across the wings, with the flight feathers being blue. The tail feathers are olive, usually with bluish tips. A bare area of white skin encircles the eyes, and the bill is black. Young birds show a greater range of coloration than adults, with more extensive green feathering.

Red-headed Conure (*Aratinga erythrogenys*). Originating from Peru and Ecuador, this is one of a number of *Aratinga* conures with red feathering on the head. In this species, however, it is extensive—covering almost all of the head apart from the back of the cheeks. Red is also present on the edge of the wings and under the wings—these features help identify young of this species, which also have green heads.

Petz's Conure (*Aratinga canicularis*). This species occurs in western Central America, from Mexico to Honduras. It is mainly green, being a grayer shade on the head and upper chest. There is a prominent orange area above the bill with a pale blue area behind, above the eyes.

Nanday Conure (*Nandayus nenday*). Originating from the southern part of South America, these conures can be instantly identified by their black heads. There is an area of red feathering at the top of the thighs and a pale blue band across the chest, with the remainder of the plumage being predominantly green.

Care and Conditions

These conures make attractive aviary occupants, although their calls can be quite shrill and penetrating, with this situation likely to be worse if a number of pairs are being housed together in adjacent flights. If one pair is disturbed they are likely to set all the others off, too. *Aratinga* conures are often seen in flocks in the wild, and they can be housed in a

◄ *Sun Conures originate from northern South America. They were largely unknown in aviculture until 1971, although they were first bred in France in 1883.*

Fact File

Family name:	Psittacidae
Length:	9–14in (23–36cm)

Distribution: From Central America southward over much of South America.

Color variant availability: None available

Compatibility: Best kept as individual pairs for breeding purposes.

Pet potential: Friendly by nature but can be noisy.

Diet: Complete diet or a quality parrot mix with seeds such as groats, canary seed, and millet added should be offered. Daily offerings of fruit and green-stuff required.

Health problems: May be at risk of feather-plucking.

Breeding tips: Nest box often preferred in the aviary shelter rather than in the flight.

Nesting needs: Nest box about 12in (30cm) square x approximately 18in (46cm) high, with a thick lining of coarse shavings on the base.

Typical clutch size: 3–4 eggs

Incubation: 26–28 days

Rearing requirements: Softfood may be eaten when there are chicks in the nest.

Fledging: Will leave the nest at 7–8 weeks of age.

Lifespan: Can exceed 25 years.

Red-headed Conure

Petz's Conure

Peach-fronted Conure

◀ *Red-headed Conures make attractive, if somewhat destructive, aviary occupants. They are one of the largest members of the genus. The prominent orange area above the bill of Petz's Conure gives rise to its alternative name of Orange-fronted Conure.*

Q&A...

● **How can I distinguish Petz's, or the Orange-fronted Conure, from the Peach-fronted Conure?**

The upper bill of the Orange-fronted Conure is ivory in color, whereas that of the similarly colored Peach-fronted, or Golden-crowned, Conure (*Aratinga aurea*) is black. The young birds of both species can be identified by their darker irises, and by the fact that the orange area of feathering on their heads is also reduced.

● *How often will Aratinga conures breed?*

They will usually nest once or twice in succession, although this depends partly on the individual pair. Generally speaking, smaller species such as Peach-fronted Conures are likely to prove more prolific than larger conures such as the Red-headed. When conures start to use the nest box during the day, this is a sign that the birds are ready to nest.

● *Where should I site the nest box?*

Site the nest box in a position so that it gives the pair seclusion—for example, by being hidden away from conures in neighboring aviaries.

● *Can Aratinga conures be kept on a colony basis?*

Yes, these conures are frequently seen in flocks in the wild, and they can be housed in a similar way in large aviaries. For breeding purposes, however, it is usually better to accommodate pairs separately.

similar way in large aviaries, but for breeding purposes it is usually better to accommodate pairs separately.

Feeding presents no particular problems, although birds may develop individual tastes.

Conures should be provided with a nest box throughout the year, and they will use this for roosting purposes when they are not breeding.

Other Conures

GENERA: PYRRHURA, CYANOLISEUS, ENICOGNATHUS

CONURES OF THE GENUS *PYRRHURA* ALL FEATURE lighter edging on the feathers of the chest, which has led to their being called scaly-breasted conures. Slender-billed Conures resemble them, although they are larger. Patagonian Conures can be noisy and somewhat destructive. These are all friendly birds with a willingness to breed.

Popular Varieties

Some of the most popular species among aviculturists are described below.

Maroon-bellied Conure (*Pyrrhura frontalis*). This species has rich, jungle-green plumage on the head and wings. The ear coverts are brown, with yellowish edging to the breast feathers. The abdomen and undersides of the tail feathers are maroon. These conures are tame and confiding even in aviary surroundings, swaggering up and down the perch when in a displaying mood, but are not especially social with their own kind.

Patagonian Conure (*Cyanoliseus patagonus*). Predominantly dark olive-brown, this species

◄ *Sometimes also known as the Red-bellied Conure, the Maroon-bellied Conure is one of the best-known of the* Pyrrhura *species.*

Fact File

Family name:	Psittacidae
Length:	9–20in (23–51cm)

Distribution: From Central America down to the tip of South America.

Color variant availability: Exceedingly uncommon

Compatibility: Pairs are usually accommodated individually for breeding purposes.

Pet potential: Lively, affectionate companions. Some can be noisy.

Diet: Provide either a complete diet or a quality parrot mix with seeds such as groats, canary seed, and millet added. Greenstuff, fruit, and carrot are usually eaten readily.

Health problems: Susceptible to feather-plucking.

Roundworms can be a problem in Slender-billed Conures.

Breeding tips: Provide nest box in the shelter, giving easy access to the interior.

Nesting needs: Nest box about 10in (25cm) square x approximately 18in (46cm) high for *Pyrrhura* species; up to 15in (38cm) square for Patagonian Conures.

Typical clutch size:	4–6 eggs
Incubation:	24–26 days

Rearing requirements: Soaked seed and softfood recommended.

Fledging:	Will leave the nest at 7–8 weeks old.
Lifespan:	May live for 25 years or more.

▶ *Originating from parts of Argentina and Chile, the Patagonian is the largest of the conures. It displays a variable band of white feathers across its chest.*

▼ *The Slender-billed Conure is unmistakable in appearance, thanks to its elongated upper bill that it sometimes uses to dig for roots.*

has a grayish-brown chest, golden-yellow thighs, and red in the center of the abdomen. The bill is black in adults but partly white in young birds. **Slender-billed Conure** (*Enicognathus leptorhynchus*). The predominant plumage color of this species is green, with red around the cere and a similar patch in the center of the abdomen. The bills of young birds are shorter than those of adults on fledging, and the bare skin around the eye is whitish at first, rather than gray.

Care and Conditions

While *Pyrrhura* species can be housed in a standard aviary, the other two species need a more sturdy enclosure with a few adaptations. For the Patagonian Conure, which roosts and nests in vertical limestone cliff faces, try to arrange nest boxes so that the entrances are easily accessible. For Slender-billed Conures, include a small area of lawn on the ground where the birds can dig with their bills or, failing this, cut up a square of untreated turf and place it on the floor of the aviary on a seed tray. These conures also need a relatively deep drinking container.

Q & A ...

● **Can any of these conures be sexed by sight?**

Unfortunately not. The behavior of the birds may be confusing, too, because two birds of the same sex may engage in mutual preening, suggesting that they are a true pair. If you cannot acquire a proven pair, surgical or DNA sexing is your only reliable guide.

● **What is the best food for these birds?**

Pyrrhura species will sample almost any food, and can be weaned easily onto a complete diet in most cases. Slender-billeds are more conservative feeders, but they often display a taste for blackberries, whereas spinach beet (especially stems) is a favorite of many Patagonian Conures. Corn-on-the-cob will be taken readily as well.

● **Can Slender-billed Conures talk?**

These conures are rather undervalued as pets, with hand-reared birds proving to be not only talented talkers but affectionate companions as well.

● **Are the chicks at risk from attack in an aviary?**

Hand-reared *Pyrrhura* chicks can be aggressive from an early age toward other birds being reared with them, so beware of this. In aviary surroundings, there is usually no need to remove the young of Slender-billed or Patagonian Conures as soon as they are feeding independently—especially if the aviary is large—because they are unlikely to be attacked by adult birds.

Brotogeris Parakeets   GENUS: BROTOGERIS

Tovi Parakeet

White-winged Parakeet

Canary-winged Parakeet

▲ Brotogeris *parakeets are highly sociable birds, and breeding results are often better if a group is housed together in a large aviary. There are seven species in this genus, all predominantly green in color with distinguishing markings on the head and wings.*

PARAKEETS OF THE GENUS *BROTOGERIS* HAVE been kept both as pets and aviary birds for over a century, but they have never proved to be ready nesters compared with most conures, for example. This may be due to the fact that they cannot be sexed visually and also because of their strong colony instincts.

Popular Varieties

Color mutations are exceedingly rare among *Brotogeris* parakeets, although occasional blues have been recorded, notably in the case of the Brazilian All-green Parakeet (*Brotogeris tirica*).
White-winged Parakeet (*Brotogeris versicolorus*). Two subspecies exist, of which the White-winged itself is less common in collections. It is a relatively dark shade of green, with white markings most apparent on the edges of the wing. In contrast, the Canary-winged Parakeet (*B. v. chiriri*) is a brighter color and has rich, canary-yellow patches on the sides of its wings. The White-winged race occurs over northern parts of South America, while the Canary-winged is found farther south.
Tovi Parakeet (*Brotogeris jugularis*). Also known as both the Bee-bee and as the Orange-chinned Parakeet, thanks to a distinctive orange spot under the chin, its coloration is quite dull, being mainly green with a brown area extending across the wings. There are traces of blue on the head and near the rump. This species ranges from the southwest of Mexico down into parts of Colombia and Venezuela in South America.

Care and Conditions

Young *Brotogeris* parakeets are very tame and settle well as pets, but they are likely to prove noisy as they grow older. Adults birds often tend to be shy, and will remain so no matter how hard you try to tame them in aviary surroundings. Their powerful bills mean they can, and will, inflict damage on exposed parts of the aviary woodwork. Providing a plentiful supply of fresh

● *What other Brotogeris parakeets are likely to be available?*

... The Orange-flanked Parakeet (*Brotogeris pyrrhopterus*) is the most colorful member of the genus, with blue on the head and orange under the wing coverts. It originates from Ecuador and Peru. The other species most likely to be seen is the Golden-winged Parakeet (*Brotogeris chrysopterus*). In this species the wing coverts are orange, with a blackish-brown band above the cere.

● *What is the best way to breed Brotogeris parakeets—by housing them in individual pairs or on a colony basis?*

Unless you can provide a very large aviary, best results for breeding are likely to be achieved by housing pairs within sight and sound of each other. Ensure that the double-wiring between the flights is secure, so that there is no risk of birds grabbing neighbors' toes as they clamber over the two layers of mesh separating them.

▲ *This Canary-winged Parakeet in flight shows clearly the bright, canary-yellow wing patches that give it its popular name. This subspecies is found in Argentina, Paraguay, and Bolivia.*

perches should help to divert their interest, but these will be rapidly destroyed from the ends, so it is best to cut branches slightly longer than those required at the outset. The branches can then be angled slightly when being fixed up in the flight and straightened as the ends are gnawed away. These birds are avid bathers, so provide a bowl of water daily for this purpose. They also need plenty of fruit in their diets, but they often avoid greenstuff.

Pairs grow increasingly destructive as they come into breeding condition. In a group, it may only be the dominant pair that nest. Under no circumstances should birds be removed from, and then returned to, the colony, since it will upset the social structure of the flock. It is also likely to make breeding birds desert their nests.

Fact File

Family name:	Psittacidae
Length:	7–9in (18–23cm)

Distribution: From Mexico southward to Bolivia, Paraguay, and Argentina.

Color variant availability: Occasional blues known.

Compatibility: Social by nature; will live well in established groups.

Pet potential: Chicks can be tame. Not talented mimics.

Diet: Complete diet or parakeet mix of small cereal seeds and a good-quality parrot food. Fruit should also be provided daily.

Health problems: Foot injuries need to be prevented.

Breeding tips: Offer a range of nest boxes in a secluded part of the aviary.

Nesting needs: Nest box about 7in (18cm) square x 12in (30cm) deep, lined with thin battening which the birds can whittle down to make a nest lining.

Typical clutch size:	3–4 eggs
Incubation:	26 days

Rearing requirements: Soaked millet sprays and groats plus fruit, greenfood, and softfood may all be eaten.

Fledging: Young will leave the nest when 10–11 weeks old.

Lifespan:	May live for 20 years or more.

Parrotlets GENUS: FORPUS

SIX SMALL, SQUARE-TAILED PARROTS COMPRISE the *Forpus* genus. All are predominantly green, with blue and occasionally yellowish markings. They are ideal for a backyard town aviary, since they can be housed easily in these surroundings, and their calls are unlikely to upset neighbors.

Popular Varieties

Several color mutations have been documented, but it is the blue form of the Celestial Parrotlet that is most widely kept today. Its color is the result of an autosomal recessive mutation. In Brazilian collections, however, a wider range of colors are bred, including lutino, yellow, and pied forms of the Blue-winged Parrotlet (*Forpus xanthopterygius*), as well as a blue mutation of this species.

Celestial Parrotlet (*Forpus coelestis*). Cocks have blue plumage extending back behind the eyes, with an area of blue feathering at the edge of the wings. The facial plumage is bright green. Hens, in comparison, are much duller, with perhaps just a hint of blue on the head and rump. The Yellow-faced Parrotlet (*F. c. xanthops*) is sometimes considered to be a separate species. It is even more brightly colored, with yellow facial feathering and is slightly larger in size. Cocks of

▲ *Originating from Ecuador and Peru, the Celestial Parrotlet is sometimes also described as the Pacific Parrotlet. Sexing is straightforward in this variety, as it is with most parrotlet species.*

Fact File

Family name:	Psittacidae
Length:	5–6in (13–15cm)
Distribution: From Mexico southward to Paraguay and Argentina.	
Color variant availability:	Blues and lutinos.
Compatibility:	Pairs need to be kept apart.
Pet potential:	Can settle well if hand-reared.
Diet: Mixture of smaller cereal seeds such as millets and plain canary seed, augmented with some sunflower and small pine nuts. Greenstuff and fruit should also be provided, even when rearing young.	
Health problems: Injuries due to fighting through the aviary mesh.	

Breeding tips: Avoid housing pairs in adjoining flights to prevent disputes.

Nesting needs: A Budgerigar-type nest box can be used, lined with shavings rather than concave, but a smaller box may be preferable. A box measuring 5in (13cm) square x 7.5in (19cm) is ideal.

Typical clutch size:	4–6 eggs
Incubation:	18–20 days

Rearing requirements: Offer soaked millet sprays and softfood.

Fledging: Young will leave the nest at 4–5 weeks of age.

Lifespan: May live for 20 years or more.

▶ *A pair of Green-rumped Parrotlets. The cock is the lower bird. Unusually for parrots, hens are more colorful than their mates.*

this species have a more brightly colored blue rump than hens. These parrotlets are restricted to the upper Marañon Valley in northern Peru. They have proved reasonably prolific in aviculture.

Green-rumped Parrotlet (*Forpus passerinus*). Sometimes described as the Guyana Parrotlet since it originates from this part of South America, as well as Trinidad, cocks have bright emerald-green coloration on the back and rump. Their facial feathering is of a similar shade, with dark blue wing coverts and blue also evident at the edge of the wing. The wing coverts of hens are bright green with yellowish plumage evident in the vicinity of the forehead. Again, a variety of color mutations of this parrotlet have been developed in Brazilian collections, including blue, lutino, and cinnamon forms, but none of these is common elsewhere.

Care and Conditions

Parrotlets are long-lived birds, with individuals known to have bred successfully at 18 years of age. Even so, it may be better to start with unrelated young birds, especially as they can be sexed visually soon after fledging. This should lessen the likelihood of acquiring a cock in particular that may have strong aggressive tendencies toward his offspring—even to the extent of attacking and killing them soon after fledging. Parrotlets mature quickly and can be expected to breed by the time they are a year old. It is not advisable to encourage them to nest at an earlier stage, since this may leave them more vulnerable to egg-binding. Parrotlets will normally rear two rounds of chicks in succession.

Feeding is straightforward. Parrotlets need a seed-based diet augmented by fruit and greenstuff, plus a vitamin and mineral supplement. As always, do not forget to provide both grit, to aid the digestive process, and cuttlebone to serve as a source of calcium—this is especially important when hens are about to lay.

Q & A

● **Can I keep parrotlets with other birds?**

... Unfortunately, in view of their aggressive natures, it is better not to mix them with other birds. They may even harass larger, non-aggressive companions such as Cockatiels.

● **Are parrotlets hardy?**

In spite of their small size, parrotlets can generally be kept without any artificial heat over the winter months in temperate climates, provided that they are properly acclimatized. In fact, they usually ignore a nest box provided for roosting purposes, but they should have a snug shelter forming part of the aviary so they can escape from the worst of the weather.

● **Do parrotlets make good pets?**

Young birds can develop into attractive pets, although they are not talented talkers. Their small size means that they can be accommodated quite easily in the home, and their calls will not be disturbing there.

● **Will parrotlets nest satisfactorily in breeding cages?**

Yes, but the likelihood of the young being attacked around fledging time is increased. Watch for signs of aggression. As always, it is vital to separate the young from their parents at fledging time, but the risk of attack is greater in a breeding cage.

Pionus Parrots GENUS: PIONUS

THESE MEDIUM-SIZED PARROTS ARE NOT BRIGHTLY colored compared with some species, but the subtle hues in their plumage are highlighted by shafts of sunlight, transforming their appearance. Eight species are recognized, with none being either especially noisy or destructive by nature. Visual sexing is not possible.

▶ *Maximilian's Parrot has a range in the wild that extends from Brazil to northern Argentina.*

Popular Varieties

Color mutations are very rare, although Blue-headed Parrot mutations are occasionally seen.

Maximilian's Parrot (*Pionus maximiliani*). This species is predominantly green, with individual feathers often having a bronzy hue. There is a patch of blue or red feathering (depending on the subspecies) under the chin and over the upper breast, with the undertail coverts again being red. A bare area of white skin encircles the eyes, with the bill itself being horn-colored. It is often possible to recognize young birds by the reduced blue feathering on the chest and by the presence of a red frontal band. In common with the other *Pionus* species, Maximilian's Parrots settle well as pets when obtained as youngsters, especially if they have been hand-reared. They are also much quieter than the better-known Amazon parrots.

Blue-headed Parrot (*Pionus menstruus*). One of the most widely available species, it has an extensive area of deep blue plumage on the head and upper breast, with black ear coverts. There is pink feathering on the throat, while the majority of the rest of the body is green—being of a duller shade on the underparts. Bronze patches are present near the shoulder, while the bill is blackish with some reddish-pink coloration at its sides.

Fact File

Family name:	Psittacidae
Length:	10–11in (25–28cm)
Distribution: From Mexico southward to Bolivia and Argentina.	
Color variant availability:	None
Compatibility: Breeding pairs should be housed on their own.	
Pet potential: Hand-reared chicks will settle well as companions.	
Diet: Complete diet or seed-based mix comprised of sunflower, safflower, pine nuts, peanuts, and some smaller cereal seeds such as millet sprays. Greenstuff and fruit should also be provided.	

Health problems: Susceptible to the fungal disease aspergillosis.	
Breeding tips:	Seclusion is important.
Nesting needs: Nest box about 8in (20cm) square x 18in (46cm) deep, with coarse shavings or wood inside to whittle away.	
Typical clutch size:	3–4 eggs
Incubation:	26 days
Rearing requirements: Soaked millet sprays and softfood can be offered.	
Fledging: Young will emerge from the nest at about 10 weeks old.	
Lifespan:	May live for 25 years or more.

▲ *Young Blue-headed Parrots have duller plumage than adults, although they often display a reddish front band above the cere that disappears when the birds are about a year old.*

Care and Conditions

Pairs need to be sexed, because these parrots can be very aggressive toward each other, flaring their tails to display the red plumage here as a warning sign. Adults can also be nervous, especially in unfamiliar surroundings. Therefore you should aim to minimize the stress by leaving them to settle down undisturbed.

In spite of their size, *Pionus* parrots often display a particular fondness for the smaller cereal seeds such as plain canary and millets. Be sure to offer a selection of fruit and greenstuff regularly.

Serious disputes can sometimes even break out among compatible pairs, so that as breeding time approaches you need to be aware of the danger signs. Feather-plucking of the hen by the cock can become intense and persistent at this time.

● My hen Pionus is wheezing, but she appears generally in good health. Is this a cause for concern?

Not necessarily, because these parrots will wheeze and gasp when frightened, particularly after being caught and handled. Nevertheless, she could be suffering from the chronic fungal disease aspergillosis, for which there is no reliable treatment. Consult a veterinarian specializing in birds to ascertain the cause of the problem.

● What can I do to help reduce nesting aggression?

Although the pair will only start to use the nest box when breeding is imminent, it should be constantly available in a secluded part of the aviary. Otherwise, a hen may be reluctant to accept a strange nest site just before the breeding season commences, and this may cause her intended mate to attack her. The greatest danger period is just before egg-laying begins. Equally, it is important to avoid disturbances in the vicinity of the nest once the chicks have hatched, because disturbances at this time can cause nervous pairs to kill their offspring.

Amazon Parrots GENUS: AMAZONA

THE TWENTY-SEVEN SPECIES IN THIS GROUP ARE sometimes described simply as "green parrots," because this color often predominates in their plumage. Visual sexing is impossible in all but the White-fronted Amazon, and even here it may not be entirely infallible. The main drawback of these attractive looking parrots is their loud, raucous calls, which are mostly heard at dawn and dusk. Such noise will inevitably cause neighbors to complain.

Popular Varieties

The Caribbean Amazons include the largest member of the group—the Imperial Amazon (*Amazona imperialis*) of Dominica. Some species are endangered in the wild and are rarely seen in private collections. Color mutations are also rare, although occasional blues and lutinos have been recorded. These are being bred in small numbers, particularly in the United States.

Blue-fronted Amazon (*Amazona aestiva*). This species has a relatively southerly distribution, extending into northern Argentina. As with other Amazons, it often takes several years for the bright yellow-and-blue coloration on the head to develop to its maximum extent.

Orange-winged Amazon

Blue-fronted Amazon

▲ ▶ *The Blue-fronted Amazon has been popular as a pet for many years. The markings are highly individual, and help to distinguish particular birds. The similar-looking Orange-winged Amazon is smaller.*

Fact File

Family name: Psittacidae	**Health problems:** Can suffer from viral papillomas.
Length: 10–18in (25–46cm)	**Breeding tips:** Pairs can become aggressive when breeding.
Distribution: From Mexico southward to Bolivia and Argentina. Also present on various Caribbean islands.	**Nesting needs:** Nest box about 10in (25cm) square x 18in (46cm) deep, and lined with wooden battening that can be whittled away by the birds to form a nest lining.
Colour variant availability: Scarce	
Compatibility: Breeding pairs should be housed on their own.	**Typical clutch size:** 3–4 eggs
	Incubation: 26–28 days
Pet potential: Hand-reared chicks are likely to develop into lively but noisy companions.	**Rearing requirements:** Soaked sunflower and softfood may be eaten readily.
Diet: Complete diet or seed-based mix comprised of sunflower, safflower, pine nuts, and peanuts. Will also eat pumpkin seeds and flaked or kibbled maize. Fruit and greenstuff must also be offered.	**Fledging:** Young will emerge from the nest at about 9–10 weeks old.
	Lifespan: May live for 80 years or more.

● My Amazon has become rather withdrawn and is far less friendly than before. He is now three years old. What have I done wrong?

Probably nothing. The temperament of cocks in particular can change dramatically as they mature and come into breeding condition. Hopefully, before long, this phase will pass.

● Will my Amazons need artificial heating over the winter period?

No. Assuming they are well established in their quarters, and have a snug shelter attached to their flight, no heating will be necessary for Amazons kept in temperate areas.

Orange-winged Amazon (*Amazona amazonica*). Originating from further north in South America, this bird can be confused with the preceding species in general appearance. But the lighter horn color of the upper bill, coupled with the orange rather than red markings on the wings and tail, help distinguish them.

White-fronted Amazon (*Amazona albifrons*). This is the smallest member of the genus and is confined to Central America. It can usually be sexed visually; males have red feathering down the edges of the wings. Unfortunately, it is very noisy, too.

Mealy Amazon (*Amazona farinosa*). Several different races of this bird are recognized, differing mainly in terms of the extent of blue plumage in the vicinity of the head. They range from Central America into parts of South America (where their coloration is greener). The Mealy Amazon is often considered to be among the noisiest of all the Amazon parrots.

Care and Conditions

Housing these parrots can be relatively costly due to their destructive natures—which will become especially apparent when they come into breeding condition. A brick, or block-built, shelter may prove better than one made of wood.

Feeding is straightforward, but it is particularly important that greenstuff, vegetables, and fruit feature prominently in the diet of these parrots.

● How can I recognize a young Amazon parrot, and when is the best time to buy one of these birds?

If you are seeking an Amazon parrot as a pet, start out with a hand-raised youngster, which can be recognized by its dark irises. The availability of chicks is closely linked with the breeding season of these parrots, which is restricted to the summer months in northern temperate areas. This means that you are likely to find the widest selection available from late summer onward.

▲ *Provide Amazon parrots, like this lively Blue-fronted, with a good supply of stout perches. This will help divert their attention away from any timber used in the construction of their flight.*

A diet consisting primarily of dry seed will inevitably lead to a vitamin A deficiency and is also likely to cause poor breeding results.

Although it can take a year or so for a pair to settle after a move, they are likely to breed consistently once established in their quarters. Like most larger parrots, Amazons generally only breed once a year, with the hen sitting alone. Site the nest box in a secluded part of the flight, where you can inspect the interior easily without arousing the anger of the adult birds, because they can resent intrusions during this period.

Senegal and Related Parrots
GENUS: POICEPHALUS

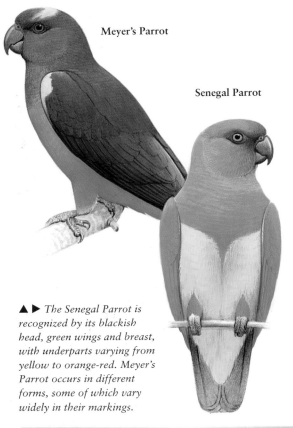

Meyer's Parrot

Senegal Parrot

▲ ▶ *The Senegal Parrot is recognized by its blackish head, green wings and breast, with underparts varying from yellow to orange-red. Meyer's Parrot occurs in different forms, some of which vary widely in their markings.*

THERE ARE NINE DIFFERENT SPECIES FORMING the genus *Poicephalus*, all of which are found in mainland Africa. These parrots have variable coloration, stocky bodies, and square tails. They also have powerful bills, so they must be kept in aviaries with 16-gauge mesh. Although these parrots can be destructive, they are not noisy and have been undervalued as aviary birds. Now, however, the signs are that they are growing in popularity, since the smaller species in particular are unlikely to disturb neighbors with their calls, and successful breeding represents a challenge.

Popular Varieties
The largest member of this group is the Cape Parrot (*Poicephalus robustus*), which is endangered in some parts of its range. The following species are, however, widely available.

Senegal Parrot (*Poicephalus senegalus*). Originating from west Africa, this is the best-known member of the group. Its color scheme is unique. The sexes cannot be distinguished visually.

Meyer's Parrot (*Poicephalus meyeri*). The markings on this parrot vary quite widely, displaying yellowish plumage on the head in some cases. The underparts are bluish-green, with yellow

Fact File

Family name:	Psittacidae
Length:	9–12in (23–30cm)
Distribution: Widely distributed across Africa to the south of the Sahara.	
Color variant availability:	Essentially unknown
Compatibility: Pairs usually housed individually for breeding purposes.	
Pet potential: Hand-reared chicks are highly underrated as companions, being easier to manage and less costly than larger species.	
Diet: Offer a complete diet or a seed-based mix comprised of sunflower, safflower, pine nuts, and smaller cereal seeds. Peanuts are usually a particular favorite. Provide fruit and greenstuff daily.	

Health problems: Eye infections can be a problem.	
Breeding tips: Be sure to locate the nest box in the dark part of the shelter.	
Nesting needs: Nest box about 10in (25cm) square x 18in (46cm) deep, lined with coarse wood shavings or thin battening that can be whittled away to form a nest lining.	
Typical clutch size:	3–4 eggs
Incubation:	26–28 days
Rearing requirements: Soaked sunflower seed and softfood may be eaten readily.	
Fledging: Young will emerge from the nest at about 10–12 weeks old.	
Lifespan:	May live for 50 years.

● *How do these parrots rate as pets?*

Although adult birds are shy and will not settle well in the home—even remaining shy when kept in aviary surroundings—young poicephalid parrots can develop into very affectionate pets. They are quiet and gentle by nature, and can be taught readily to whistle, with this sound being similar to their natural call. They can also mimic a few words as well.

● *Can any poicephalid parrots be sexed visually?*

The Red-bellied (*Poicephalus rufiventris*) is easy to sex, since only cocks have the orangish-red underparts, with those of hens being green. Distinguishing other species is much harder. Do not be fooled by slight differences in markings; they simply indicate birds belonging to different subspecies.

● *I've had a true pair of Senegal Parrots for five years now, but they've never tried to breed. How can I encourage them?*

It can take a year or so for a pair to settle in new surroundings before they go to nest, but by this stage they should have made some attempt. Try giving a wider choice of nesting sites, especially in the shelter. The site at present could be too close to the window, allowing the sun to illuminate the interior of the box. Also, provide a more varied diet if necessary.

▲ *Unlike the other species in this group, Jardine's Parrot inhabits more densely forested areas in the wild, rather than scrubland. Young birds are less colorful than adults.*

plumage at the shoulder, offset against brown wings. Young birds have dark irises.

Jardine's Parrot (*Poicephalus gulielmi*). This bird also varies in color, being a combination of dark green and orange overall. In some cocks the iris is reddish-brown. Hens' irises are brown.

Care and Conditions

All these parrots are hardy once acclimatized, but they may start nesting in cold weather. This obviously reduces the likelihood of success, since both eggs and any chicks hatching at this time of year are at risk of being fatally chilled in outdoor surroundings. When the hen is in breeding condition, she flares her tail feathers—especially in the proximity of the nest box—indicating her readiness to breed. Over-preening by the cock can cause a bald patch on her neck at this stage, but these feathers will regrow. Established pairs may continue nesting for well over a decade.

Offer these parrots a varied diet, for if fed on little more than sunflower seed they are likely to develop upper respiratory infections due to vitamin A deficiency. Infections are usually indicated by blocked nostrils and may be accompanied by swelling of the bald area of skin around the eyes.

Grey Parrot SPECIES: PSITTACUS ERITHACUS

PROBABLY THE MOST FAMILIAR OF ALL PARROTS, and undeniably the most talented talker of the entire family, the Grey Parrot has an unmistakable appearance. In terms of character, however, Greys can prove to be rather shy—particularly when kept as pets—lacking the brash confidence of Amazon parrots. Nevertheless, they will become very attached to people they know well. The natural sounds made by these parrots are not especially loud or disturbing—being comprised mainly of a series of whistles—although they have a harsher call warning of danger.

Color Forms
The Grey Parrot exists in two distinctive forms. The slightly smaller Timneh subspecies (*P. e. timneh*) comes from Sierra Leone, Liberia, Ivory Coast, and Guinea. It is also a significantly darker gray color, with maroon rather than bright red feathering on the tail and a horn-colored area on the upper bill—an area which is black in the case of the Grey Parrot itself. Cocks have darker plumage than hens from the same area.

◀ *There can be some variance in coloration between individuals, particularly in the Grey Parrot itself, with some birds being of a lighter, more silvery shade than others.*

Fact File

Family name: Psittacidae

Length: 11–13in (28–33cm)

Distribution: Ranges in a broad band across central Africa, from islands off the west coast to Tanzania and Kenya in the east.

Color variant availability: Virtually unknown

Compatibility: Pairs usually housed on their own for breeding purposes, but can also be kept on a colony basis if the aviary is large.

Pet potential: Highly valued as a pet. Hand-reared chicks are easier to manage and are less costly than larger individuals.

Diet: A complete diet or seed-based mix comprised of sunflower, safflower, pine nuts, plus smaller cereal seeds. Peanuts are a favorite but must not be fed to excess. Also provide fruit, greenstuff, and vegetables ranging from corn-on-the-cob to carrot daily.

Health problems: Feather-plucking in pet birds housed indoors is not uncommon.

Breeding tips: Compatibility is vital for success.

Nesting needs: Nest box measuring about 12in (30cm) square x 18in (46cm) deep. Provide some thin battening that can be whittled away to form a nest lining inside, or coarse wood shavings for the same purpose.

Typical clutch size: 3–4 eggs

Incubation: 28–30 days

Rearing requirements: Offer soaked millet sprays, sunflower, and softfood.

Fledging: Young will emerge from the nest at about 10–12 weeks old.

Lifespan: May live for 70 years or more.

▲ *Ten-week-old Grey Parrots. The dark irises distinguish juveniles from adults (whose irises are yellow). Greys are relatively slow to talk; a six-month-old bird may still not be speaking well at this age.*

Care and Conditions

Grey Parrots need careful acclimatization before being placing in a sheltered outdoor aviary throughout the year. They are highly social birds, and for breeding the ideal is to start with several birds of opposite sex, and allow them to pair up themselves to ensure compatibility. Although the tendency in recent years has been to house breed pairs indoors to maximize their breeding potential (they will nest through much of the year), it is quite possible to breed them satisfactorily in an outdoor aviary on a colony system.

When Grey Parrots are housed indoors, they must be sprayed on a regular basis to keep their plumage sleek. Otherwise, they are likely to start plucking their feathers, and this problem soon becomes habitual.

A varied diet is also important, since Greys can become addicted to sunflower seed, which does not provide a balanced diet on its own.

● **Is it worth paying extra for a proven pair of Greys?**

Yes, because in the case of these parrots simply picking out two adult birds of opposite sex will not guarantee that you will have a compatible pair. They are choosy about their partners, normally forming a lifelong bond together.

● **What are King Greys?**

In Africa, Grey Parrots with abnormal feathering are highly prized by tribal rulers. The most frequent color aberration is the appearance of pinkish feathering among areas that are normally gray. Such birds have become known as King Greys. This change is not very stable, however, with such feathers sometimes appearing at one molt and disappearing at the next. It can be the result of a metabolic problem, which in the case of young Greys is often linked with an excessive amount of cod-liver oil in the rearing food. It is not wise to buy one of these birds at an exorbitant price.

● **Are there any other color variants known?**

Grey Parrots that have no melanin in the plumage have been recorded occasionally, but they are rare. Such birds have white feathering on their bodies and retain their red tail feathers.

Ring-necked and Alexandrine Parakeets

GENUS: PSITTACULA

THESE PARROTS WERE PROBABLY THE FIRST representatives of the group to be kept, about 2,500 years ago. The name of the Alexandrine Parakeet commemorates Alexander the Great, whose soldiers returned to Greece bringing psittaculid parakeets of this type home from India after the campaign of 327 B.C.

Popular Varieties

Both species are well represented in collections, but as aviary occupants rather than as pet birds. The Ring-necked is more widely kept.

Ring-necked Parakeet (*Psittacula krameri*). This species occurs in two distinctive populations. The African race (*P. k. krameri*) can be easily recognized when compared with its Indian relative (*P. k. manillensis*) by the color of its bill, which is much darker, with the upper mandible being blackish rather than red.

Color varieties are now established in the Indian Ring-necked. Both the blue and lutino forms are descended from wild birds that were highly valued by Indian princes. It has proved

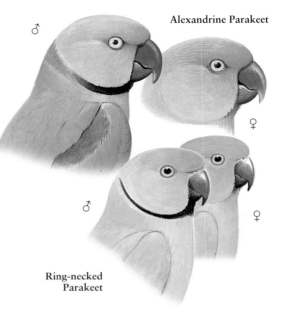

Alexandrine Parakeet

Ring-necked Parakeet

▲ *The Alexandrine Parakeet is significantly larger than the Ring-necked Parakeet, with a further distinguishing feature being the presence of red patches of plumage near the top of the wings.*

Fact File

Family name: Psittacidae

Length: Ring-necked 15in (38cm); Alexandrine 20in (51cm).

Distribution: Ring-necked ranges across northern Africa south of the Sahara, plus southern Asia into China. Alexandrine ranges from India to Thailand.

Color variant availability: Well established, particularly in the Ring-necked.

Compatibility: Pairs usually housed on their own for breeding purposes. Can also be kept on a colony basis in a large aviary.

Pet potential: Not even hand-reared birds make particularly good companions.

Diet: Complete diet or a quality seed-based mix of sunflower, safflower, peanuts, and pine nuts, plus other items such as flaked maize and pumpkin seeds. Greenstuff, vegetables, and fruit eaten readily.

Health problems: Both varieties very vulnerable to frostbite.

Breeding tips: Pair a young hen with an older cock, rather than vice versa.

Nesting needs: Nest box about 12in (30cm) square x 18in (46cm) deep. Battening on the floor will be whittled to form a nest lining.

Typical clutch size: Ring-necked 4–5 eggs; Alexandrine 2–3 eggs.

Incubation: Ring-necked 24 days; Alexandrine 30 days.

Rearing requirements: Offer greenstuff, softfood, and soaked sunflower seed.

Fledging: Young leave the nest when about 7–8 weeks old.

Lifespan: May live for 25 years or more.

▶ *The gray form is a widely kept variety of the Indian Ring-necked Parakeet. In the wild, the Ring-necked Parakeet has the widest distribution of any species of parrot.*

possible to create an albino variety from these colors, with birds of both sexes having snow-white plumage and being visually indistinguishable—even when mature—since the cock has no neck collar. Widely kept variants also include gray, gray-green, pied, and cinnamon forms.

Alexandrine Parakeet (*Psittacula eupatria*). Alexandrine and Ring-necked hens lack the characteristic pink nuchal collar seen across the back of the cock's neck. The Ring-necked is also known as the Rose-ringed Parakeet due to this collar.

Color variants in the Alexandrine are scarce, and it can be difficult distinguishing between those that are pure and other birds created by hybridization involving Ring-neckeds—although these tend to be smaller. There is a genuine lutino mutation, however, that is sex-linked, and a stunning blue form as well. Cinnamons are also known in this species.

Care and Conditions

A stout aviary is required for both these species, because they are potentially destructive, particularly near breeding time. Ring-neckeds will start nesting earlier than most parakeets in temperate areas, with hens often laying as early as February in the northern hemisphere. It is therefore vital that the nest box is positioned in a snug location to avoid losses of eggs and chicks during a sudden cold snap. Adequate protection from the elements at this time is also essential, because although hardy, these parakeets can easily suffer from frostbite.

Alexandrines tend to nest slightly later than Ring-neckeds, and if their first clutch of eggs fails to hatch, the hen may lay again. Otherwise, they will normally only rear one round of chicks in a season. Once established in their quarters, Alexandrines in particular often prove to be very reliable parents, with pairs being known to produce chicks annually over two decades.

Q&A

● *Why don't these parakeets make good pets?*

... This is related directly to the fact that cock and hen do not have a strong pair bond, and they do not appreciate close contact. Indeed, for much of the year, the hen is dominant and only as the time for breeding approaches will the cock cautiously approach her. Mutual preening is confined to this brief period.

● *How can I protect these birds against frostbite?*

Always try to ensure that they roost under cover when the temperature is likely to fall below freezing. Covering the front and sides of the aviary at this time of year will help to reduce the wind chill factor. Providing a nest box for roosting purposes is also recommended.

● *How long does it take for young cocks to be recognizable?*

It may not be until their third year that the distinctive plumage emerges around the neck of cocks. Yet today, thanks to DNA sexing, young birds can be sexed when they leave the nest—or even beforehand if required.

Moustached and Plum-headed Parakeets   GENUS: PSITTACULA

THESE MEMBERS OF THE PSITTACULID GROUP ARE widely represented in aviculture, particularly the attractive Plum-headed Parakeet.

Popular Varieties

Both species described below are easy to look after, but they need to be accommodated so as to minimize any risk of frostbite in temperate areas. **Moustached Parakeet** (*Psittacula alexandri*). Approximately eight races are recognized throughout the range of this species. Although it is generally possible to sex these parakeets on the basis of upper bill color (red in males), this does not apply to the Javan Moustached Parakeet (*P. a. alexandri*). The grayish feathering on the head tends to be a bluer shade in the hen, however, so visual sexing is possible. While acquired coloration has been recorded in the Moustached, genuine mutations have yet to emerge.

Plum-headed Parakeet (*Psittacula cyanocephala*). These parakeets are so-called because of the color of the cock's head. The hen has a grayish head and lacks the maroon wing patch seen in the cock. The subspecies known as the Blossom-headed Parakeet (*P. c. rosa*) has pale yellow, rather than white, tipping to the cock's central tail feathers. Hens have maroon wing patches.

One of the most beautiful color mutations is the lutino, in which the body of the cock is a rich yellow, offset against a red head, with the black stripes being replaced by white. Blues have also been recorded, along with cinnamons. Acquired coloration is not uncommon, with yellow pieds and individuals with mottled red and green plumage being documented. Such coloration tends to be transitory and may vary in distribution from one molt to the next, compared with a genetic mutation where the markings are fixed.

Care and Conditions

These parakeets need similar care to that recommended for their relatives (see pages 182–183). Although Plum-headeds tend to nest later in the

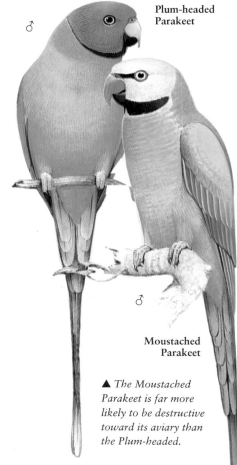

Plum-headed Parakeet

Moustached Parakeet

▲ *The Moustached Parakeet is far more likely to be destructive toward its aviary than the Plum-headed.*

year—often not until April in temperate areas—the hen has an unfortunate tendency to stop brooding her young before they are fully feathered, and this behavior can leave them vulnerable to hypothermia overnight. Even if their eggs are fatally chilled, a pair of Plum-headed Parakeets will probably show no further signs of breeding activity until the following year.

As with other psittaculids, compatibility between a pair cannot be guaranteed. Provide a choice of feeding sites—especially if housed in an indoor flight at any stage—in case the hen should dominate one feeding station.

Fact File

Family name:	Psittacidae
Length:	13in (33cm)

Distribution: Plum-headed mainly found in India and Pakistan. Moustached ranges further east to China and south to islands such as Java and Bali.

Color variant availability: Very rare in the Plum-headed; unknown in the Moustached.

Compatibility: Pairs are not mixed with others of their kind for breeding purposes.

Pet potential: Essentially aviary rather than pet birds.

Diet: Complete diet or parakeet-type seed mix of sunflower, millets, pine nuts, safflower, groats, etc. Offer carrot, greenstuff such as chickweed, and fruit including apple and pomegranates regularly, too.

Health problems:	Very vulnerable to frostbite.
Breeding tips:	Provide a stout nest box.

Nesting needs: Nest box about 7in (18cm) square x 18in (46cm) deep. Add a layer of coarse wood shavings as a nest lining, or short strips of wooden battening for Moustached, which tend to be more destructive.

Typical clutch size:	3–4 eggs
Incubation:	24 days

Rearing requirements: Softfood, soaked millet sprays, and greenstuff.

Fledging: Young will emerge from the nest when about 7–8 weeks old.

Lifespan:	May live for 25 years or more.

● **When will my young Plum-headeds molt for the first time?**

On leaving the nest these parakeets are virtually completely green in color, with yellow bills. They molt at between 12 and 20 weeks of age, with both sexes acquiring a silver-gray head color at this stage. Odd plum-colored feathers emerging after this stage confirm young cocks, but they will not acquire the full adult plumage until they are two years old.

● **Are these birds noisy?**

Plum-headeds have a pleasant, musical call that is not heard particularly frequently outside the breeding season. The calls of the Moustached are relatively loud, however—like those of most larger psittaculid parakeets—and could disturb near neighbors.

▼ *Plum-headed Parakeets, like this pair, can sometimes be kept with finches and softbills in an aviary. Color mutations have been recorded, but none is common.*

Peach-faced Lovebird

SPECIES: AGAPORNIS ROSEICOLLIS

THIS SPECIES IS NOW THE MOST POPULAR OF ALL the lovebirds, thanks to the wide range of color mutations. There is, unfortunately, no reliable way of sexing these birds visually. At the start of the breeding season, however, the pelvic bone test can give a reliable indication of their gender, since the gap between these bony prominences just above the vent enlarges at this stage in hens, to allow the passage of eggs. This can also be confirmed by behavioral signs, with hens usually undertaking much of the task of nest-building without assistance from their partners.

Popular Varieties

The first color variant was a yellow form, bred in 1954, in which the colors are diluted, giving rise to what has been called the Japanese Golden Cherryhead. The lutino, characterized by its red eyes and white rump, is pure yellow in color with the pink coloration on the face being retained. A variety which does not have a direct counterpart in the Budgerigar is the sea-green or pastel blue, in which some of the yellow and red pigment is

◀ *The bird on the left is the attractive sea-green, or pastel blue, mutation of the Peach-faced Lovebird. The other two birds show the normal form of plumage.*

Fact File

Family name:	Psittacidae
Length:	6in (15cm)
Distribution:	Southwestern Africa
Color variant availability: Wide choice now being bred.	
Compatibility: Pairs usually housed on their own for breeding purposes but can also be kept on a colony basis in a large aviary.	
Pet potential: Hand-reared chicks can develop into lively companions.	
Diet: Millets, canary seed, groats, and some sunflower, with greenstuff and fruit plus a supplement. A complete food can be used instead.	

Health problems: Susceptible to injured toes from fighting and frostbite.	
Breeding tips: Twigs and other materials required for nest building.	
Nesting needs: Nest box measuring about 6in (15cm) square x 9in (23cm) deep.	
Typical clutch size:	4–6 eggs
Incubation:	23 days
Rearing requirements: Soaked millet seeds, softfood, and greenstuff.	
Fledging: Young leave the nest when they are about 6 weeks old.	
Lifespan:	May live for 15 years or more.

retained, so the facial feathering in this case is reduced to a pale salmon shade, with the body being greenish-blue in color. By combining this with the lutino, the creamino has been created, which is a pale, creamy shade overall.

A pied mutation has also been developed. This can be combined with other mutations, resulting in olive pieds, for example, where the green plumage is darker than usual. The single factor green form of the dark factor mutation is better known as the jade rather than as the dark green, although both names are used. A gray mutation is also now well established, as is a cinnamon variant among others.

Care and Conditions

Peach-faced Lovebirds are very easy to look after, although if they are housed in adjoining flights, the panels must be double-wired to ensure that the birds cannot reach each other's toes through the mesh.

When breeding, hens will cut off pieces of bark (see page 189) which they fold up and carry back to their nest box tucked in among the feathers of their rump. This probably allows them to build their nest more rapidly than if they were carrying material in their bills. The chicks hatch with a layer of dense, red down and develop rapidly, being recognizable by dark markings on the beak when they first leave the nest. Remove them as soon as they are independent, because the adult birds are likely to be nesting again and may resent the presence of their earlier brood.

At the end of the breeding season in temperate areas, provide a clean nest box for roosting. Do not include nesting material, however, otherwise hens may continue laying and will then risk becoming egg-bound.

▲ *The pied can be combined with other color mutations to produce additional varieties. A pied mutation has been crossed with a sea-green mutation to produce this sea-green pied mutation.*

Q & A

● *How can I keep these lovebirds successfully in colonies?*

... By providing a large aviary where they have plenty of space and a good choice of nest boxes widely spaced around the enclosure at the same height. It is also very important to introduce all the lovebirds at the same time, since later additions will be treated as intruders by the flock and are very likely to be attacked and even killed.

● *Do Peach-faced Lovebirds make good show birds?*

These birds are a relatively common sight at shows, although the different color varieties are not generally standardized for judging purposes, as in the case of Budgerigars, for example. These lovebirds may be shown in pairs rather than individually. Condition is very important for judging purposes, with missing claws or molt birds being heavily penalized.

● *Why do my green Peach-faced Lovebirds keep producing offspring of other colors?*

This is the result of domestication and the emergence of new color varieties. It is actually very difficult now to acquire true-breeding Peach-faced Lovebirds of the normal green color. Repeated crossings have led to the situation where such birds are usually masking colors such as pastel blue, and these then emerge when the lovebirds produce their own offspring.

Masked and Fischer's Lovebirds

GENUS: AGAPORNIS

THESE TWO SPECIES OF LOVEBIRDS ARE CLOSELY related, originating near to each other in East Africa. They are very adaptable birds, nesting in gaps under roofs in towns where natural tree holes are not available. These species form part of the white eye ring group of lovebirds—recognizable by the broad area of white skin encircling each eye.

Popular Varieties

Color varieties are more common in the Masked Lovebird. The blue strain is a pure blue mutation with grayish-white plumage replacing the yellow coloration of the normal, and blue evident on the

Q&A...

● **Is it safe to keep my Fischer's Lovebird alongside my Masked?**

This is not necessarily a good idea, because the birds may start to breed. This is then likely to result in the production of hybrid offspring that could harm existing strains—although such birds tend to be recognizable by having darker heads than true Fischer's.

● **At what age will my young Masked Lovebirds be ready to breed?**

The likelihood is that they will be sexually mature at six months old, but generally it is better to wait until they are a year old before allowing them to start breeding. In effect, this means that chicks hatched in the early summer in temperate areas can be allowed to breed in the following year.

● **How can I stop my lovebirds nesting over the winter months if they need a nest box for roosting purposes?**

The simplest solution is to swap the position of the box in the autumn after the breeding season. First wash it out with a suitable avian preparation to kill any parasites that may be lurking inside. Once it has dried and can be replaced in the aviary, withhold nesting material and line the interior instead with just a thin layer of shavings.

● **I would like a Masked Lovebird as a pet. How will I be able to recognize a young bird?**

As in many other species of birds, the bill is the most obvious indicator of age. At about eight weeks old, there may still be dark tip to the upper bill. Young birds are also duller than adults in overall coloration.

◀ *A blue mutation of the Masked Lovebird. The blue strains seen today are all descended from a single cock of this color brought from Africa to England in 1927.*

wings and lower part of the body, while the black feathering on the head is retained. There is also a yellow variety that is a dilute form of the normal. The yellow variety has also been combined with the blue to create a white form; this variety still has dark plumage on the head and a very pale hint of blue elsewhere on the body. Similar mutations exist in Fischer's Lovebird, but they are less common.

Masked Lovebird (*Agapornis personata*). The blackish head, yellow chest, and green plumage on the wings merging into yellow on the underparts make identifying these lovebirds quite an easy task. Like the other three closely related species displaying white skin around their eyes, the Masked constructs a large nest. This is usually the responsibility of the hen, who collects strips of material and carries these to the nest box in her bill. It is not possible to distinguish pairs on the basis of differences in their plumage.

Fischer's Lovebird (*Agapornis fischeri*). Again, it is impossible to distinguish the sexes visually, in spite of the fact that some individuals may show a greater suffusion of black on the back of their heads than others. Pairs usually nest very readily, once they have become established in their quarters.

Care and Conditions

These lovebirds are hardy, and in most parts of the world they can be housed outdoors without artificial heat throughout the year, provided that

Masked Lovebird

Fischer's Lovebird

▲ *Both species of lovebirds are very popular, being attractive and easy to accommodate in an aviary of modest dimensions.*

they have a snug shelter as part of their quarters.

Provide a good choice of thin branches at the start of the breeding period that the birds can use to provide a basis for their nest. Willow is traditionally used for this purpose, but any branches —such as those cut from apple trees that have not been treated with chemicals—will also be suitable. These lovebirds may also collect feathers and even use millet sprays to augment their rather bulky nest, having eaten the millet seeds beforehand. The hen sits alone on the nest, although the cock may join her on occasion.

Fact File

Family name:	Psittacidae
Length:	6in (15cm)
Distribution:	Tanzania. Introduced to Kenya.
Color variant availability: Greatest in the Masked Lovebird.	
Compatibility: Pairs should be accommodated on their own for breeding purposes.	
Pet potential: Hand-reared chicks usually prove to be very tame.	
Diet: Smaller cereal seeds, augmented with some sunflower, groats, and a little hemp, plus fruit and greenstuff.	

Health problems:	Can suffer from intestinal worms.
Breeding tips:	Provide nesting material.
Nesting needs: Nest box measuring about 6in (15cm) square x 9in (23cm) deep.	
Typical clutch size:	4–6 eggs
Incubation:	23 days
Rearing requirements: Soaked millet seeds, softfood, and greenstuff.	
Fledging: Young leave the nest when they are about 6 weeks old.	
Lifespan:	May live for 15 years or more.

Black-cheeked and Nyasa Lovebirds
GENUS: AGAPORNIS

THESE OTHER TWO MEMBERS OF THE WHITE EYE ring group are less commonly seen in aviculture, although breeders specializing in these birds find them to be quite prolific under suitable conditions. Both have very restricted ranges in the wild, which is one reason why the Black-cheeked was one of the last species of parrot in the world to be discovered, with its existence only being documented in 1904.

Popular Varieties
Color mutations are scarce in both these lovebirds, although there was once a fairly common lutino form of the Nyasa Lovebird. This was unusual for a mutation of this type because it was an autosomal recessive characteristic, rather than being sex-linked in its mode of inheritance.

▲ *Black-cheeked Lovebirds often bathe when housed in outdoor aviaries. If housed indoors, they should be sprayed regularly to help maintain their plumage in good condition.*

It originated in Australia in 1930, and stock was brought to Europe. A few individuals are still found in mainland Europe and elsewhere, but this variant has effectively vanished. A blue mutation of the Black-cheeked occurred in Denmark during the 1980s, but it has not become common.

Black-cheeked Lovebird (*Agapornis nigrigensis*). These lovebirds are typified by a blackish head, with orangish suffusion on the upper chest and green plumage elsewhere. This color is darker on the wings.

Nyasa Lovebird (*Agapornis lilianae*). Slightly smaller in size than Fischer's Lovebird, which it resembles. The upper tail coverts are green, rather than blue, however, and there is no trace of black markings on the head.

Care and Conditions

Neither Black-cheeked nor Nyasa Lovebirds appear to be as hardy as related species, and it is best to house them in indoor flights over the winter in temperate areas. It has also proved possible to breed these lovebirds in spacious flight cages, once they have been sexed, which helps to explain why Black-cheeked Lovebirds are well represented in Scandinavian collections. The Nyasa in particular is a relatively docile species, compared with its relatives, and colony breeding with these birds can often give excellent results.

One of the problems that breeders in northern Europe found with this species was that breeding often occurred during the winter months. Suitable accommodation for this purpose should be provided at this time of year, with artificial lighting being essential to allow the adult birds to obtain adequate food for themselves and their chicks. In the tropics, including Zimbabwe, close to the natural range of these lovebirds, they have been found to breed successfully throughout most of the year. A similar pattern of breeding has been recorded in Australia where conditions are also equable for them. Like other members of their group, both Black-cheeked and Nyasa Lovebirds construct a nest, carrying material in their bills for this purpose.

● *My pair of Nyasa Lovebirds have started to pluck their chicks. What is likely to be the reason?*

Unfortunately, behavior of this type is quite common in these birds and may be an inherited problem. It certainly seems to be more associated with some bloodlines than others, but there could be other aspects involved, such as the birds' diet.

● *How can I prevent feather-plucking?*

Feather-plucking usually takes place just as the feathers cover the body, typically in the vicinity of the shoulders. Once you have a pair that have previously plucked their offspring, it is worth offering the hen the choice of a second nest box as well, when breeding is likely. Sometimes it can be a frustrated desire on the part of the adults to nest again that causes them to pluck the plumage of their chicks. A second box will allow them to start preparing to breed again, and may divert them from attacking their offspring in this way.

● *Will Black-cheeked Lovebirds hybridize with Masked Lovebirds?*

Unfortunately, yes, and particularly with a parrot that has such a restricted range in the wild, every effort should be made to keep existing Black-cheeked bloodlines pure. Hybrids have more yellowish plumage in the vicinity of the throat, although individuals differ in this respect.

● *Should I remove the chicks from my colony of Nyasa Lovebirds as they become independent?*

This partly depends on the number of birds in the aviary. Outbreaks of aggression are most likely if the birds start to become overcrowded, but reintroducing them can be difficult as well.

Fact File

Family name:	Psittacidae
Length:	5.5in (14cm)

Distribution: Black-cheeked southwest Zambia; Nyasa found in Malawi.

Color variant availability: Essentially unknown in the Black-cheeked; very rare now in the Nyasa.

Compatibility: Pairs often housed on their own for breeding purposes but can be kept successfully in breeding colonies.

Pet potential: Hand-reared chicks are friendly, but not talented as talking birds.

Diet: Smaller cereal seeds such as millets with some sunflower, groats, and a little hemp, plus fruit and greenstuff. A complete diet can also be used.

Health problems:	Fertility can sometimes be low.
Breeding tips:	Nesting material required.

Nesting needs: Nest box approximately 6in (15cm) square x 9in (23cm) deep.

Typical clutch size:	4–6 eggs
Incubation:	23 days

Rearing requirements: Soaked millet seeds, soft-food, and greenstuff.

Fledging: Young leave the nest around 6 weeks old.

Lifespan:	May live for 15 years or more.

Eclectus and Hanging Parrots

GENERA: ECLECTUS, LORICULUS

BOTH THESE GROUPS OF PARROTS HAVE RATHER specialized requirements, particularly in their diet, and are not good choices as pets, although they thrive in suitable aviary surroundings. Pairs will breed readily—particularly the Eclectus.

Popular Varieties

These parrots make rewarding aviary occupants. The female Eclectus is striking in appearance, and, as their name suggests, the hanging parrots spend much of their time hanging upside down. **Eclectus Parrot** (*Eclectus roratus*). Approximately ten races of this species have been identified, and the differences between them are clearest in the hens, with their predominantly reddish plumage. The Red-sided Eclectus (*E. r. polychloros*) from New Guinea and nearby islands, the Moluccan race (*E. r. vosmaeri*), and the

◀ *A colorful hen Eclectus Parrot. Eclectus Parrots do not have a fixed egg-laying season. Instead, the hen may lay eggs at virtually any time of the year—except when she is molting.*

Fact File

Family name: Psittacidae

Length: Eclectus 12–14in (30–36cm); hanging parrots 5in (13cm).

Distribution: India, Sri Lanka, and southeast Asia. Eclectus is confined to offshore islands here, and its distribution extends to the far north of Australia.

Color variant availability: None

Compatibility: Eclectus should be housed in pairs on their own. Hanging parrots are quite social.

Pet potential: Eclectus are less confiding than other parrots, even if hand-reared, while hanging parrots are generally regarded as too messy.

Diet: About a third of the diet of Eclectus should consist of fresh foods such as vegetables and greenstuff rather than seed. Hanging parrots need a daily supply of nectar, as well as fruit, some greenstuff, and softbill food. Millet sprays also eaten readily.

Health problems: Feather-plucking in Eclectus. Overgrown claws in hanging parrots.

Breeding tips: Always site nest boxes under cover.

Nesting needs: Nest box about 12in (30cm) square x 3ft (90cm) deep (Eclectus); 5in (13cm) square x 6in (15cm) deep (hanging parrots).

Typical clutch size: Eclectus 2 eggs; hanging parrots 3–5 eggs.

Incubation: Eclectus 28–30 days; hanging parrots 20 days.

Rearing requirements: Soaked millet seeds, softfood, and greenstuff. Hanging parrots need livefood such as mealworms or waxmoth larvae.

Fledging: Eclectus 11 weeks; hanging parrots 5 weeks.

Lifespan: Members of both groups may live for 20 years or more.

▶ *When the Eclectus Parrot was first discovered, it was thought that the cock and hen were different species of birds, due to the extreme differences in their plumage.*

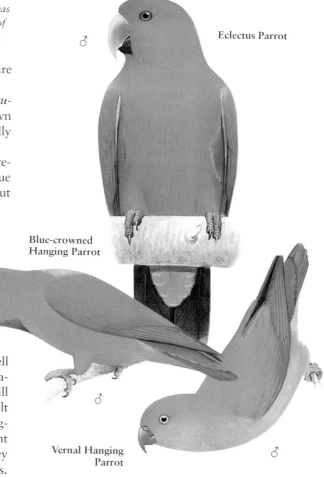

Eclectus Parrot

Solomon Islands form (*E. r. solomonensis*) are most widely kept.

Blue-crowned Hanging Parrot (*Loriculus galgulus*). The distinctive blue marking on the crown helps to identify this species, with hens normally lacking the red throat spot.

Vernal Hanging Parrot (*Loriculus vernalis*). Predominantly green as its name suggests, with blue suffusion on the throat. Sexing is difficult, but hens may have less blue on their throats.

Blue-crowned
Hanging Parrot

Vernal Hanging
Parrot

Care and Conditions

In view of their size and powerful bills, Eclectus require strong aviaries. They also prefer a shady environment. They have loud calls but are not generally too noisy unless several pairs are housed in the same area. Their daily diet must incorporate plenty of vegetables and other greenstuff, as well as some fruit. Eclectus Parrots have a high vitamin A requirement, and the deficiency that will arise on a seed-based diet is also likely to result in the fungal illness known as candidiasis. Hanging parrots are quite at home in a planted flight in the company of softbills and finches, but they require wintertime warmth in temperate areas. These parrots will cut leaves and other vegetation at the start of the nesting period to make a nest lining. Hens carry this material tucked in among the feathers over the rump.

▲ *The quiet natures and predominantly green coloration of the Blue-crowned Hanging Parrot and the Vernal Hanging Parrot mean that they can sometimes be hard to spot in a well-planted aviary.*

● My Eclectus have now nested successfully on four occasions, rearing six chicks, all of which have been male. Is this a record?

At Chester Zoo in Britain, a pair hatched approximately 30 chicks before producing a hen! No one is sure why this happens, but it may be linked with the temperature during the incubation period. It is now known that in many reptiles just a fraction of a degree can influence the sex of the young. A similar phenomenon may apply in this case. Alternatively, it might be that males have a more hazardous existence in the wild, and so nature compensates by producing more male chicks.

● I bought what is supposed to be a proven pair of Eclectus, but the hen is very aggressive toward her partner. Are they likely to breed successfully together?

This is not uncommon. Provide extra feeding bowls to lessen the likelihood of bullying, and house them in a spacious aviary where there is less potential for conflict.

● One of my hanging parrots has difficulties when flying off the aviary mesh. Can you suggest a reason?

Catch the bird and examine its feet. Almost certainly, one or more claws will be overgrown, being hooked at the tip and making it difficult for the parrot to free itself easily. Trim back the claw carefully with suitable clippers.

Seed-eating Doves

GENERA: GEOPELIA, STREPTOPELIA, CHALCOPHAPS, COLUMBINA

THESE DOVES ARE POPULAR IN BIRDKEEPING circles, although few breeders specialize in them. Instead, the birds tend to be housed as part of a mixed collection. Planted aviaries are recommended, because the bushes here will not only provide cover but can also serve as nesting sites.

Popular Varieties

Color mutations are only well known in the Diamond Dove. They include silver, fawn, red (actually auburn), cream, blue (a steely-gray), plus variants such as pied and white-rumped.

Diamond Dove (*Geopelia cuneata*). Justifiably popular, they are easy to care for and steady by nature. Can be kept with finches, non-aggressive softbills, and Cockatiels. These doves have white, diamond-shaped markings over their wings. The remainder of the upperparts are brownish-gray, with the underparts bluish-gray. They are relatively easy to sex at the start of the breeding period especially, when the red orbital skin of the cock becomes more pronounced. Pairs will breed readily if provided with a canary nesting pan, rearing several clutches of chicks in succession. They are far less aggressive than many other doves and, if kept in a spacious

▼ ▶ *In spite of their reputation as birds of peace, doves can be very aggressive toward each other, and so it is advisable to keep only a single pair in an aviary. They can also be rather nervous, especially until they are settled in their quarters. Feeding these doves is relatively straightforward, however.*

flight, several pairs can be kept in harmony.

Zebra Dove (*Geopelia striata*). Ranging over a wide area of southeast Asia to Australia, there are distinctive differences in appearance between the various populations of these doves. Their bodies are barred, with the orbital skin around the eye being blue. Sexing is difficult, but hens may be a slightly duller shade.

Laughing Dove (*Streptopelia senegalensis*). Another widely distributed species with a corresponding variance in appearance. Hens typically have grayer upperparts than cocks.

Green-winged Dove (*Chalcophaps indica*). A brownish-purple head and underparts, coupled with a white shoulder patch and green wings, are characteristic features of the cock. The white areas are grayer in hens, with the rump being brownish rather than black. These doves are

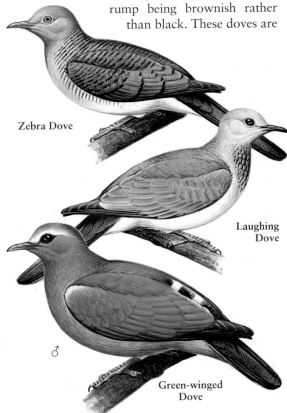

Zebra Dove

Laughing Dove

Diamond Dove

♂

♂

Green-winged Dove

Fact File

Family name:	Columbidae
Length:	7–10in (18–25cm)

Distribution: Diamond Dove Australia; Laughing Dove Africa and the Middle East; Gold-billed Ground Dove northwestern South America; others Australasia.

Color variant availability: Well established in the Diamond Dove.

Compatibility: Breeding pairs should be housed on their own.

Pet potential: Usually too nervous, although young Diamond Doves can become finger-tame.

Diet: Complete diet or seed-based mix comprised of smaller cereal seeds such as mixed millets. Will also eat chopped up greenstuff. May also sample softbill food, eggfood, and chick crumbs.

Health problems: Can be susceptible to the protozoan infection trichomoniasis.

Breeding tips:	Seclusion is important.

Nesting needs: Nesting platform with sides at least 1in (2.5cm) high, to provide support for the nest.

Typical clutch size:	2 eggs
Incubation:	13 days

Rearing requirements: Offer soaked millet sprays and softfood.

Fledging: Young leave the nest when they are about 14 days old.

Lifespan:	May live for 10 years or more.

forest dwellers and must be kept in planted aviaries, being nervous in open enclosures.

Gold-billed Ground Dove (*Columbina cruziana*). One of a group of South American doves, this species is instantly recognizable due to the golden-yellow area visible on the bill, which is brighter in the case of the cock.

Care and Conditions

These doves are reasonably hardy once properly acclimatized, but need a well-lit, dry shelter into which they can retreat during bad weather. A dry sand area for dust-bathing is also important, since these birds are very reluctant rain-bathers.

Cocks can sometimes be very aggressive to their intended mates at the start of the breeding season—particularly the Green-winged Dove—harassing them relentlessly. Providing several feeding stations can help, as will a densely planted flight, allowing the hen to escape from her suitor. Once she has laid, harmony is restored, with both birds sharing the incubation. The young should be removed once they are feeding independently, since the adult pair are likely to breed again. The cock in particular will soon actively resent the presence of his previous offspring. Pairs should be restricted from rearing more than three rounds of chicks in succession.

▶ *Gold-billed Ground Doves are often called Pygmy Doves because of their small size. In spite of their name, they spend most of the time perching.*

● *How can I distinguish between doves and pigeons?*

Unfortunately, it is not possible. They all belong to the same family, and there are no clearcut differences between them. The only guide is that the description "pigeon" is usually reserved for larger species, with doves being the smaller members of the group.

● *My Diamond Doves are very wasteful when feeding. Any suggestions?*

Try a plastic quail feeder divided into sections to prevent the birds from scattering the seed so easily. By standing the feeder on a clean newspaper, you can also tip the spilt seed back into the container each day.

Imperial Fruit Pigeons
and Fruit Doves GENERA: DUCULA, PTILINOPUS

▼ *The Green Imperial Pigeon. Both cock and hen of this species share the tasks of incubation and caring for the young.*

SOME FRUIT DOVES HAVE PLUMAGE RIVALING that of the most beautifully colored softbills or parrots. Imperial fruit pigeons are less colorful, but look very impressive in a spacious, planted aviary—being suitable companions for larger, non-aggressive softbills such as touracos. Visual sexing is usually impossible, but cocks tend to be slightly bigger, with larger heads.

Popular Varieties

These birds are only sporadically available to birdkeepers, but they have become better known over recent years, and breeding results are now being obtained more consistently. Not surprisingly, no color varieties have been recorded.

Green Imperial Pigeon (*Ducula aenea*). The head and body are usually gray, with the wings and tail being dark green and the undertail coverts dark chestnut. The subspecies diverging most significantly from this coloration are to be found on some Indonesian and Philippine islands. They have patches of contrasting color on the nape. They are highly scarce in collections.

Pink-spotted Fruit Dove (*Ptilinopus perlatus*). There are two distinctive forms of this fruit dove, occurring on New Guinea and smaller neighboring offshore islands. The distribution of the most widely kept subspecies (*P. p. zonurus*) is centered on southern New Guinea. Its head is greenish-yellow, with upperparts being green, suffused with bronze, broken by the distinctive pink spots over the upper area of the wings. A grayish collar encircles the neck and extends up to the bill, with the upper breast being golden-bronze and the remainder of the underparts being a dark shade of yellowish-green. In contrast, the north-eastern population (*P. p. plumbeicollis*) has a grayish head and broader collar.

Care and Conditions

Fruit doves and pigeons need particular care when first obtained, particularly if they are not acclimatized to living in an outdoor aviary. They

Q & A...

● **Do I need to cut up grapes for my fruit doves?**

Thanks to their amazing gape, these birds will swallow large fruits whole—which is probably just as well because their bills do not allow them to nibble off chunks of fruit. The stones of large-stoned fruits, such as cherries, are often regurgitated instead of passing through the digestive tract.

● **The color of the droppings of my fruit doves is quite variable. Is this a sign of illness?**

Not usually. The fruit that the birds have been eating can have a dramatic effect on their droppings, with blackberries or red grapes turning them purplish-red in color, whereas green grapes will not have this effect. Whitish droppings alone are more indicative of illness, suggesting that the bird has not been eating properly.

● **My hen Pink-spotted Fruit Dove has started to lay, but from the perch onto the floor. What I can do?**

This is not uncommon at first, and hopefully she will soon adopt a nesting basket or platform to lay her eggs. Such behavior can be a sign that the existing breeding sites are not sufficiently secluded, or there may be a shortage of twigs and moss for nest-building.

are likely to need artificial heat over the winter months but will then prove to be relatively hardy. In spite of the name of these birds, they cannot be maintained in good condition on fruit alone. They will rapidly lose condition if offered little more than grapes and diced apple, requiring much more protein in their diet. Protein can be introduced either by means of avian pellets or a complete maintenance dog food of the appropriate size. These items should be soaked in water to improve their palatability when introducing them to the birds. Any of the feeding mix that remains should always be discarded at the end of the day before it starts to turn moldy.

Some cocks, particularly those of imperial pigeons, can be aggressive toward hens at the start of the breeding period.

It is normal for chicks to leave the nest before their plumage is fully developed, but keep a close eye on them at this stage, since they will not be able to fly properly and the adults will not normally descend to the ground to feed a youngster. As they start to become independent, the young tend to become very wild, and they should be transferred to a secluded aviary where they can settle down. Established pairs may lay two or three times in the course of a year.

▲ *The pink spots on the wings of Pink-spotted Fruit Doves enable them to be identified easily. These markings may differ slightly in size and distribution, enabling individual birds to be recognized.*

Fact File

Family name:	Columbidae
Length:	10–18in (25–46cm)

Distribution: Green Imperial Pigeon southeast Asia, including offshore islands such as the Philippines; Pink-spotted Fruit Dove New Guinea.

Color variant availability:	None

Compatibility: Pairs should be kept apart from others of their kind.

Pet potential:	None

Diet: Fruit such as diced apple and grapes sprinkled with softbill food. Mynah pellets or a maintenance dry dog food also required.

Health problems:	Vulnerable to tapeworms.

Breeding tips: Allow pairs sufficient time to become established; can take 2–3 years.

Nesting needs: Provide a nesting platform with sides at least 2in (5cm) high, as a basis to support the nest.

Typical clutch size:	1 egg

Incubation: 28 days (Green Imperial Pigeon); 14 days (Pink-spotted Fruit Dove).

Rearing requirements: Nothing specific. Pigeons and doves produce their own "crop milk" for this purpose.

Fledging:	Similar to incubation periods.
Lifespan:	May live for 15 years or more.

Pheasants
GENERA: CHRYSOLOPHUS, SYRMATICUS

▲ A cock Lady Amherst's Pheasant. Red feathering on the legs of cocks suggests a past hybridization with Golden Pheasants. Hybrid hens usually have yellowish, not blue-gray, legs.

MEMBERS OF THIS MAJESTIC GROUP OF BIRDS make spectacular aviary occupants, although they should be housed in large enclosures located in seminatural settings. Pheasants can be prolific when breeding, but the potentially aggressive nature of cocks means extra accommodation is often needed, particularly at this time.

Popular Varieties
The species listed here are widely bred, therefore obtaining stock is usually straightforward. It may be better to start with young birds rather than older birds—particularly in view of the highly aggressive nature of some cocks.

Such is the beauty of these pheasants that there is little interest in color varieties, although there is an attractive dilute form of the Golden Pheasant. This is distinguishable by its paler overall body coloration, with yellow, rather than reddish, underparts. Other recorded variants include a strain with darker throat coloration and another with salmon-colored underparts.

Lady Amherst's Pheasant (*Chrysolophus amherstiae*). This bird is a close relative of the Golden Pheasant, but cocks differ significantly in coloration, having a black-and-white tippet, dark green chest and wings, plus white underparts. Yellow and red feathering is confined to the back and tail. Females are larger than hen Golden Pheasants, with blacker barring and a greener sheen on their upperparts.

Golden Pheasant (*Chrysolophus pictus*). The deep, orangish-red underparts of cocks contrast with the ruff or tippet of feathers around the neck (used for display purposes), which are orange with black edging. Golden-yellow plumage is present on the head and back. Hens are much duller, being predominantly brownish.

Reeves' Pheasant (*Syrmaticus reevesi*). Shades of brown, mixed with areas of black-and-white plumage, are characteristic of cocks of this large species. Hens are again predominantly brown.

Care and Conditions
Pheasants spend much of their time on the floor and need a large, well-drained aviary to prevent their plumage becoming muddy. The design usually features a well-planted central area offering

▶ The colorful plumage of the cock Golden Pheasant is unmistakable. It takes approximately two years for young cocks to acquire full adult plumage.

Fact File

Family name: Phasianidae	**Health problems:** Vulnerable to intestinal parasites.
Length: 30–84in (76-213cm); cocks always have significantly longer tail plumes than hens.	**Breeding tips:** Do not keep a cock with a single hen.
Distribution: China	**Nesting needs:** Good cover in flight to provide security, so hen can lay undisturbed on the ground.
Color variant availability: Established in the Golden Pheasant.	**Typical clutch size:** 7–15 eggs
	Incubation: 23–25 days
Compatibility: Cocks are aggressive, especially toward other males.	**Rearing requirements:** Softfood and greenstuff important.
Pet potential: None	**Fledging:** Young are mobile immediately after hatching.
Diet: Seed mix containing grain, plus greenstuff and some invertebrates.	**Lifespan:** May live for 15 years or more.

cover, and a gravel area laid around the inner perimeter where the birds can walk freely, with the main floor covering being grass. Perches in the shelter must be positioned higher than those in the flight, to encourage the pheasants to roost under cover where they will be less vulnerable to frostbite on cold nights.

Cock pheasants are very territorial and fight savagely, so if they are to be housed in adjacent flights, there will need to be a solid barrier here, taller than the birds, so they cannot see each other. These pheasants are polygamous when breeding, which means that a cock must be housed with two or three hens. Even so, a close watch should be kept for signs of aggression. It may be better to introduce the cock to the hens and then remove him again as egg-laying starts, leaving the hens to rear their chicks on their own.

Q&A...

● *Do pheasants hybridize together?*

Yes, with cross-breeding of this type having taken place in the past between Golden and Lady Amherst's. Be sure not to mix species for this reason, and remember that two cocks of any species are still likely to fight and must therefore be kept apart.

● *One of my hen Golden Pheasants keeps eating her eggs. What can I do to prevent this?*

Take the eggs away as soon as they are laid and transfer them to an incubator or place under a broody bantam. Some breeders place old, infertile eggs under hens that behave in this way in the belief that the awful taste of the eggs will deter the hen, but this could cause illness. Dummy eggs may break this habit, however.

● *Can I allow the pheasants out of their aviary to roam around the garden?*

This is not generally recommended, because the birds are likely to stray, even if the flight feathers on one wing are clipped back to just above the shaft. Trimming both wings in this way is more effective but leaves the birds increasingly vulnerable to predators such as cats.

Quails

GENERA: EXCALFACTORIA, COLINUS, CALLIPEPLA

QUAILS ARE CLOSELY RELATED TO PHEASANTS, BUT are much smaller and far less brightly colored, with shades of brown generally predominating in their plumage. They have a rather dumpy body shape, with inconspicuous tail feathers.

Popular Varieties

Color variants are best known in the Chinese Painted Quail, with the silver form being the most widely kept. Cocks retain the distinctive chestnut markings on their underparts in this bird, so that sexing is straightforward, but the predominant color in the plumage is silver.

Chinese Painted Quail (*Excalfactoria chinensis*). The small size of these quails has helped ensure their popularity among birdkeepers. Cocks are more colorful than hens, with slaty-blue coloration extending from head to lower chest, whereas hens are mottled brown in color.

Bobwhite Quail (*Colinus virginianus*). Slight variations in plumage are not uncommon in these quails, with over 20 different races being recognized. Overall, cocks are more brightly colored than hens and can be identified by their white, rather than buff-colored, throats.

Californian Quail (*Callipepla californica*). Brown wings and a buff-colored forehead help to distinguish cocks of this species from the closely related Gambel's Quail. Cocks have a black crest, whereas hens have a smaller, brown crest, with their heads being entirely grayish-brown and lacking any white stripes.

Care and Conditions

While Chinese Painted Quails can be housed in an aviary with finches or softbills, the larger species can be much more disruptive. They will fly up readily if alarmed and will also seek to roost off the ground. You will need to cut a quail door in the main area linking the shelter and flight, to give these birds access back and forth. The door should be fixed so that it cannot be accidentally closed, leaving the quail trapped in the flight. Their food and water containers should be placed on the shelter floor, so that they cannot be soiled from above by the other birds. Since quails can be messy feeders, special quail feeders that help to prevent seed from being scattered around the floor are recommended.

Do not house these birds with larger softbills, such as laughing thrushes or starlings, since they may prey upon the young quails—which in the case of the Chinese Painted are little bigger than bumblebees when they emerge from their eggs. They can easily slip out through any gaps in the aviary structure, and possibly even the mesh itself, so it may be necessary to fix some plastic screening around the base of the enclosure at first to prevent escapes. Once the chicks are feeding independently they should be removed from the aviary, because the hen will often be starting to lay again by this stage.

◄ *Chinese Painted Quails will not cause a disturbance in an aviary and do not roost on the perches—unlike some larger relatives.*

Q&A...

● *What can I do to prevent my Bobwhite Quails from flying up and colliding with the aviary roof?*

These birds are often very nervous when first transferred to new quarters, but will settle down in time, particularly if there is good cover in the aviary. String lightweight plastic mesh, similar to that used in fruit cages, to form a taut barrier below the wire mesh in the aviary.

● *Why do my Chinese Painted Quails keep scattering their eggs round their aviary, rather than incubating them?*

It seems that over the generations, incubator-hatching has affected the maternal instincts of hens, so that many will not incubate their own eggs. Other possible causes may include persistent attention from the cock and lack of cover, resulting in the hen being unable to find a secluded area for a nest.

● *If I use an incubator to hatch the eggs, what temperature setting will be required?*

The figure should be 100–102°F (38–39°C). The chicks will then need to be moved to a brooder once they hatch, with the temperature being slightly reduced and lowered further as they grow.

● *How should I pair up cocks and hens for breeding purposes?*

Cock quails are extremely aggressive, and it is very important to house a cock with several hens, rather than keeping them in individual pairs. if you do not do this, a single hen is likely to be seriously attacked by her potential partner in these circumstances.

Californian Quail

Bobwhite Quail

▲ *These North American quails are widely kept and bred, but in many cases it is necessary to invest in an incubator and brooder to ensure that the eggs are hatched and the chicks reared successfully. The adult birds should be provided with as much privacy as possible to increase the likelihood that they will carry out these tasks.*

Fact File

Family name:	Phasianidae
Length:	5–10in (13–25cm)

Distribution: Chinese Painted Quail southern Asia, from India eastward; Californian Quail western coast of the United States; Bobwhite Quail more widely distributed in the United States, south to Mexico.

Color variant availability: Well established in the Chinese Painted Quail

Compatibility: Cocks must not be housed together.

Pet potential:	None

Diet: Cereal seeds—millets most suitable for Chinese Painted Quail—plus softfood, invertebrates, and greenstuff such as chickweed.

Health problems: Hens vulnerable to being feather-plucked or even injured by cocks. Action must be taken without delay to prevent this.

Breeding tips: Keep cocks apart from each other.

Nesting needs: Secluded area under a bush where the hen can excavate a scrape for her eggs.

Typical clutch size:	10–16 eggs

Incubation: 16 days; Chinese Painted Quail 23 days.

Rearing requirements: Starter crumbs, softfood, chick crumbs, and soaked millet sprays beneficial.

Fledging: Young able to leave nest immediately after hatching.

Lifespan:	May live for 8 years or more.

Glossary

Acquired melanism Abnormal darkening of the plumage seen in FINCHES—usually linked with a poor diet or liver failure.

Albino A MUTATION in which all color pigment is missing, resulting in a pure white body, red eyes, and pink legs.

Autosomal recessive mutation A MUTATION linked with the autosomes (chromosomes that have no influence over the bird's gender). The recessive nature of such mutations means that their characteristics will not emerge in the offspring if paired with a pure, normal individual of the same species.

Aviary An outdoor unit for housing birds, consisting of a FLIGHT and a SHELTER.

Aviculture The keeping and breeding of birds in controlled surroundings.

Backcross A term used to describe the pairing of a bird with one of its parents, in the hope of duplicating a desirable feature, in terms of TYPE or coloration.

Birdroom An enclosed indoor area where birds are kept and frequently bred.

Buff A relatively coarse feather with slightly paler edges, seen particularly in Canaries.

Cap The top of a bird's head. Of particular significance in the lizard Canary, whose markings here are critical when showing.

Cere The largely unfeathered area at the top of the upper bill. Most apparent in PARROTS, particularly the Budgerigar, and providing the basis for sexing.

Chromosome One of the threadlike, normally paired structures present in the nucleus of all living cells. Chromosomes contain the GENES.

Clear egg An egg that is infertile or fails to develop.

Cloaca The internal chamber into which the digestive, urinary, and reproductive tracts enter, prior to voiding their contents.

Closed ring A continuous, circular ring, or band, applied to the leg of a chick when it is still in the nest. Provides a permanent record of details such as the bird's age or sex.

Clutch size The number of eggs laid by a hen in succession over a short time span.

Cobby Of thick-set appearance.

Colony system The practice of keeping birds of the same species together in an AVIARY for breeding purposes.

Color feeding An artificial means of improving the coloration of certain FINCHES and SOFTBILLS by using a food or additive containing special coloring agents.

Crop The saclike organ in the avian digestive tract between the esophagus and the proventriculus, used for the storage of food.

Dead-in-the-shell The term used to describe fully formed chicks which fail to hatch, dying toward the end of the incubation period.

Dilute coloration A paler version of the NORMAL coloration.

Dominant characteristic A genetic characteristic that should emerge in a first generation pairing with a pure, normal individual of the same species.

Double-buffing The pairing together of two buff-feathered individuals to increase the size of the offspring. Increases the risk of FEATHER CYSTS.

Down Fluffy plumage which serves to insulate the body. Most evident in chicks.

Egg-binding The inability of a hen to expel an egg from her body.

Estrildid Relating to the family Estrildidae.

Fancying The selective breeding of birds for particular traits such as coloration.

Feather cyst A swelling, seen typically in buff-feathered Canaries, resulting from the failure of a feather to emerge properly through the skin. Also known as a feather lump.

Feather plucking The removal of feathers by a bird, resulting in areas of baldness. Often associated with PARROTS.

Finch In birdkeeping terms, one of the group of birds that feeds mainly on seed.

Flecking Unwanted dark markings on the clear head area of Budgerigars. Particularly associated with opalines.

Fledging The period during which a chick leaves the nest.

Fledgling A bird that has left the nest but is still being fed by its parents.

Flight The part of an AVIARY or large cage where birds can fly.

Flight cage A spacious cage that enables the occupants to fly freely within it.

Flight panel One of the wire-covered frames that form the outer part of an AVIARY.

Foreign finch Any non-domesticated species of FINCH.

French molt A feather disease caused by a virus. Most common in young Budgerigars.

Frugivore An animal that depends on fruit for a significant part of its diet.

Gene The part of a CHROMOSOME that carries the information which is responsible for determining the body's inherited characteristics.

Genotype The genetic makeup of an organism.

Gizzard The part of the avian digestive tract where seeds and other foodstuffs are ground up into smaller particles.

Going light The term used to describe weight loss across the breastbone, causing this to appear more prominent than normal.

Gut loading Feeding special food to invertebrates to benefit the birds which then eat them.

Hand-rearing The artificial rearing of chicks (usually PARROTS).

Hybrid An individual created by the breeding together of animals of two different species.

Inbreeding Mating between very closely related animals—such as between parent and offspring.

Insectivore An animal that depends on insects for a significant part of its diet.

Insectivorous food A food prepared for SOFTBILLS containing a relatively high proportion of dried invertebrates.

Iris The colored area of the eye surrounding the dark pupil. Can provide a means of identifying young PARROTS, which usually have darker irises than adults.

Iron storage disease A condition in which excessive levels of dietary iron are absorbed in the body, causing liver damage.

Jabot The curled plumage on the chest of frilled breeds of Canary.

Lethal factor A genetic abnormality responsible for the death of chicks during incubation or very soon after hatching.

Melanistic plumage An area of black feathering.

Molt The replacement of old feathers with new ones.

Mule A HYBRID resulting from the mating between a Canary and a species of FINCH.

Mutation A sudden change in the genetic character. In birds, this may cause offspring to appear showing an unexpected alteration to the color of the plumage, for example.

Nectivore An animal that depends on nectar for a significant part of its diet.

Normal The usual coloration associated with a species—such as light green in the Budgerigar.

Nuchal collar An area of plumage around the back of the neck of some species of birds, giving the appearance of a collar.

Nuptial plumage The colorful breeding plumage of some birds.

Papilloma A wart-like growth, most common in the CLOACAS of larger PARROTS.

Parasite An organism that lives on (ectoparasite), or in (endoparasite), another organism (the host) and depends on it for nutrition. Some parasites may cause serious diseases.

Parrot A general term used to describe either members of the order Psittaciformes, or a specific group within this order.

Phenotype The observable traits displayed by an organism, such as plumage color in birds.

Pied In birds, plumage that has contrasting areas of light and dark feathering.

Plainhead A bird belonging to a crested variety, but which itself has no crest.

Posture breed A type of Canary judged partly on its stance.

Preening The process of grooming the plumage by a bird.

Probiotic A product containing beneficial bacteria.

Psittaculid Relating to members of the PARROT family.

Quail door An opening near the bottom of the aviary SHELTER door, to allow quails to enter and leave easily.

Race A localized form of a species.

Recessive characteristic A genetic characteristic that will not emerge in a first generation pairing with a pure, normal individual of the same species.

Scaly leg An illness caused by the same parasitic mites responsible for scaly face.

Self A single, basic color.

Sex-linked character A genetic character linked with the pair of sex CHROMOSOMES.

Sexual dimorphism Possessing clear, visual means of distinguishing the sexes—usually by means of plumage differences.

Shelter The enclosed part of an AVIARY.

Softbill One of the group of birds that feeds mainly on fruit, invertebrates, and/or nectar.

Split ring A ring that can be applied to a bird at any age.

Standard A list of the points deemed desirable in a particular variety of bird. Used for judging purposes at shows.

Subspecies A taxonomic division below the level of species, indicating slight differences in appearance between birds from different populations.

Surgical sexing A means of determining the gender of a bird by using an endoscope.

Ticked Having a small mark which contrasts with the color of the rest of the bird's plumage.

Tight feather Sleek plumage.

Type The "official" appearance of a bird, as set out for exhibition and judging purposes.

Unflighted A young bird that has yet to molt its flight feathers.

Vent The posterior body opening connecting with the CLOACA.

Yellow Both a color and a feather type (the opposite of BUFF)—being more brightly colored and softer.

Birds and the Law

A number of regulations apply in respect to keeping birds—often emanating from the Convention on the International Trade in Endangered Species of Wild Fauna and Flora (CITES), to which more than 120 countries have now signed up. CITES regulates the international trade in wildlife, irrespective of whether the subjects are bred in captivity or caught in the wild. Its regulations are then incorporated into national legislation. Both the United States and the European Union have stricter regulations than those of CITES. Since the species listings and the requirements change from time to time, advice on

the current situation should be sought from your country's CITES management authority, and from the agricultural department for advice on health and quarantine requirements. There may also be local state restrictions, including the need to obtain permission to advertise and sell endangered species. These apply even if the birds have been bred in collections. Today, the shipment of birds internationally is also tightly regulated, and in spite of the very occasional disasters which are reported, the vast majority of birds usually reach their destinations without coming to harm.

Further Reading

Alderton, D. *You & Your Pet Bird* (Dorling Kindersley, London, UK 1992)

Alderton, D. *The Complete Guide to Bird Care* (Howell Book House, New York, USA 1998)

Alderton, D. *A Birdkeeper's Guide to Budgies* (Interpet Publishing, Dorking, UK 1999)

Alderton, D. *A Birdkeeper's Guide to Parrots & Macaws* (Interpet Publishing, Dorking, UK 1999)

Alderton, D. *A Birdkeeper's Guide to Breeding Birds* (Interpet Publishing, Dorking, UK 1999)

Alderton, D. *The Complete Book of Finches and Softbills: Their Care and Breeding* (TFH, Neptune, USA 2000)

Brown, D. *A Guide to Pigeons, Doves & Quail: Their Management, Care & Breeding* (Australian Birdkeeper, South Tweeds Head, Australia 1995)

Burgmann, P. *Feeding Your Pet Bird* (Barron's Educational Series, Inc., New York, USA 1993)

D' Angieri, A. *The Colored Atlas of Lovebirds* (TFH, Neptune, USA 1997)

Goodwin, D. *Estrildid Finches of the World* (British Museum [Natural History], London, UK 1982)

Haupt, T. *Cockatiels* (Barron's Educational Series, Inc., New York, USA 1999)

Howman, K.C.R. *Pheasants: Their Breeding and Management* (K & R Books, Leicester, UK 1979)

Low, R. *Parrots: Their Care and Breeding* (Blandford Press, London, UK 1986)

Robbins, G.E.S. *Quail: Their Breeding and Management* (World Pheasant Association, Reading, UK 1984)

Trollope, J. *The Care and Breeding of Seed-eating Birds* (Blandford Press, London, UK 1983)

Vince, C. *Keeping Softbilled Birds* (Stanley Paul, London, UK 1980)

Von Frisch, O. *Canaries* (Barron's Educational Series, Inc., New York, USA 1999)

Vriends, M. *The New Bird Handbook* (Barron's Educational Series, Inc., New York, USA 1989)

Walker, G.B.R. & Avon, D. *Coloured, Type & Song Canaries* (Blandford Press, London, UK 1987)

Wellstead, G. *Cage and Aviary Bird Survival Manual* (Barron's Educational Series, Inc., New York, USA 1997)

Websites:

American Federation of Aviculture
http://www.afa.birds.org

The Avicultural Advancement Council of Canada
http://www.islandnet.com/~aacc/intro.htm

Acknowledgments

David Alderton 15l, 19cl, 19cr, 19bl, 19br, 29b, 36; **Dennis Avon** 20, 22, 23, 28, 32, 33r, 41t, 41b, 43, 46b, 50, 51, 52, 53, 57, 58, 61, 64, 83, 84, 88t, 88b, 91, 97, 101, 102, 105, 107, 108l, 111, 113, 116, 127l, 127r, 130, 131, 132, 137, 150, 154, 155, 162, 168, 169l, 169r, 181, 200; **Jane Burton** 199; **Hans Reinhard/Bruce Coleman Collection** 49; **Juniors Bildarchiv/F. Aschermann** 24; **Juniors Bildarchiv/M. Wegler** 2, 7, 21, 128, 129; **Juniors Bildarchiv/J. & P. Wegner** 120-121; **Cyril Laubscher** 10t, 10b, 11, 15r,

16, 25, 29t, 31, 33l, 34, 37, 46t, 54, 59, 67, 69, 73, 74, 77, 79, 86, 87, 89, 92, 94, 96, 99, 100, 106, 114, 121, 123, 124, 136, 140, 142, 145, 147, 149, 151, 152, 157, 159, 160, 161, 165, 166, 171, 173, 175, 177, 179, 180, 183, 185, 187, 188, 190, 192, 195, 197; **Cyril Laubscher/Eliot Lyons** 108r; **Kim Taylor** 135, 186.

Artwork: Robin Budden, Robin Carter/Wildlife Art; Malcolm Ellis, George Fryer, David Thelwell/Bernard Thornton Artists; Michael Loates/Linden Artists.

Index

Page numbers in *italics* refer to illustrations